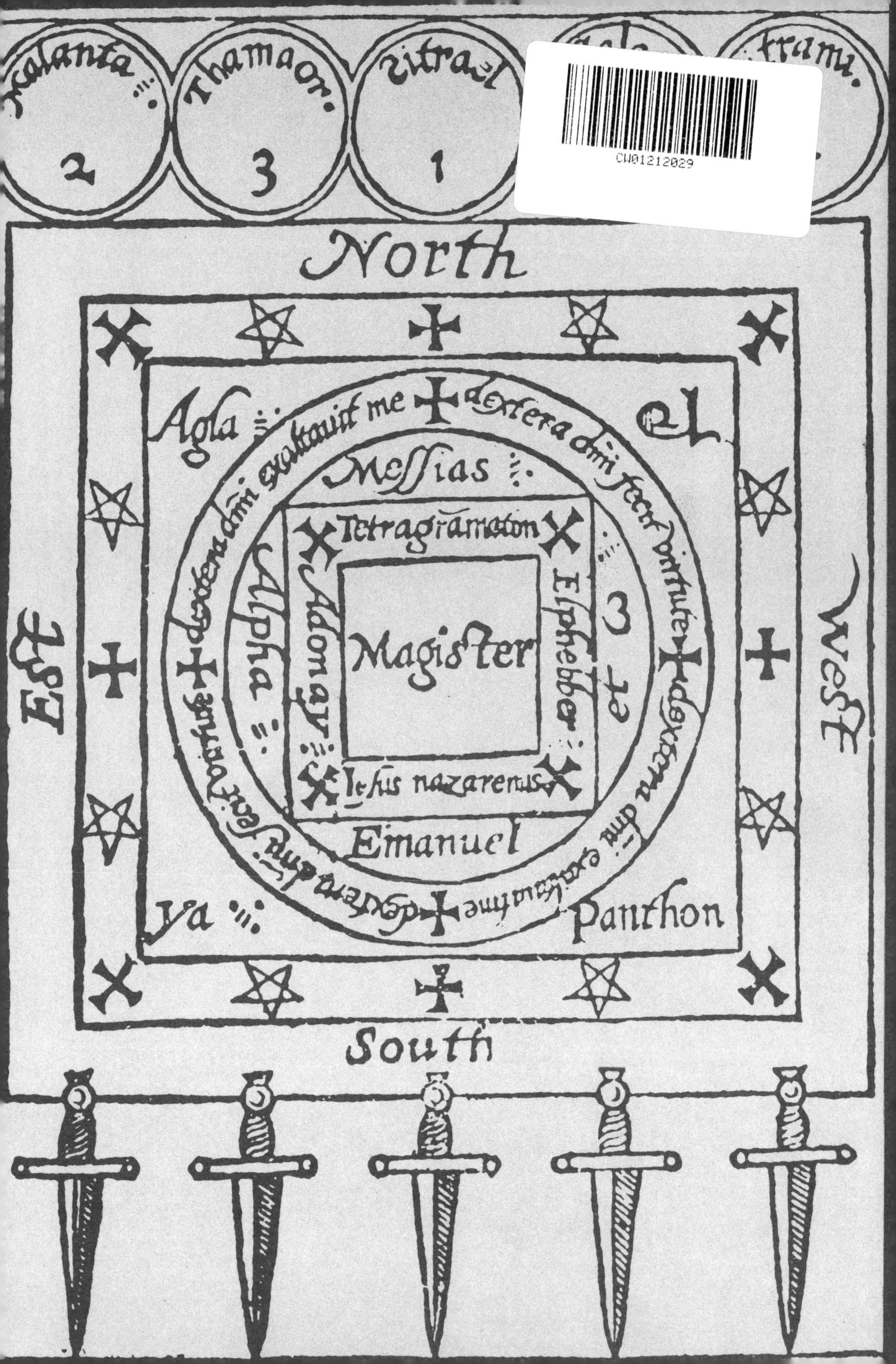

Thamaor
2
3
1
North
Agla
Messias
Tetragramaton
Magister
Alpha
Adonay
Emanuel
ya
Panthon
South
East
West

WITCHCRAFT, MAGIC AND THE SUPERNATURAL

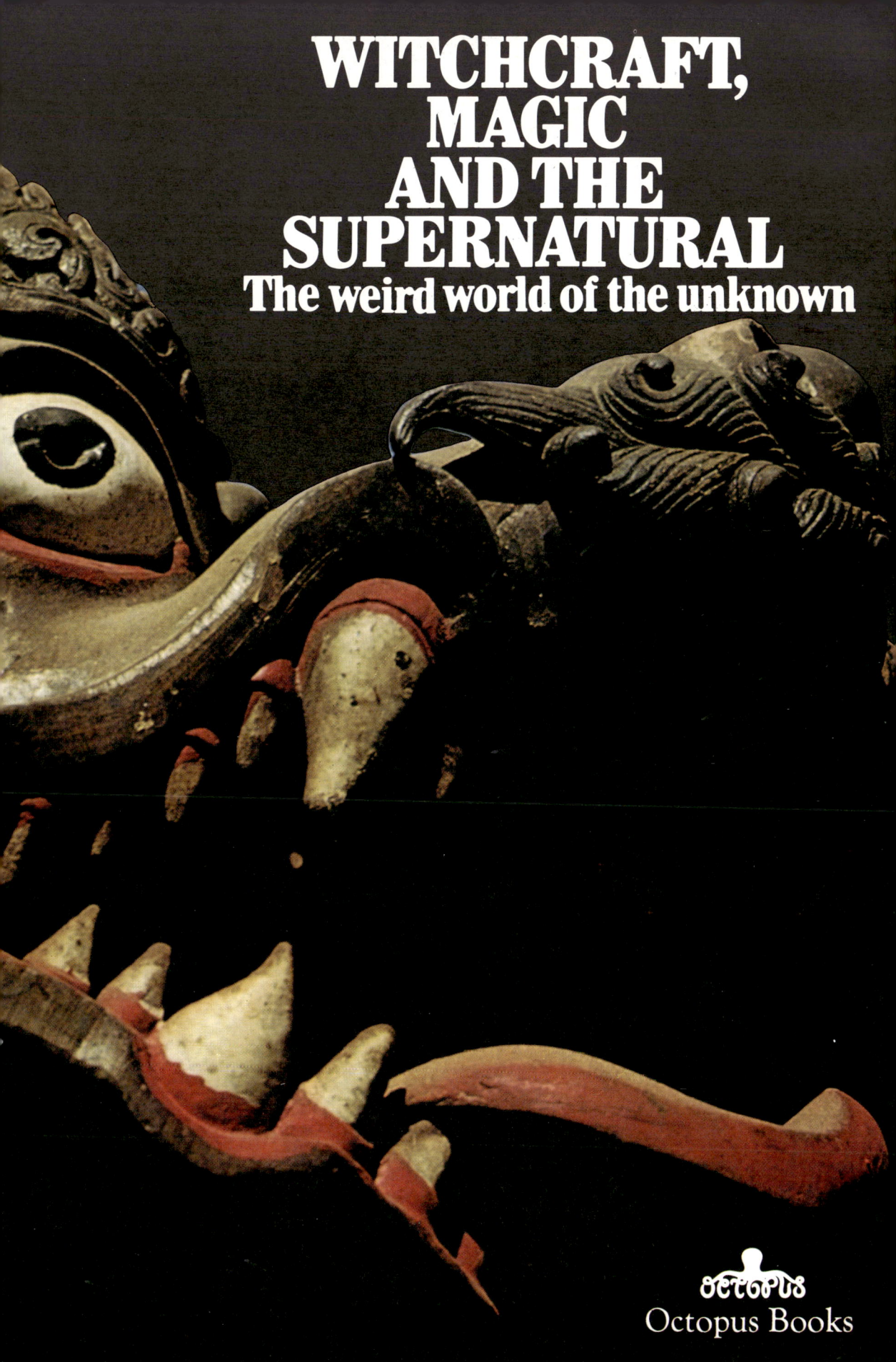

WITCHCRAFT, MAGIC AND THE SUPERNATURAL
The weird world of the unknown

Octopus Books

First published 1974 by
Octopus Books Limited
59 Grosvenor Street, London W1

ISBN 0 7064 0351 7

© 1974 Octopus Books Limited

Produced by Mandarin Publishers Limited
14 Westlands Road, Quarry Bay, Hong Kong

Printed in Hong Kong

Contents

6   **The Supernatural at Work**
Douglas Hill

46   **Devils, Demons and Evil Spirits**
Tessa Clark

62   **The Practice of Magic and Witchcraft**
Pat Williams

108   **The Forces of Nature**
Tessa Clark

116   **Ritual and Ceremony**
Frank Smyth

148   **Magic in the Modern World**
Frank Smyth

173   **Further Reading**

174   **Acknowledgments**

175   **Index**

The Supernatural at Work

Previous pages *living in a hostile and inexplicable environment, ancient man peopled his world with supernatural forces. Even today some of his descendants still believe that the universe is a complex of mysterious powers.*

These pages *witch-doctors, the priests of primitive societies, use magical techniques to contact the spirit world, and are set apart by their costume.* Above *and* centre *witch-doctors in the Cameroons and Nigeria* Above right *an aboriginal dancer relies on body markings for magical effect, while the witchdoctor* (right) *is shrouded in his robe, his face hidden by a sinister horned mask*

At the beginning of human history, ancient man peopled every perceptible inch of the world around him with spirits, demons, inexplicable supernatural forces. Even today, hundreds of thousands of years later, some of his descendants still believe that every tree, stone, pool, cloud and creature contains a supernatural being or power.

Of course, the primitive would not understand the concept behind the word 'supernatural', meaning above or beyond Nature. To him there was, and still is, no distinction. Nature and the universe were quite clearly marvellous, if mysterious, complexes of forces and powers. He embodied these entities in narrative explanations of natural phenomena. We call these myths. And he developed a complicated array of techniques to deal with these forces and powers so that he could protect himself from their more dire effects, or call up, direct and control their beneficial ones. We call these techniques magic.

Magic and myth arose out of primitive man's confrontation with the unknown; but although we know a great deal more about the objective natural

world than did our ancestors we must try not to be too self-congratulatory or condescending to the Stone Age wielder of magic, shivering from more than the cold in his draughty cave.

We know that lightning is not a bearded god in a cloud flinging spears of flame at the earth, but the result of a charge of static electricity leaping across a space. But the fact remains that a great many intelligent and grown-up people today, who know all about static electricity, nonetheless feel a trifle nervous during an electrical storm.

It is the old atavistic response of our primitive ancestor, and like many similar responses it shows that he is still very much with us, or within us. Apparently the immense modern progress in scientific knowledge has not been of much help in subduing these instinctive reactions.

In fact modern science has in some regards merely opened up new areas of the unknown to summon atavistic terrors. Scientists have developed a bomb that works in a way totally incomprehensible to the layman, yet that is able to wipe out people in their

Previous pages *the ancient belief in demons and spirits inspired many colourful rituals which are still practised today. A dragon mask* (left) *symbolizing good luck and benevolence, leads dancers during a Hong Kong festival. The monkey is often regarded as having supernatural powers, probably because of its resemblance to man; a dancer in Singapore* (right) *portrays a sacred monkey*

Facing page *superstitions, based on the belief that good or bad luck, health or illness, can be attracted or warded off, are a form of modern magic. Pieces of cloth are left at the Cloutie well in Scotland* (above) *by people who have come to be healed. Breaking a mirror* (below) *is popularly believed to bring seven years bad luck; the reflected image was thought to be the soul, and damaging the glass would harm the soul and therefore the person who had broken the mirror*

millions. Science makes manned thrusts into the unbearably vast unknown that is space. Science penetrates into the unacceptably small region beyond the atom, where particles of matter actually cease to be matter, and cease also to obey the usual laws of Nature. Science probes into the black mud of the unconscious mind, stirring up all kinds of nightmare monsters. For reasons such as these, mankind has failed to slough off the old involvement with the supernatural, as he has progressed towards civilization.

Modern man no longer sees a spirit or a demon in every rock or tree, nor does he invent narrative myths to explain phenomena he does not understand. But the belief in spirits of one kind or another remains as powerful as ever. There are plenty of people who reject scientific explanations of how the earth was formed, for example, or how man came to be, preferring the older, 'mythic' answers. (It is a sobering thought, but worth remembering, that one man's religion is another man's mythology.)

Much modern involvement with the supernatural may arise out of a wish to escape the modern world and all its attendant fears and horrors. Whatever the reason, this involvement generally parallels the old primitive use of the supernatural, especially of the portion called 'magic' which is regarded as a means of coping with the world.

This statement may seem sweeping. A man living a normal life in the 1970s may not be ready to believe that he knows many people who try to cope with the world through magical means.

But magic is not only the power in the fairy godmother's wand that changes pumpkins into coaches, nor yet the muttered spell by which the evil old witch changes the prince into a frog. These examples, taken from popular fiction and instantly recognizable, are of miraculous changes wrought by beings who are themselves supernatural or have supernatural endowments. More usefully, magic can be seen as the poor man's (the primitive man's) science. Like science, it is believed to provide the power by which the ordinary human being can exercise some control over the outside world, if he has the knowledge.

Traditionally this power is manifested in as many forms, and for as many possible purposes, as modern electricity. But where ancient man had only magic, modern man seems to insist on having technological as well as magical power, dual means of dealing with the world.

Some forms of modern magic are so familiar that it is possible to forget that that they are essentially magical. Common superstitions, the 'folk beliefs' beloved of practising folklorists, are an example. The civilized world's richest treasure hoards of these beliefs, together with other traditional lore and old wives' tales, are found in areas more or less isolated from the mainstream of social development – areas like the Ozark Hills of the United States, the outer isles of Scotland, the mountain villages of Europe. But it would be wrong to think that ordinary superstitions now hold sway only in 'backward', 'ignorant', underprivileged communities. It may be, as many folklorists and other experts think, that such people merely admit more readily to holding such beliefs. Certainly, a post-war study of a group of American college students revealed that over 60 per cent were willing to admit that they were to some degree super-

All over the world sacred figures or buildings are associated with spirits, gods or the souls of people who have died. They are part of man's armoury of magical techniques for coming to terms with the unknown
Far left *figure in a shrine near Katmandu* Above left *Melanesian mask representing the spirit of a dead man*
Left *these chalk figures are honoured as the abodes of spirits in Melanesia*
Above *a Buddhist* stupa *near Katmandu; stupas symbolize Buddha's earthly body*

17

Primitive man's close association with the spirit world is reflected in many artifacts Previous pages *totem poles in British Columbia* (far left and centre); *these carved posts with grotesque human and animal heads depict the myths of North American Indians who believed that their ancestors had the magical ability to take either human or animal shape. A carved dish from Canada* (below right); *the linear design reflects its American Indian origin. Wood and ivory divining tablets from Rhodesia* (above); *the various patterns have a magical significance for the fortune teller*

stitious. Other experiments hint that the proportion of superstitious young people might be much higher.

There are many people who will not walk under a ladder, who carry a rabbit's foot or some other personal 'lucky piece' wherever they go, who touch wood when they utter some assurance about the future. When pressed about these actions, they may be slightly embarrassed and insist that they do them only 'for fun'. But they would be even more uncomfortable if they had to omit doing them. These are superstitions; they are also a widely-practised type of magic.

Many everyday superstitions take the form of omens. Seeing a black cat is lucky, or unlucky, depending on whether one lives in Britain or in North America. Stumbling at the beginning of a journey means ill luck. A red sky at night foretells a pleasant day, sunshine on a wedding party presages a happy marriage. Other superstitions are taboos. Don't light three cigarettes with one match, or break a mirror, or put shoes on a table, or whistle on a sailing ship.

A third category is made up of practices, positive actions – simple magical rituals. The practices are magic because they try actively to alter external reality, or the course of events, or both. They are rituals because they do not 'work' unless always done the same way. Some of these little magics are intended to offset an evil omen or an inadvertently broken taboo. For instance, some people, if forced to walk under a ladder, will cross their fingers while doing so. This is one form of a very ancient gesture made to ward off evil forces. If salt is spilt, an ill omen, a pinch of it should be flung over the left shoulder – because evil approaches from the left, according to tradition.

The ritual of touching wood is intended to counteract a danger that is important and widespread in superstition, the danger of 'tempting fate'. In older times the gods or evil spirits were the fates tempted. Tempting fate occurs when a person voices a certainty about the future – that he or she will pass an examination or win a race, achieve promotion or avoid illness. Fate, or the gods or spirits, will be tempted to puncture spitefully that over-confidence, and it is necessary to placate these beings, keep the ill luck at bay, by touching wood (or knocking on wood, in the United States). This will be most effective if the wood is from one of the traditionally sacred trees of ancient northern European religion such as the oak, ash and rowan.

These examples, and most ordinary folk beliefs that exist today embody a considerable amount of ancient myth and magic. Other parallels are found among primitives (especially so far as placating potentially harmful spirits is concerned, an act which has been at the root of all 'propitiatory' sacrifice to the gods, throughout history.)

Anyone interested in the persistence and prevalence of magic in the modern world could therefore do worse than start by making a note of the various little superstitions, especially rituals, that his friends and acquaintances give credence to.

Another widespread and familiar set of practices is also rooted in ancient magical lore. Today's favourite group label for these practices is 'fortune telling'; but they would once have been called divination.

The proponents of these practices, those people who believe that the future and other 'hidden' matters can be divined, do not in fact accept that all forms of divination are magical. They claim some are merely perceptions of correspondences that exist within the universe, and are relatively plain to see for anyone with the requisite training and experience. In ancient Greece and Rome and other civilizations the diviners 'knew' that the markings on a sacrificial animal's liver could indicate the future if interpreted correctly. This particular practice may have died out now, but the idea of correspondences continues – between a person's palm, for instance, and his character and potential; or between the fall of cards (or tea-leaves) and the future.

Astrology, another form of divination, has as its basic principle the belief that the cosmic positions of planets and distant constellations will reveal, if read properly, the character and future of a human being on earth.

Astrologers reject the idea that magic is involved in the art of the horoscope, and insist that it is not a ritual but a scientific process. But it may seem less than scientific to draw up a 'star map' – for that is what a horoscope is – that places the earth at the centre of the universe, and the constellations in positions they have not held for thousands of years. The traditions of astrology hark back to its beginnings in ancient

The shipboard ceremony of 'crossing the line' has its roots in the ancient need to placate the all-powerful gods and spirits. The ritual daubing and drenching of anyone who is crossing the Equator for the first time, under the direction of King Neptune, is a carefree modern version of ancient sacrifices to the gods

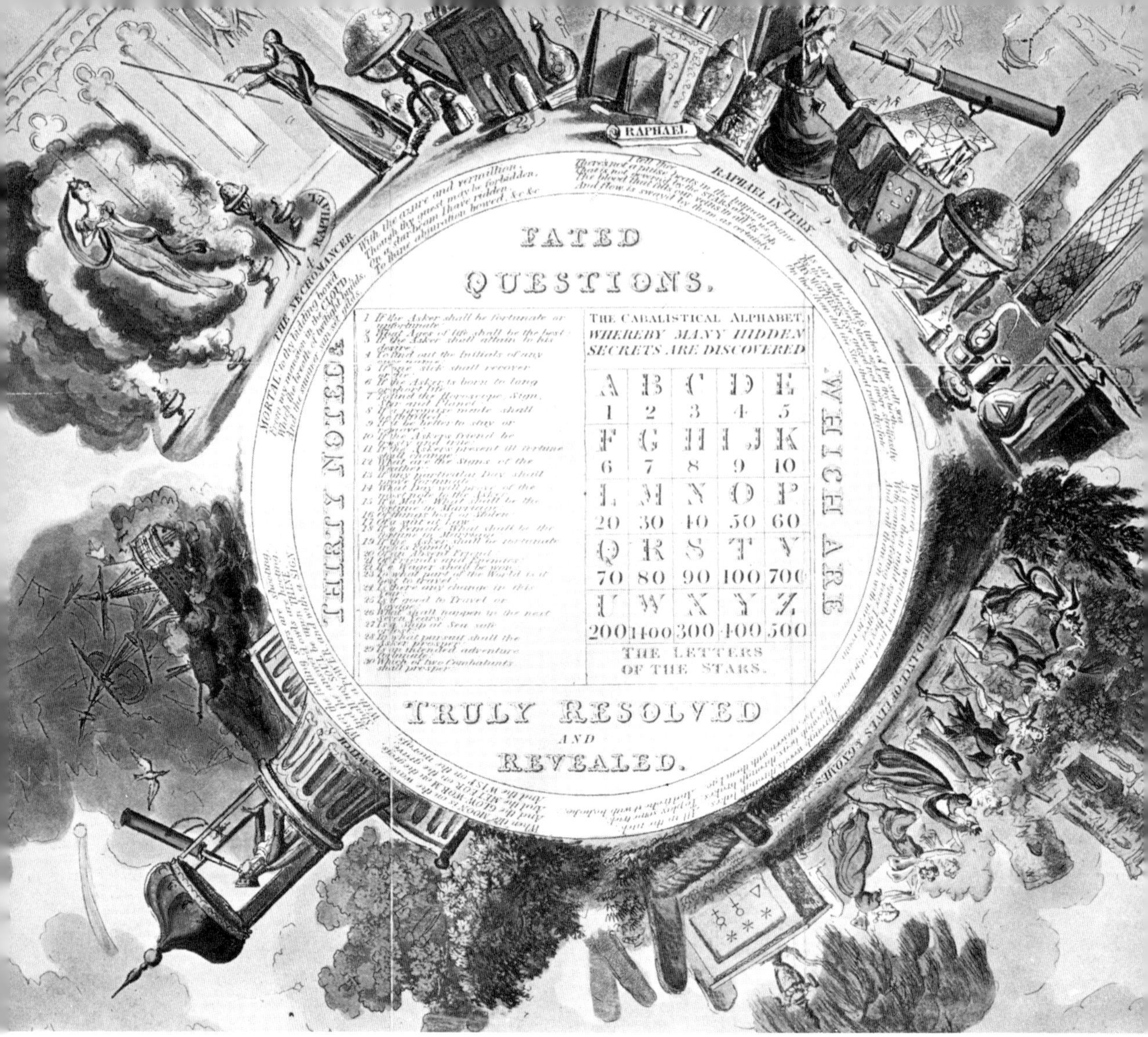

Mesopotamia when astronomy and astrology were one and the same, and wholly the concern of the priest-magicians. Later astronomy was divided from astrology and became the province of scientists. However, no scientific doubt deters the millions of people today who have made astrology a mighty industry worth $200 million a year in the United States alone.

Although astrologers refuse to have the image of their science or art tarnished by any magical association, other forms of divination more obviously involve magic.

The magical influence is clearly apparent in divinatory practices which demand some sort of rite or ceremony before the future can be foretold. In theory, the future then becomes directly perceptible, not just apparent through a set of correspondences or symbolic relationships that need decoding. The most obvious

examples of such divinatory magics are the various forms of scrying – a word meaning 'seeing' or 'perceiving'.

The most familiar form of scrying involves the use of a crystal ball, and is still widely practised by 'gypsy fortune tellers' at funfairs, and also by high-priced diviners, but it is possible to buy a crystal ball quite cheaply and try some do-it-yourself scrying at home. It is an ancient practice. Among the Egyptians, Greeks and others the smooth surface of water was the scryer's favourite, along with smooth reflecting surfaces – the mirror in the story of 'Snow White' is a familiar example. The ancient Merovingians, or Franks, were among the first users of the crystal ball. Their tombs, dating from about 2000 years ago, held small spheres of crystal, and small crystalline objects have been used for divining by the Incas, New Guinea tribesmen,

Many forms of divination are based on ancient magical lore, while others stem from the belief that correspondences can be perceived within the universe
Above left *a fortune-telling manual,* Raphael's Witch *or* Oracle of the Future
Left *Japanese print depicting tabletilting, a popular method of contacting the spirit world*
Above *a 19th century print,* Cup tossing; *the way the tea leaves fall is said to reveal the future*

Although methods of divination differ, fortune telling is practised throughout the world Right *a Voodoo sacrifice. In classical times diviners forecast the future by interpreting the markings on a sacrificial animal's liver* Far right *a Malayan woman in a Buddhist temple looks into the future by throwing a piece of wood* Below right *a witch gazes into a concave black mirror looking for clairvoyant images; this is a variation on the ancient practice of crystal-gazing* Below, far right *fortune telling in India*

Australian aborigines and American Cherokee Indians.

For all of these, as for modern practitioners, the process was simply to gaze at the smooth surface in the hopes of seeing something. Expectation would be heightened if a ritual preceded the gazing, a ritual which resembled nothing so much as the method of casting a magic spell.

Modern handbooks recommend that the ball should rest on a stand inscribed with ancient magical names, symbols and diagrams; the crystalgazer should prepare the scene with incense, herbal infusions and other purifying preludes; the gazing must take place at an auspicious time (sunrise or sunset under the sign of Libra is thought to be best); and may be preceded by speaking of traditional incantations.

The gazing itself may well bring on a semi-trance state. Some seers claim that the ball produces only abstract swirls and cloudy shapes which must be interpreted. In times long past some seers expected that the magical prelude would call up the image of a demon in the glass, who could then be prevailed upon to use his supernatural power to produce visions of future events. More recent belief dispenses with this middle man, and it is claimed that clear images of scenes to come (three-dimensional and often in colour) should materialize within the ball like an instant television programme on the screen.

Whether or not such scenes ever get to a level beyond the stereotyped 'I see a tall, dark stranger' of folk humour must, in the end, be left to the customer's opinion. Certainly, as with astrology, palmistry, Tarot cards, ouija boards, and other forms of divination, there seems to be no likelihood of a shortage of customers.

Clairvoyance, and that allied form of extra-sensory perception called precognition, should perhaps be classed as magic, if only because the shamans and medicine-men of primitive tribes included this power of seeing directly into the future in their armoury of magical abilities. Many of them performed a high-powered ritual to induce the trancelike state that would set the power working.

Modern spiritualist mediums do much the same, even if their 'power' seems limited to bringing messages from 'beyond' rather than from the future. Nevertheless, it seems that scientists and thinkers are becoming

Above *scientific investigation, in Rome, of precognition which is a form of extrasensory perception* Below *a medium with 'ectoplasm' issuing from her nostril* Far right *a medium and her spirit guide, Geordie* Above right *cases have been recorded of artists producing paintings or drawings apparently guided by some outer, or subconscious force: 'automatic' painting by Mrs Alaric Watts*

increasingly interested in the apparently quite hard evidence that flashes of 'second sight' do happen to people, and prove to be accurate.

The Magical Tradition
At the root of magical tradition is the certainty that the use of magic means power. Not just the passive power of seeing the future, but the active power of affecting external reality.

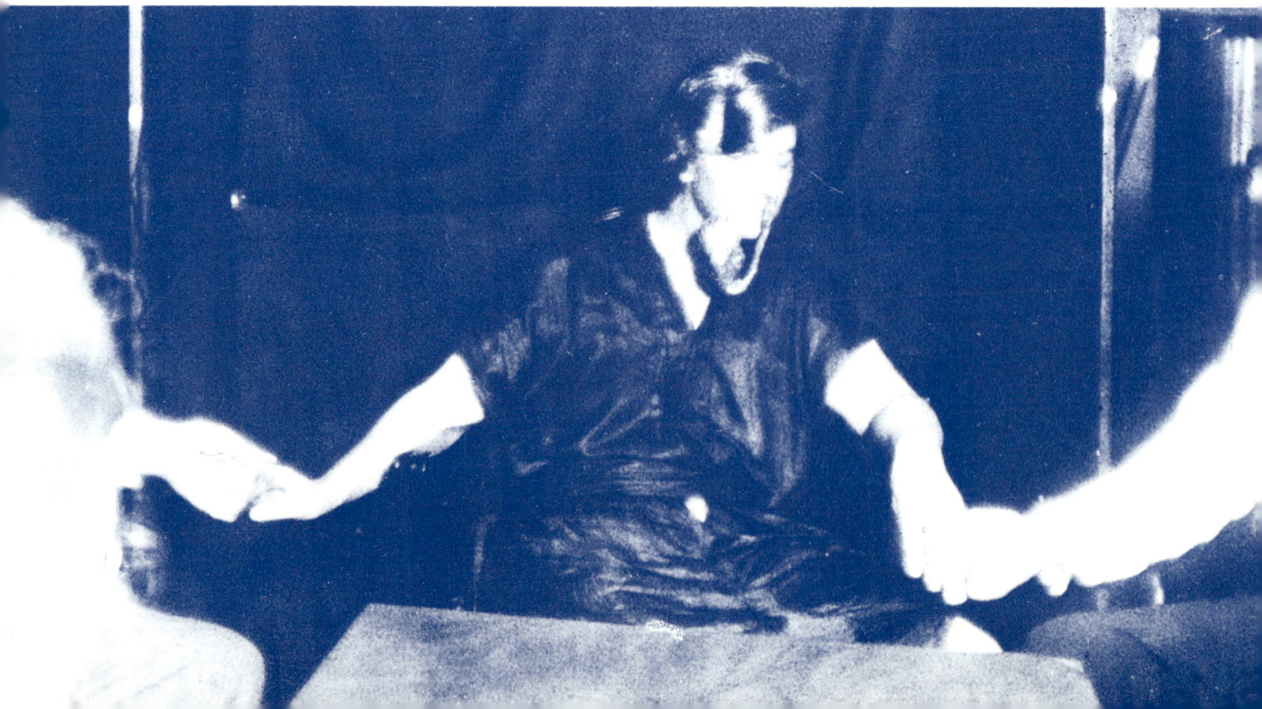

In some cases it seems to be an innate power that cannot be acquired, but is the possession of the favoured and fortunate few, in the way that our Western traditions say that clairvoyance is a 'gift' found only in the 'born psychic'. Belief in such an inborn magical ability is found in the world-wide concept of the Evil Eye – the idea that a glance from a person with the power can harm or destroy people, creatures, objects. The concept has existed since ancient times. Often in the past the power was thought to be the property of some supernatural being, but since the Middle Ages at least it has been believed to be a human power. The belief may have retreated now to those comparatively out-of-touch regions mentioned before as the repositories for superstition; but at least it still thrives there. In rural American tradition people who are cross-eyed, or have eyes of different colours are supposed to have the power. As recently as 1966, a self-proclaimed sorcerer in Italy threatened to put the Evil Eye on the next opponents of the football team he fanatically supported – the results are not recorded.

Innate magical power can also exist for the good, perhaps most notably in the belief that people can be born with the power to heal. In past centuries a reigning monarch was thought to have this gift, and even in the 19th century the diseased, especially those with scrofula, which came to be known familiarly as the King's Evil, tried to have a monarch touch them so as to be cured. There is, of course, no shortage of other examples of miraculous healing, from the New Testament to modern evangelical 'faith healers', most of whom utilize the 'laying on of hands'.

Inherent power has long been believed to reside in inanimate objects, and, as part of our heritage of magical belief from ancient times, some objects or substances are more innately powerful than others. Almost universally, salt, silver and cold iron are supposed to be magically protective against evil influences, together with a host of other substances including garlic and certain woods. Substances connected with the human body (blood especially) and with death – graveyard dirt, portions of a corpse's shroud or indeed of a corpse – feature in much magic-working because they are powerful in themselves. A stone with a natural hole is widely regarded as a luck-bringer; an Australian aborigine's 'death bone' is an object with the Evil Eye ability to destroy anyone at whom it is directed. This is similar to the European idea of the magic wand or sorcerer's staff, itself an object infused with power – although in their case the magic is not inherent, but applied. The power in the wand or staff comes from a magical charging process.

Apart from spontaneous or innate magic, the greater part of magical activity involves ritual and ceremony – whether it be the charging process mentioned above, preparing a crystal ball, or most important, setting a major spell in action. Indeed, in terms of magical tradition, it might almost be said that the ceremony is the magic. And this is true, in the sense that it sets the magic working, as if ritual was a complicated and lengthy version of throwing a switch. Essentially, though, magical ritual is a means to an end – the channelling and control of supernatural or occult forces that are central to magic.

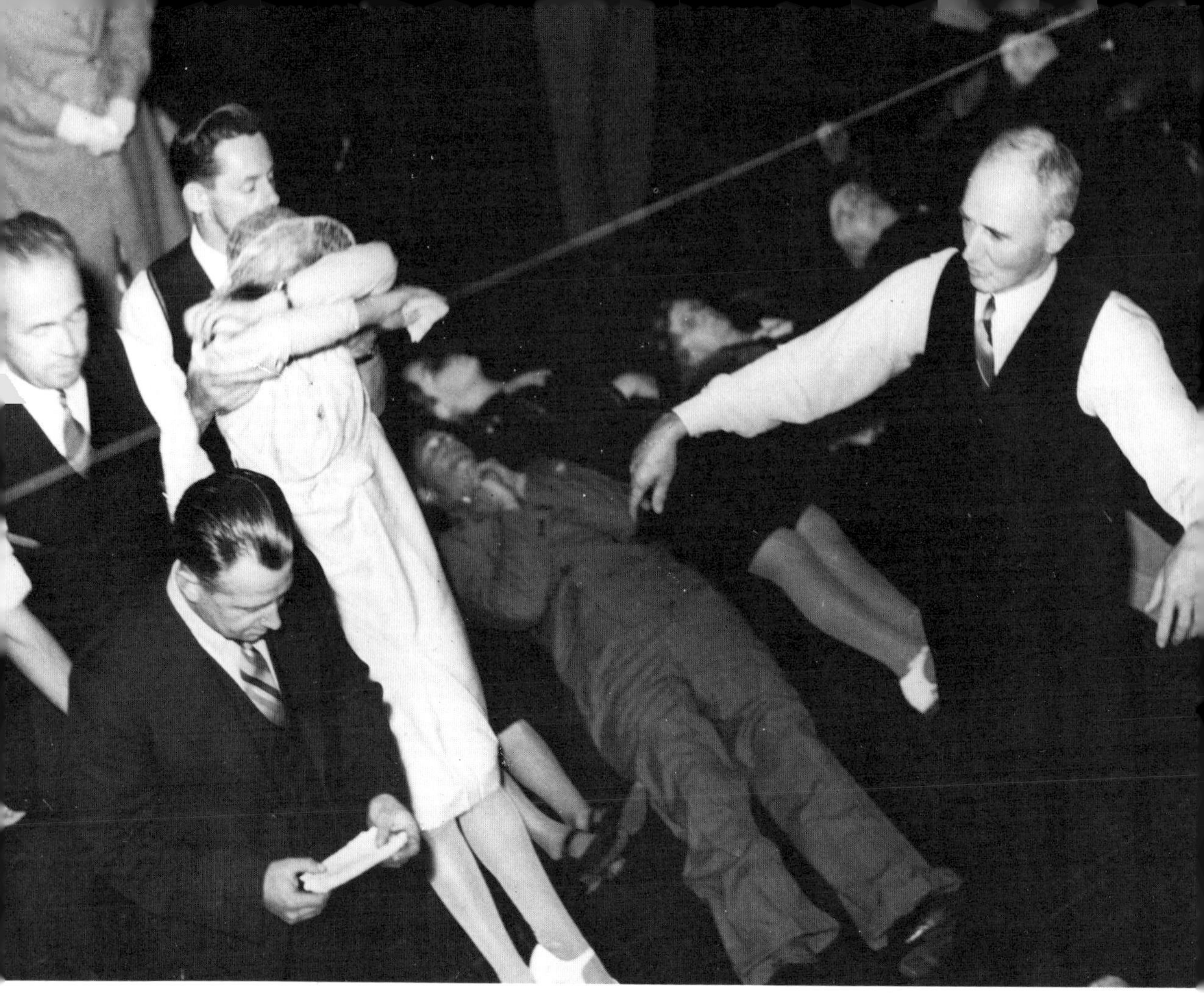

This central tradition, reaching back through European history into the classical world and perhaps into prehistory, has little interest in any concept of magic as an innate property of some humans. Instead, the magic begins with the operation of the ceremony; and the purpose of the ceremony is thought to be solely the contacting or calling up of a supernatural being, in order to obtain its magically powerful services.

The being may not be anthropomorphic, such as a horned and hoofed but otherwise humanoid demon; it may merely be, in the usual vague terms, an 'essence' or a 'force'. But whatever its shape, its presence seems crucial to ceremonial magic.

The ceremony, in short, does not make the magician himself a magical being. The magician has no innate power and acquires none. What he has is secret, occult knowledge of the correct ceremonial, which will enable him to harness the power of the supernatural being.

At its simplest, this knowledge may consist of rubbing a certain lamp to cause a genie to appear who will magically carry out his every bidding. But ritual magic is never as straightforward as that. Acquiring the necessary knowledge involves years of learning and training; and performing a magical ceremony requires strict self-discipline and concentration. Every step must be 100 per cent perfect, for every action, every word, every object that is used, has a specific meaning in magic. And this applies as much to the North American Indian medicine-man calling upon the spirits to make rain for the harvest, as to the European magician invoking the mighty demon who rules the north.

The end result, however, must be the same, for European adept or North American medicine-man: if the ritual is correctly performed, the beings are compelled to go into action. But the Indians, like other tribal people, were not always concerned with conjuration: the Pueblo rain dance calls upon the spirits to send rain, it does not invite them to the dance. The European magician, on the other hand, wants his spirit or demon to be present, perhaps because he does not always feel that his control is secure.

And he is often right. In post-Christian traditions, at least, the spirits who are there to be summoned seem to have minds of their own. Any obedience they show to the magician is usually due to whatever

Facing page *the belief that some people are born with innate magical powers exists in both Western and primitive societies. Western faith-healers are an example. A girl collapses in a trance* (above) *at the touch of A.H. Dallimore an evangelical faith healer* (also below left). *The wife of an African medium is honoured for her husband's supernatural ability to contact the gods* (below right) Top *and* above *magical force may also reside in inanimate objects. The shaman's rattle from Vancouver Island, and the magician's ceremonial staff are both charged with supernatural power: head from a magician's wand*

For centuries man has believed that certain charms will protect him from supernatural influences. This late 18th century statuette, with the head of a cock and a man's body, was often found on charms used by members of Gnostic sects from c200 AD. The cock is thought to save the world from darkness every day by crowing to bring the dawn

compulsion exists in the spell that summoned them. So the magician becomes like the wild-animal trainer who makes his tigers jump through hoops but always guards against the breakdown of control.

The more dangerous sort of being would not be summoned by most practitioners of ceremonial magic. But some adepts work especially towards such conjuration – and this introduces that ancient separation of magic into its two extremities, black and white.

To the primitive, who sees unity and correspondence where we see separation and compartmentalization, the difference is simple. To the Papuan tribesman, white magic is what your shaman does to an enemy tribe, black magic is what an enemy shaman does to you. And this clear-cut view holds true through history. According to this, the distinction lies in the magician's intention, in whether he wields magic's impersonal power for good or ill – in the same way as man can harness electricity beneficently to run machinery, or malevolently to kill by electrocution.

But Christianity confused the issue by introducing a whole army of supernatural beings whose powers are not impersonal, who could never be compelled by a ceremony to do good. These beings of evil, Satan and his legions of devils, imps and demons are the supernatural forces on whom the black magician calls. Ever since the Christian theorists of the Middle Ages spent their energies determining and naming the demonic hordes of Hell, black magic has been twice evil – by the magician's intention, and by the beings he summons to bring it about.

Much modern writing, both fiction and sensational journalism, consistently misuses the term 'black magic', together with the even more tangled term 'witchcraft'. Newspaper reports dealing with vandalism in cemeteries or the desecration of churches with occult symbols speak of black magic when what in fact occurred was some variant on the worship of the Devil, called the 'Black Mass'.

This unholy ritual, which happens in fiction more often than fact, ostensibly offers an ugly parody of the real Mass, with plenty of gruesome and obscene additions. Its essence is the element of blasphemy. During the 18th century an elegant version of Devil-worship was practised by members of the 'Hell Fire Club', a

Parts of the human body are thought to be inherently powerful, and play an important part in magic-making. The skull is especially significant because it is traditionally the dwelling place of the soul
Left *a sinister red-eyed skull from New Guinea*
Below *a human skull used as a ceremonial drum in South America*

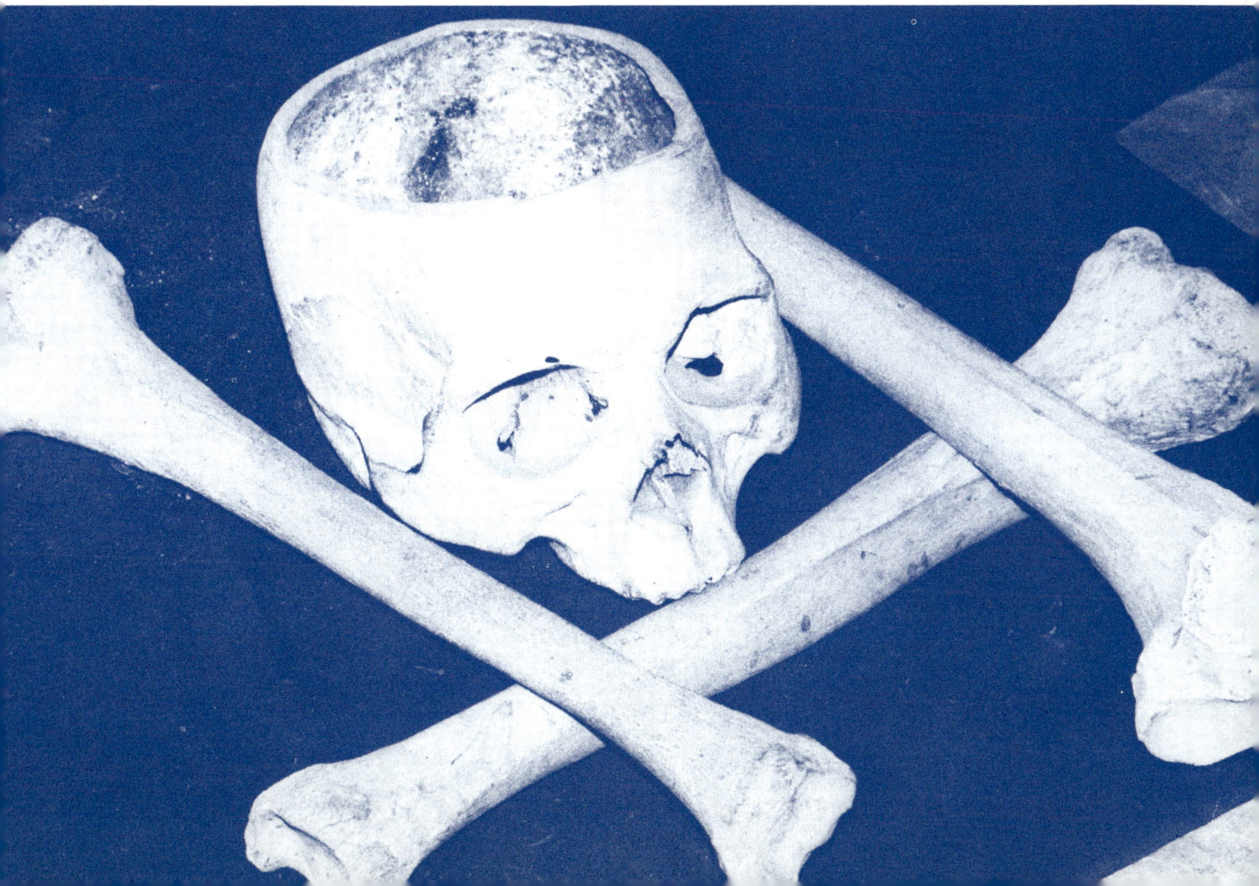

group of rakes, politicians and dandies led by Sir Francis Dashwood. Their Satanism took place in the suitably gothic surroundings of Medmenham Abbey, near London; and the form of their ritual was innocuous in comparison to that practised by other less privileged worshippers of Satan. The recent practices of the Black Mass have been very different to those early rituals, and some 200 years later in Bedfordshire, England, the worshippers left behind a chicken sacrificed on a Christian altar, and dug up graves and bones disinterred from the church-yard.

But the Black Mass and other forms of Devil-worship are not ceremonial black magic, even though the same thing – Hell may be the focus of attention in each case. The Devil-worshippers are the minions of their dark god, prostrate before him, enjoying – if it is enjoyment – the perverted ritual of worship for its own sake. The black magician performs his ritual in order to call upon the service of the dark god. In effect his object is to make the Devil into his minion.

Witchcraft engenders even more confusion. The word itself has almost as many meanings as practitioners. Pre-Christian peoples had numerous words to describe magic-workers, and modern translators may choose to say 'witch' or 'sorcerer' or 'shaman' to mention only a few; it matters little in these contexts.

But in Europe from the 15th to the 18th centuries, the definition of a witch hardened to have a special meaning. A witch was said to be a human servant of Satan, initiated into membership of a secret group – the coven – devoted to evil and to promoting the Devil's work among men. By these terms witches were Devil-worshippers. Their persecution for this heresy by a Christian society, and the lurid tales, of bewitchment of animals and crops, intercourse with the Devil, and murder by magic, that were told at witch trials have done much to perpetuate the image of the witch as an evil-working servant of the Lord of Hell.

The first known witch-hunts took place during the 14th century, but the peak of witch hysteria was from about 1450 to 1750. During that time tens of thousands of people were burned as witches as the persecutions swept Germany, Spain, Britain, France, and even colonial America.

Ingenious tortures were devised to extract confessions

Western and primitive magic-makers have a common aim: to control and manipulate supernatural powers. Most modern witches and witch-doctors use these forces to do good Facing page *the high priestess of a coven stands in front of her altar, her arms outstretched in blessing*
Above *an African witch-doctor in her robes and cap; she is said to have cured every kind of illness*

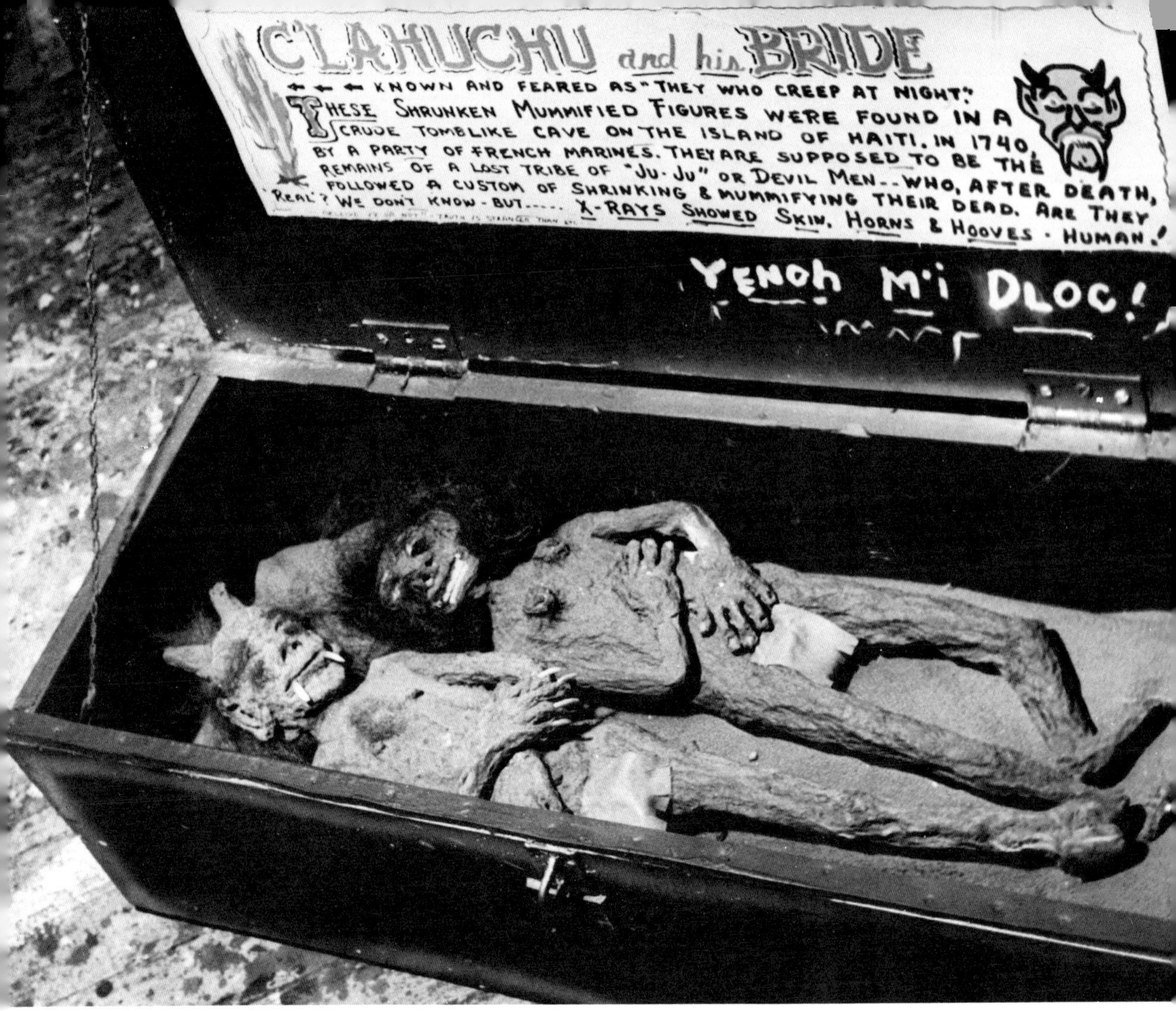
C'LAHUCHU and his BRIDE
KNOWN AND FEARED AS "THEY WHO CREEP AT NIGHT."
THESE SHRUNKEN MUMMIFIED FIGURES WERE FOUND IN A
CRUDE TOMBLIKE CAVE ON THE ISLAND OF HAITI, IN 1740,
BY A PARTY OF FRENCH MARINES. THEY ARE SUPPOSED TO BE THE
REMAINS OF A LOST TRIBE OF "JU-JU" OR DEVIL MEN.. WHO, AFTER DEATH,
FOLLOWED A CUSTOM OF SHRINKING & MUMMIFYING THEIR DEAD. ARE THEY
REAL? WE DON'T KNOW - BUT..... X-RAYS SHOWED SKIN, HORNS & HOOVES - HUMAN!
YENOH M'I DLOC!

THE SPIRIT SHALL RETURN
NTO GOD WHO GAVE IT

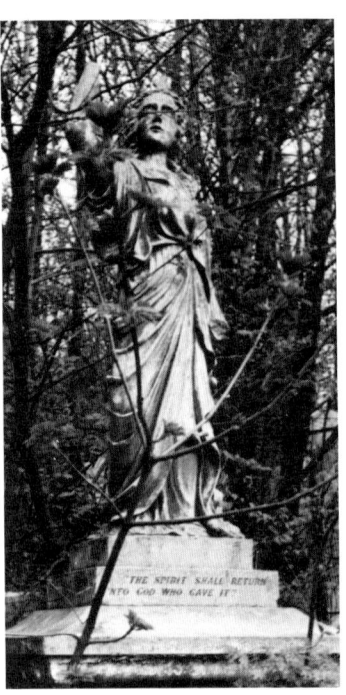

from the accused. In Bamberg in Germany, one of the more subtle methods was to feed them forcibly on herring cooked in salt, and then deny them water. In other places spikes were forced beneath their fingernails and toenails, the soles of their feet were burnt, and they were subjected to the thumbscrews, and the rack. These are only a few of the many methods used to 'persuade' supposed witches to confess.

In the atmosphere of fear and suspicion that surrounded the persecutions, the existence of a 'witch mark' – any kind of mole, scar, growth or birth-mark – could be proof of subjection to the Devil. In England and Scotland it was believed that the Devil sent familiars in the shape of dogs, cats, ferrets and even spiders to aid witches in their work. To be old and ugly, and to enjoy the company of a pet, could invite an accusation of witchcraft.

Of all the many horrors of the period, one of the most chilling was the acceptance of children's evidence. In

England a mother and daughter were executed as witches on the evidence of a ten-year-old girl; and in Salem in America young girls sparked off the notorious witch-hunt during which 200 people were arrested, and 19 put to death.

Popular hysteria grew as the persecutions continued; and although originally the Church and the learned and ruling classes had been responsible for finding witches, by the end of the 300-year period it was the common people who strove to persecute, while the judges and officials tried to restrain them.

This is the background to the belief that witchcraft is a combination of worship and magic, practised by people entered into voluntary service to Satan.

The dark side of magic therefore has a number of different aspects. It encompasses the traditional view that witches are beings who have sold themselves into slavery to the dark god, and covers also the Black Mass and Devil-worship generally. These orgiastic rituals are performed in praise of the Devil but tend to be enjoyed largely for their own sakes. Finally there is black magic which, in post-Christian times, means borrowing the power of devils to further evil intentions; its practitioners are black magicians who are not worshippers, but enacters of spells or ceremonies by which they hope to stay at least partly in control of the evil forces they unleash, so as to direct them to purposes of their own. A black magician is in business for himself, as is indicated when, in the tradition, he signs a pact with the demon he invokes.

Modern Magic-workers

With the latter-day resurgence of interest in the occult, new approaches to the old ways have developed which blur these distinctions. Today Satanism, in its many guises around the world, has a new lease of life and one or two new features. And the practice called witchcraft has taken on an entirely new meaning, although its practitioners insist that it is thousands of years old, and the only true meaning.

Satanists tend to be found in their greatest numbers in the more decadent regions of Western civilizations – the larger urban centres, and especially that haven of everything weird and unpredictable, Los Angeles. Although the label 'Satanists' could be said to in-

Facing page *a corpse, or portions of its shroud, and graveyard dirt are often essential to black magic: mummified figures* (above) *from the Voodoo island of Haiti. A battered tombstone angel in a ruined graveyard* (below)

Top *Sir Francis Dashwood, leader of the 18th century Hell Fire Club* Above *the spire of the 'church' he built in High Wycombe near London*

33

Practitioners of black magic worship Satan, and black magicians call upon devils, demons and imps in their ceremonies *Far left* Anton La Vey, leader of the Church of Satan in California; modern Satanist groups stress the wickedness and sinfulness of their activities *Left* Satan tempting Christ; 13th century stained glass window from Troyes Cathedral, France *Below* witches and devils; part of a 19th century mural in a Bulgarian monastery

clude the sick groups of thrill-seekers who find their kicks in gruesome cemetery vandalism and sadistic or fetishistic sex, the 'true' Satanists are members of organisations or sects whose practices can usually stand up to scrutiny by the light of day, or at least twilight. They rarely seem to engage in activities that are explicitly illegal, or do so, if at all, with successful secrecy. Their worship is sinful and blasphemous in the traditional Christian sense, and heretical in the Roman Catholic sense, but these facts alone are no longer sufficient to interest secular law.

Modern Satanist groups insist, by definition, on their sinfulness and wickedness. A great many of their group activities therefore take the form of actions intended as gross, outrageous, sacrilegious insults to Christian worship. The least of these insults is wearing crosses upside down. They perform versions of the Black Mass, introducing the occasional obscenity, perhaps using a nude woman as an altar. They hold Satanic parodies of traditional Christian festivals or sacraments. They take part in regular gatherings often notable for their sexual licence.

The permissiveness varies in intensity and imaginativeness depending on the group's membership, and how above ground or underground it is. The well-known 'Church of Satan' of Anton LaVey in California tends to have glamorous and Hollywoodish appurtenances. But in its more public appearances, which are frequent, it is no more socially offensive than most modern Hollywood films.

Considerably less respectable, and certainly flourishing in a less permissive time, was the Satanist group that gathered round the British occultist and black magician Aleister Crowley, whose notoriety in the 1920s earned him the title of 'the wickedest man in the world'. If he had been only a prolific writer and extensive practitioner of black magic, he would have been a major figure of modern occultism. But his excesses, practised under the Satanist slogan 'Do What Thou Wilt', ensured that in terms of sheer infamy he is probably the major figure of recent times.

In contrast to modern Satanists, witches today assert that Satan has nothing to do with them and that their worship not only existed before Christianity but probably antedates the Old Testament. They claim that the magical power that comes to them through this worship is in fact white magic, the diametric opposite of any Crowleyite evil.

A great deal of white magic is practised today. Many experts, including the British diviner and self-styled witch Sybil Leek, who now lives in the United States, have pointed out that divination is mainly white magic, as are various protective charms.

Protection is one of white magic's primary roles. According to the American magazine *Esquire*, in 1970, there are men and women in California who actively work good magic in order to offset the darker influences at large in that curious state. Healing is another main function, and includes not only faith healing but also the purely magical activities of practitioners like the legendary 'bloodstoppers' of backwoods American tradition, who are said to be able to staunch the flow of blood from a wound by muttering a secret incantation, usually involving verses from the Bible.

In the past witches were said to be human servants of Satan, who had been initiated into a secret group or coven and were dedicated to furthering the Devil's aims Above left *a witch at her evil work; her animal familiars, and a skull are nearby and a goat, symbol of the Devil, towers over her – Goya* Above *grotesque figures of witchcraft, also by Goya*

Following page *the paraphernalia of black magic used by the Church of Satan*

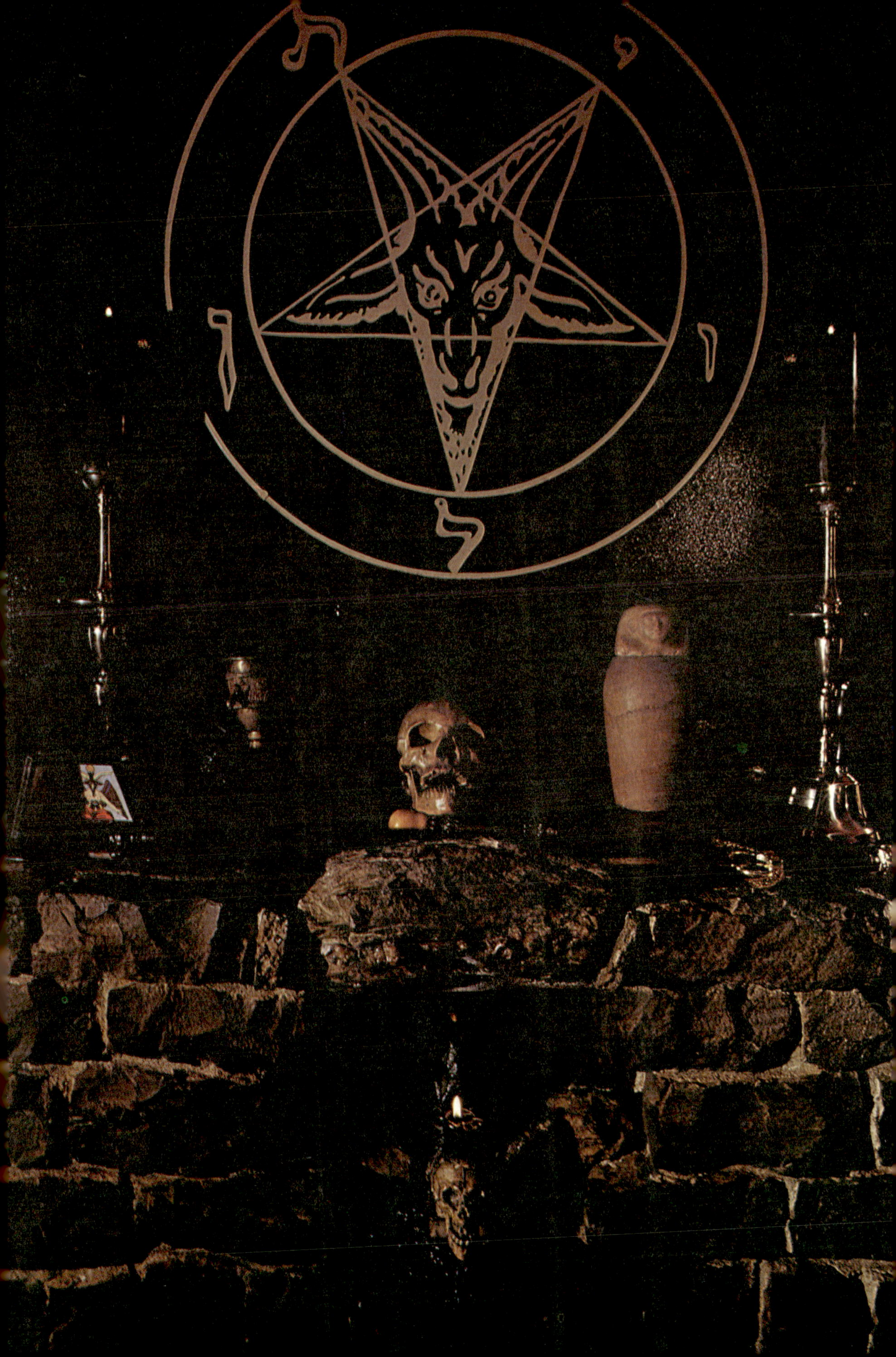

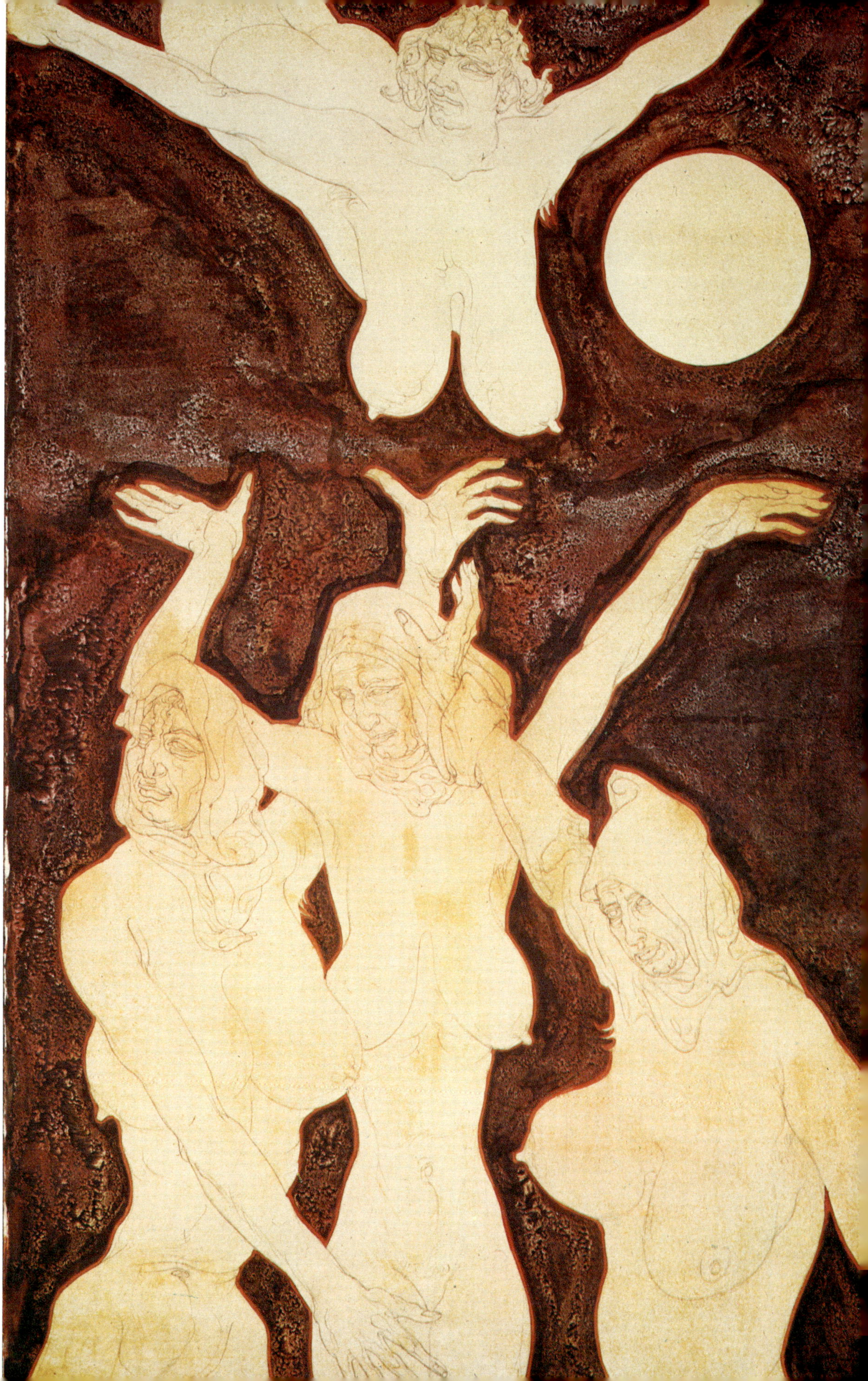

Previous page *hag-ridden witches of tradition; painting by Austin Osman Spare.*

In the past thousands of people were killed as witches, and numerous tortures were devised to force the accused to confess: Below *a 16th century German woodcut depicts the questioning, and torture, of an accused witch* Facing page *the Salem 'witch house', scene of many trials* (above), *and a Salem witch being tried* (below)

White magicians often seem to work hand in hand with Christianity, as if they are tapping and channelling a power that comes ultimately from the Christian God. For instance, a famous Spanish 'wisewoman', (the name for female magic-workers who cannot be called witches), who was still operating in post-war years had a spell which she cast on people to offset the Evil Eye which invoked the Holy Trinity.

Modern white witches may seem at first glance to have a number of features in common with the black witches who were so ruthlessly pursued in the days of the witch-burnings and persecutions. Their explanation is that many of the people who in the past suffered torture and death as servants of Satan may have been white witches whose pre-Christian practices were misinterpreted as evil. Certainly today's witches follow many of the ceremonial practices of their historical counterparts. And, of course, these white witches are primarily worshippers, as were their predecessors.

Modern witches worship immensely ancient pagan gods, in rituals handed down over thousands of years. One of their main objects of worship is a mighty goddess who in some aspects is an Earth Mother figure, resembling prehistoric European fertility deities; another is a horned god who may bear superficial resemblances to Satan, but who certainly predates him – and also predates Pan and other Greek Nature deities. Witches say their name comes from the Anglo-

Although the tarot is generally regarded as a system of fortune telling, many experts believe that the cards symbolize the occult truths that magicians and magic-workers must learn
Above *the Moon, one of the tarot trumps of Charles V of France.*

Facing page *the Magician, one of a set of cards designed for Aleister Crowley*

Saxon *wicca*, meaning 'wise'.

The pagan background of this witch-religion is vastly complicated, if all the parallels of fertility and other cults are traced through world mythology. But the importance of this religious basis cannot be over-emphasized, if only because of the confusion that arises when these worshippers are called witches.

It is then something of a shame that the white groups could not have found another name for their religion, even though it would probably have been similar to those given to the hordes of modern cults and sects and mystical-religious groups that have sprung up all over the modern world – groups with vague if occultish names like 'Society of the Inner Light' or 'Free Union of Creative Karma'. These sectarians usually profess to be seekers after mystic or occult truth, worshippers of deities or spiritual essences that represent such truth.

Many psychological and sociological theories, usually variants on the decadence of Western society, and the decline of Christianity, have been advanced to explain the abundant interest in these offbeat religions. But it is likely that some of them, like the white-witch covens, attract would-be members by offering the possibility of plugging into a meaningful source of group power.

Many modern witches are convinced that, together in their covens performing their ceremonies properly so as to build the necessary energies, they can wield magical power. And they generally use that power for good, valid purposes. The high priestess of one south London coven has asserted confidently that her group has healed the sick, even over considerable distances, when they have been asked to do so; and that they have helped members and friends to defeat enemies, find new jobs, achieve worthwhile goals and overcome various difficulties.

Occasionally witches may turn their magic to slightly discreditable ends, perhaps to cause unpleasantness or discomfort to an enemy, to a writer who has misrepresented them or a curiosity-seeker trying to spy out their secrets. But they would nevertheless argue that these operations are 'good' magic – as they are, from their point of view.

After all, there was the famous, if apocryphal,

I

The Magician ☿

A great deal of white magic is practised today Above *a 'love' sorceress in Los Angeles holding a bowl containing a lucky beetle*
Above centre *a small boy dances during a healing ritual in Ghana*
Right *at a witches' wedding or 'hand-fasting' the high priestess symbolically sweeps evil influences away from the couple, who kneel before the high priest*
Far right *one of the objectives of the Church of Satan is to free its members from feelings of guilt by encouraging carnal enjoyment, and even hate and anger*

occasion when British witches set out to use their power against one man. The man was Adolf Hitler, and the occasion was when the Nazi forces were apparently massing for an assault on England. Britain's witches, acting as one, hurled their powers against him to make him change his mind – just as, legend says, they had done when Napoleon was marshalling his armies for the same purpose.

45

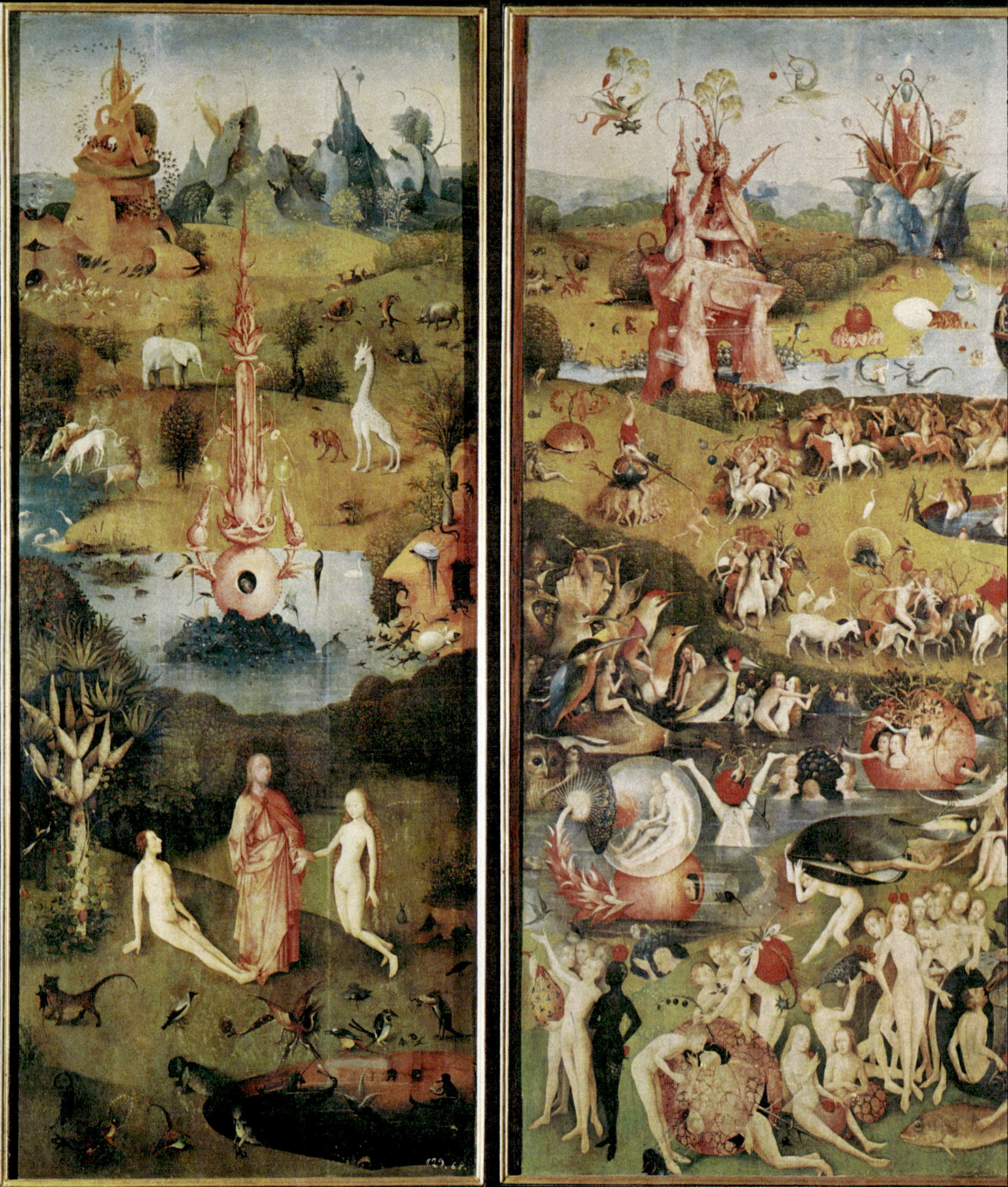

Devils, Demons and Evil Spirits

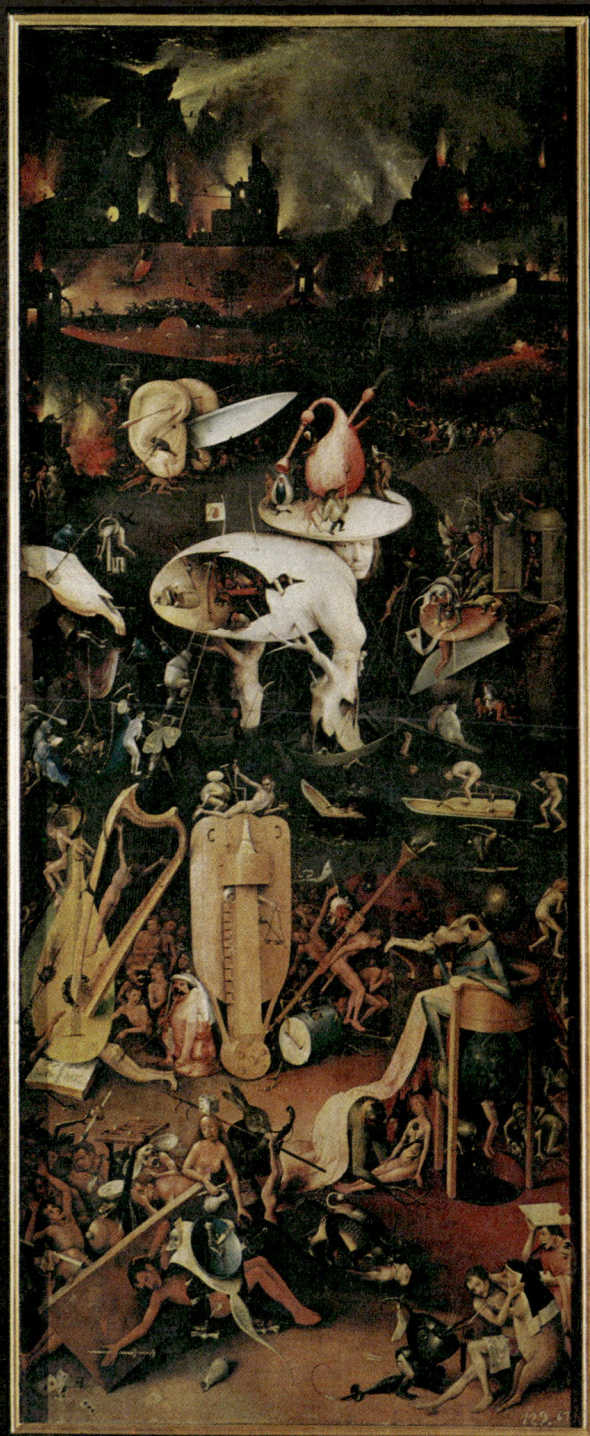

Although throughout history man has been terrified by the evil and the demonic he has nevertheless been fascinated by it and has sought to represent it in a most lurid and grotesque way. Very often an underlying theme of sexuality and eroticism is apparent
Previous pages Hieronymus Bosch's triptych, The Garden of Earthly Delights, *which depicts (from left to right) paradise, the world and hell, evokes many primitive terrors, as do the gargoyles on a Parisian church* (above)
Above right a scene from the film Dracula. *Vampires were thought to suck their victims' blood at night*

The demons which the Western magician invokes in his black magic rites are comparative newcomers to the hordes of fearful beings that have terrified men for thousands of years. The supernatural creatures he seeks to control are part of the Christian tradition. Descended from the fallen angels, they are the evil side of the religious coin whose obverse is good.

But man has lived in a threatening world since the beginning of time, feeling himself menaced by phenomena he is unable to control: the might of storm, darkness, heat and cold, drought and famine. Over the centuries, the fearfulness of this world assumed the symbolic garb of devils and demons, evil spirits who must at all costs be guarded against and placated.

Unlike Christian demons, whose evil stems from their allegiance to the Devil, the exact opposite of the Christian god, these creatures are inherently evil. Most of them owe their power to man's instinctive fears – the dread of lonely places, of disease, and above all of death.

In the East demons are often associated with deserts. The ancient Jews believed that the desolate places through which they travelled were peopled by malevolent demons of darkness who were determined to destroy human beings.

A demonic army, said to haunt the deserts of Arabia, had vampires, ghosts and phantoms in its ranks. It was so terrifying to look upon that it fled when shown its own reflection in giant mirrors.

This theme of horrifying ugliness is common to demons throughout the world. The Iroquois of North America believed in spirits who appeared in a variety of grotesque forms, including flying heads. In South

America demons often take on human shape, but they may have two heads, excessively hairy limbs, or limbs with no joints. They may look like skeletons, or skulls.

The spirits of Eskimo tradition are giants, half-human and half-animal, and Christian demons also combine human and animal characteristics to fearful and terrifying effect. Kali, the Indian goddess of warfare, pestilence, sacrifice and death, is traditionally depicted as black and emaciated. She wears a necklace of human skulls, and has protruding fangs, bloodshot eyes, and matted hair.

Kali has been described as the dark aspect of the Earth Mother who represents fertility. This ambivalent attitude towards sex is another common theme that underlies differing cultures throughout the world. It has led to the widespread belief in sexually-insatiable demons, usually female, who attempt to entice men to their own destruction.

Lilith of Jewish tradition preyed on newly-born children, and attacked men while they were asleep, seducing them then drinking their blood. Her ancestor in demonology, the *Lili* of Assyria, was believed to roam through the night hunting for mortal men.

In Western tradition these female demons were called *succubi*, and together with their male counterparts, the *incubi*, they assumed the forms of the husbands and wives of their intended partners.

The vampires of eastern Europe, night creatures who suck the blood from their victims, are in the same tradition of evil beings who use sexuality to lead human beings to their deaths.

According to another theory, demons, because they were

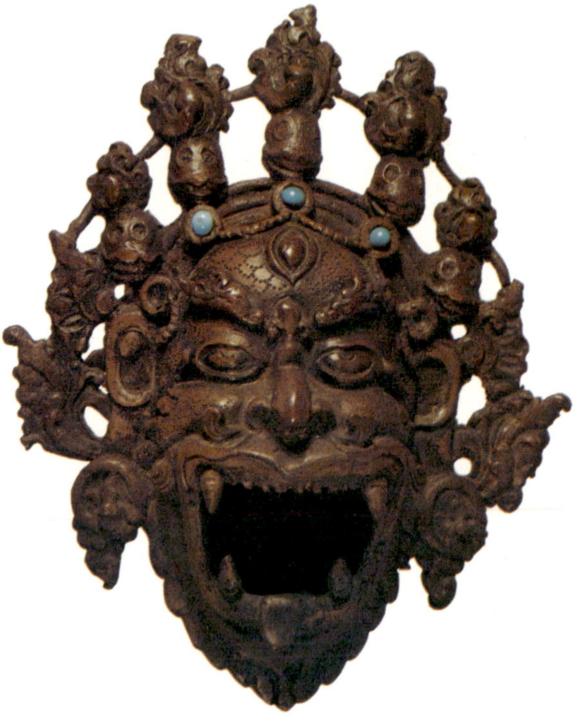
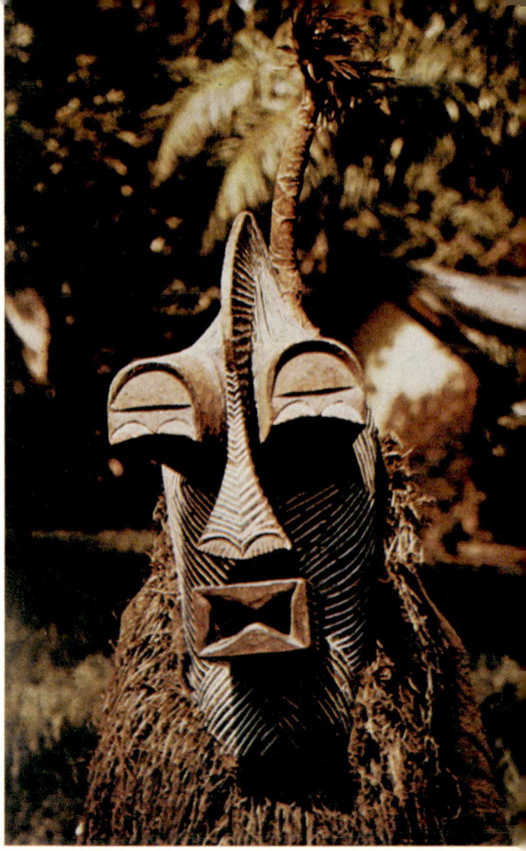
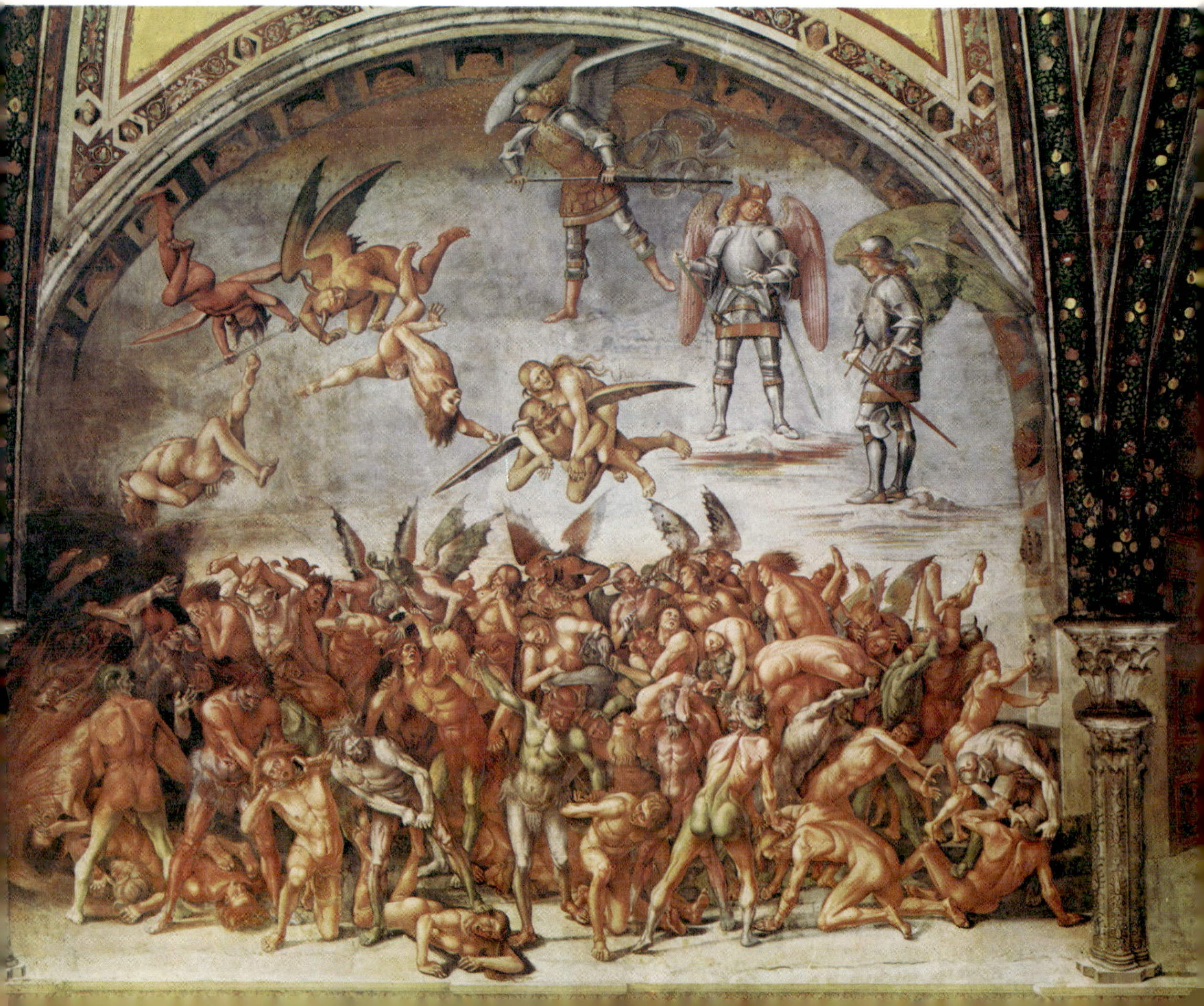

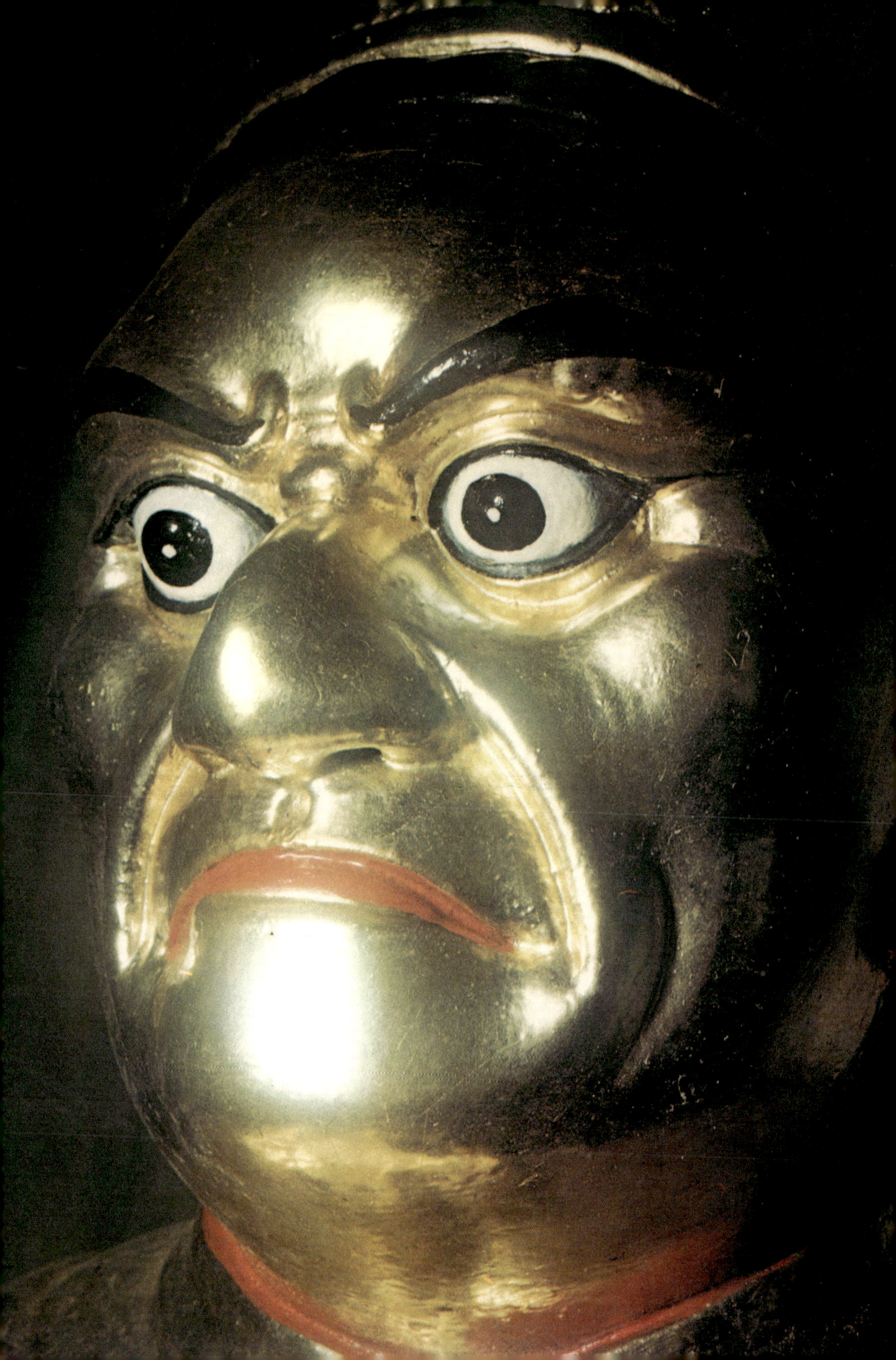

bodiless spirits, had to dress themselves in human form by entering into a corpse and re-animating it, or by creating for themselves a fleshly body and giving it life.

Death itself is haunted by demons and evil spirits. Japan, for instance, is the home of the *oni*, monstrous ghosts of the dead. In Malaya the *buso* have long bodies, feet and necks, curly hair, flat noses, two long pointed teeth, and one yellow or red eye. They live in the branches of graveyard trees, and dig up dead bodies, whose bones they eat.

According to a Zoroastrian belief which is still part of the tradition of the Parsees of India, a corpse fiend or spirit of contamination, the *nasu*, may take possession of dead bodies and spread its foul infection. Once it has entered a body the *nasu* can only be expelled by the glance of a dog. Another Indian demon, the *churel*, is the ghost of a woman who died in childbirth, or in a state of impurity. It has reversed feet, and no mouth.

Demons like these are man's imaginative response to the multiple threats of the world. Their 'religious' counterparts owe their existence to the belief that the power of good is constantly at war with evil.

The Hindu god Krishna, fount of all love, is said to have battled with demons in order to free the earth from oppressors. And Mohammedan tradition tells of two angels, Harut and Marut, who, impatient with the sinfulness of man, were sent by the Lord to live on earth. They eventually succumbed to the temptations that surrounded them and were banished from heaven. Remaining on earth, they taught man astrology and witchcraft.

This legend, in which witch-

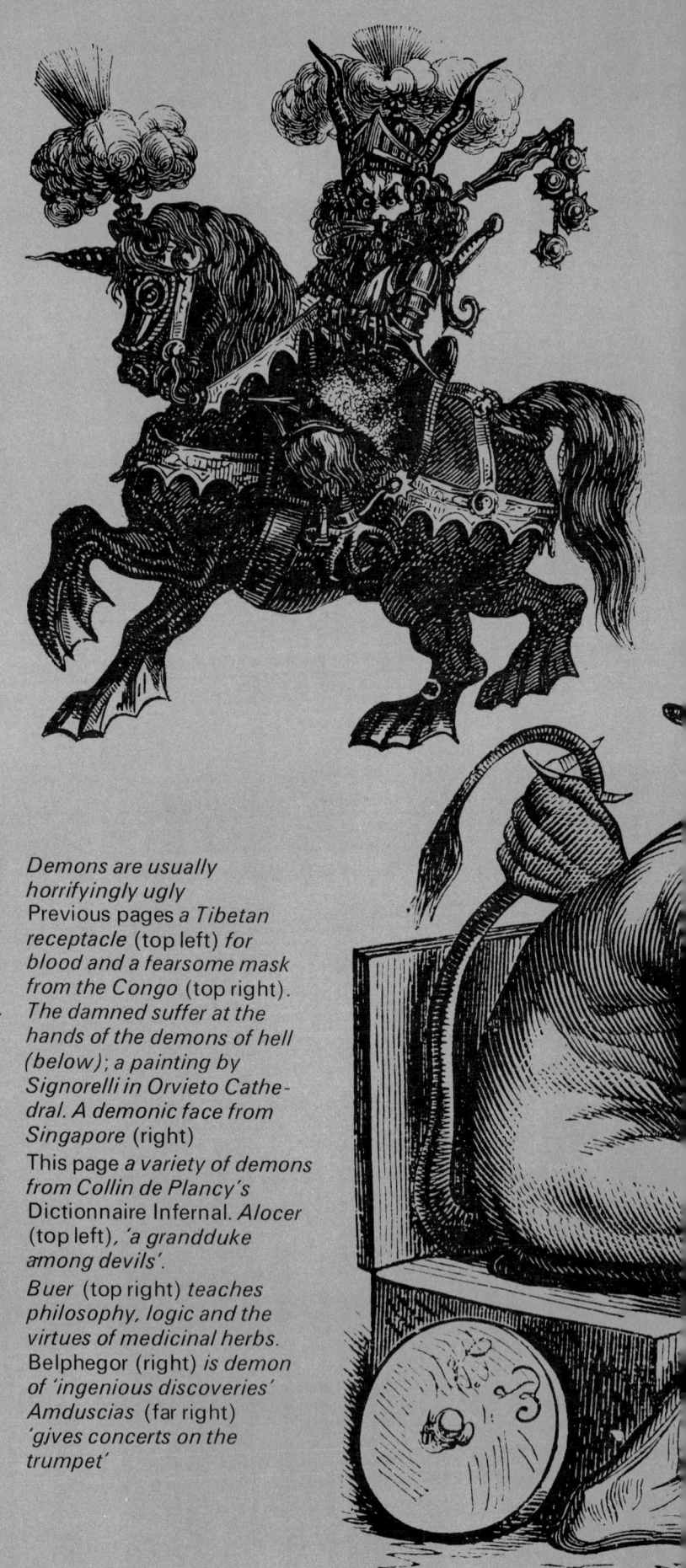

Demons are usually horrifyingly ugly
Previous pages *a Tibetan receptacle* (top left) *for blood and a fearsome mask from the Congo* (top right). *The damned suffer at the hands of the demons of hell* (below); *a painting by Signorelli in Orvieto Cathedral. A demonic face from Singapore* (right)
This page *a variety of demons from Collin de Plancy's* Dictionnaire Infernal. *Alocer* (top left), *'a grandduke among devils'.*
Buer (top right) *teaches philosophy, logic and the virtues of medicinal herbs.*
Belphegor (right) *is demon of 'ingenious discoveries'*
Amduscias (far right) *'gives concerts on the trumpet'*

53

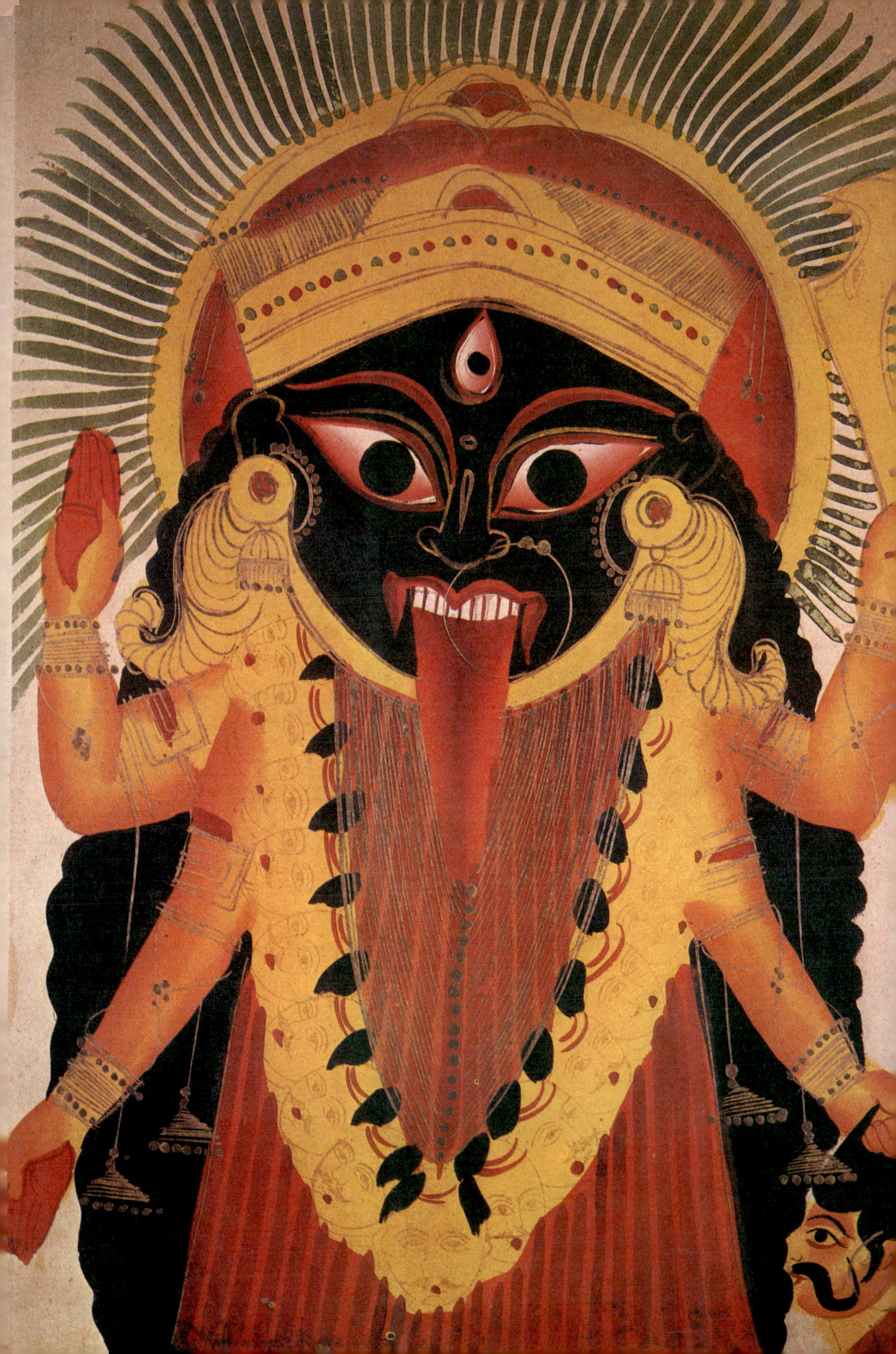

Left *a print of Kali, Hindu goddess of evil, who is shown with three eyes and four arms and wearing a*

Above *William Blake's watercolour,* Satan Arousing the Rebel Angels. *The Devil is supreme over all demons*

craft represents opposition to established religion, bears a striking resemblance to the Christian tradition. For Lucifer, the Christian angel who like his Mohammedan counterparts was expelled from heaven, became Satan or the Devil on earth, the master of the demons with which the Western magician is concerned. It is because these demons are the Devil's servants that Christianity considers them to be innately evil.

The study of demons was taken extremely seriously in past ages. It was solemnly calculated that at one time the number of demons abroad in the world was nearly seven and a half million. A 16th century demonologist allocated a demon to each of the seven deadly sins: Lucifer was concerned with pride, Mammon with avarice, and Asmodeus with lust. Satan was the devil associated with anger, Beelzebub with gluttony, and Leviathan with envy. Belphegor was the demon associated with sloth.

Another demonologist found that there were ten different kinds of devils: the Fates; poltergeists; incubi and succubi; marching hosts appearing as noisy and boisterous men; nightmare demons who emerge from the blackness of sleep; demons sprung from semen; spirits who masquerade sometimes as men, sometimes as women; those who appear only to holy men to tantalize them; and, finally, demons who deceive old women into believing that they fly to sabbats.

Hierarchies of demons were listed in the 17th century. The highest started with Beelzebub, 'next unto Lucifer'. Other powerful members of this hierarchy were Asmodeus the prince of wantons, Astaroth who tempts men to sloth and idleness, and Balberith who rules over blasphemy, quarrelling and murder.

Certain types of illness, especially what is now known to be mental illness, were said to be the result of possession by demons, and one authority listed the indications which show that a man or woman has been taken over by an evil spirit. Such a spirit would flee at the sign of the Cross, the name of Jesus or anything holy, and would blaspheme against the Catholic faith. It would exacerbate the emotions of anyone already disposed towards pride or arrogance, and would cause the person in whom it resided to

Magicians believed that every corner of the world was inhabited by a demon, and that each was assigned a specific area of activity
Left *a fearful gargoyle*
Right *Beelzebub, Lord of the Flies and Prince of Demons*

refuse to discuss his possession with a priest. The devil could be horrifying in appearance, or dejected. When it departed it would leave behind a fearful smell or noise. Grief and desolation, and mental disturbance, could result from the activities of one of these spirits.

The study of demonology was – and still is – vital to the practising magician, whose success depends on his ability to conjure up, and control, these supernaturally powerful beings. The *Lemegeton*, a 'grimoire' dating from the 16th century or possibly earlier, lists 72 demons and describes their appearance in detail – presumbably so that a magician could build up the necessary clear mental image of the spirit he was invoking.

Some demons were possessed of fearful potential. According to a 14th century astrologer, each of the beings who rules the points of the compass – north, south, east and west – commands 25 legions of spirits. McGregor Mathers, the 20th century occultist, believed that a magician could be destroyed unless he was protected by a magic circle when he summoned up one of the 'Lords of the Directions'.

Superficially, the organized and hierarchical demons and devils of Christianity bear little resemblance to the grotesque graveyard haunters of the Malayans, or to the flying heads of the Iroquois Indians. In fact, both kinds of evil spirit spring from men's similar subconscious

Good and Evil are two opposing forces, often shown in conflict Top *12th century representations of demons from a church in France* Above left *out of the body of Venu came two spirits, evil out of the left and good out of the right* Above right *a demonic face from Katmandu* Right *in Fuseli's* Nightmare *the sleeping girl is seduced by an incubus, a male demon*

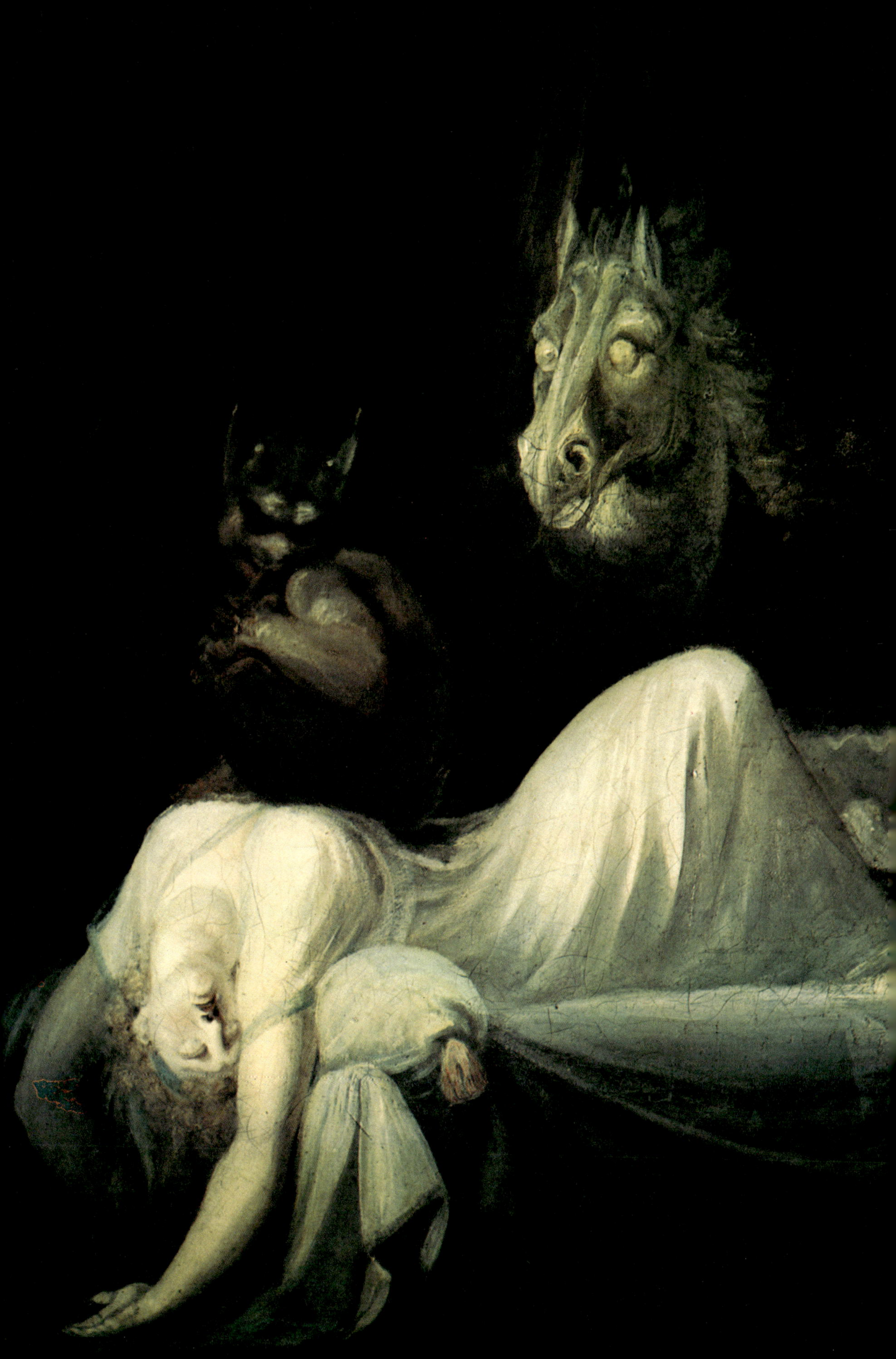

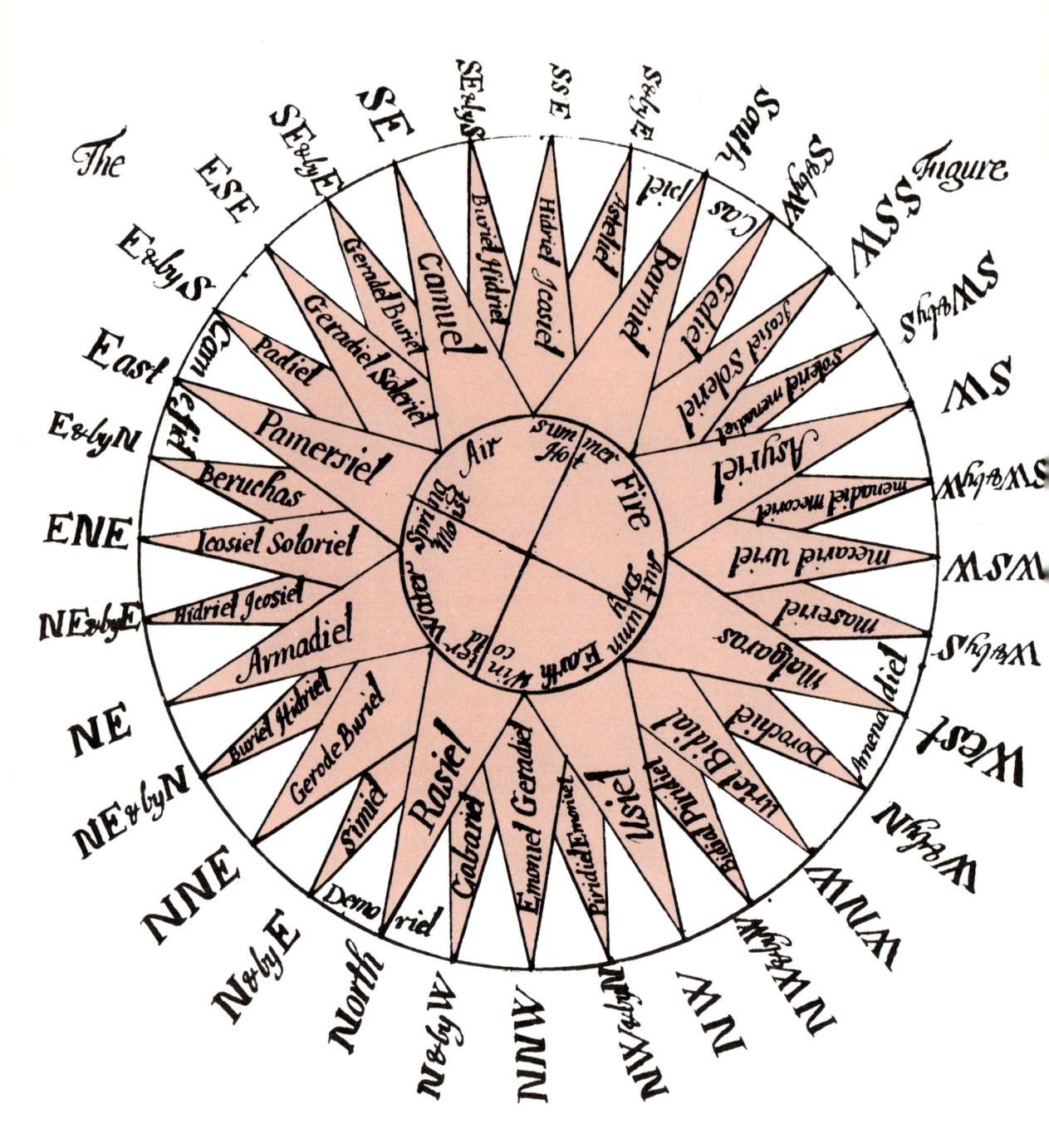

fears and terrors. The difference lies in the methods used to deal with these supernatural foes.

Primitive man concentrated on avoiding evil spirits where possible, and placating them if necessary. In Christian tradition, men classified and studied their occult enemies, believing that knowledge of the danger was their surest protection.

The magician, white or black, goes even further. He believes that an intimate knowledge of these beings, coupled with intense personal discipline, will enable him to control, and use, their magical powers.

Left *the names of demons are linked with the directions.* Above from top to bottom, left to right are: *the Incubus, Ophis, the Spirit Antichrist, Belial, Theutus, Asmodeus; demons of Western magical tradition*

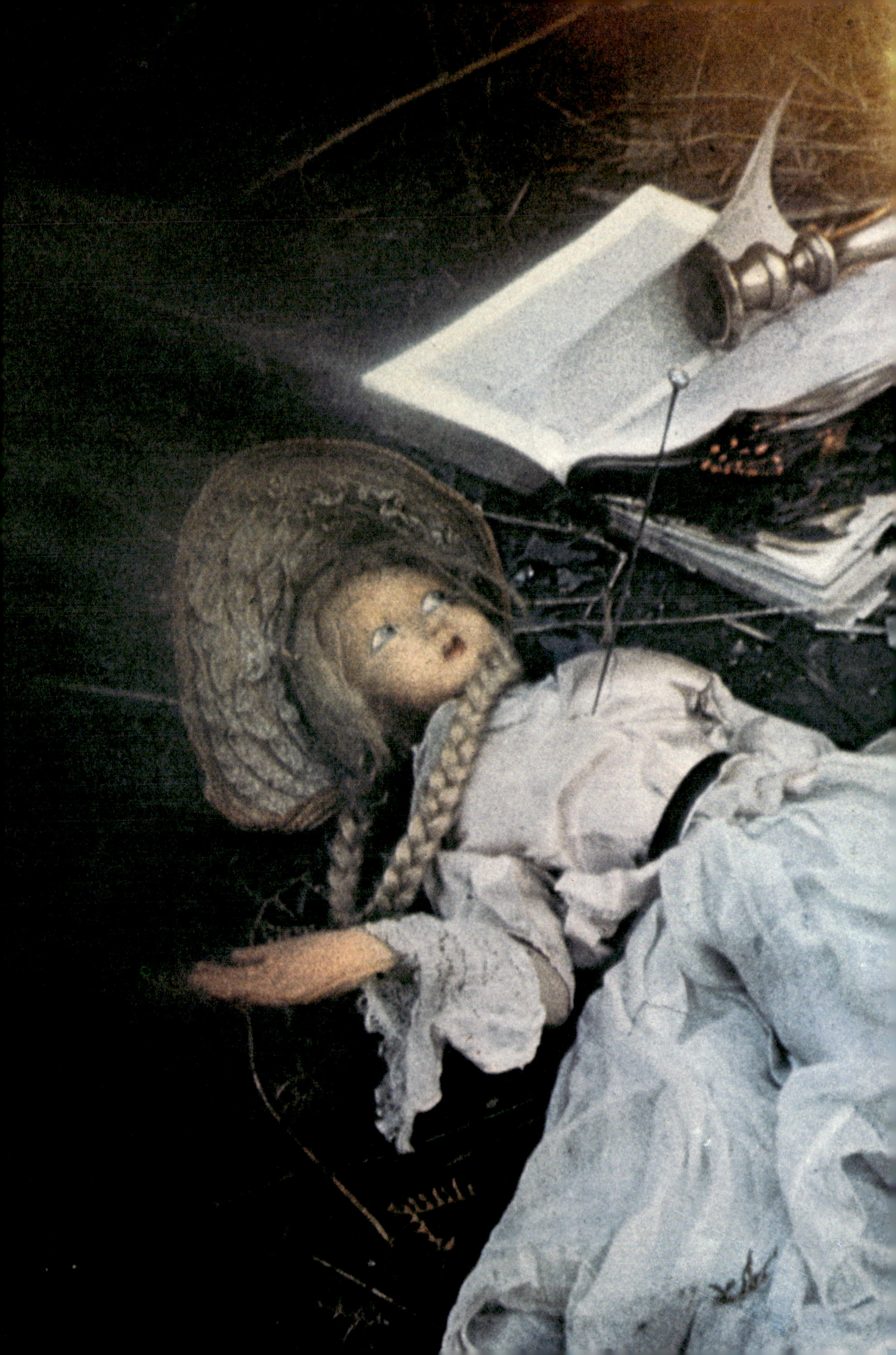

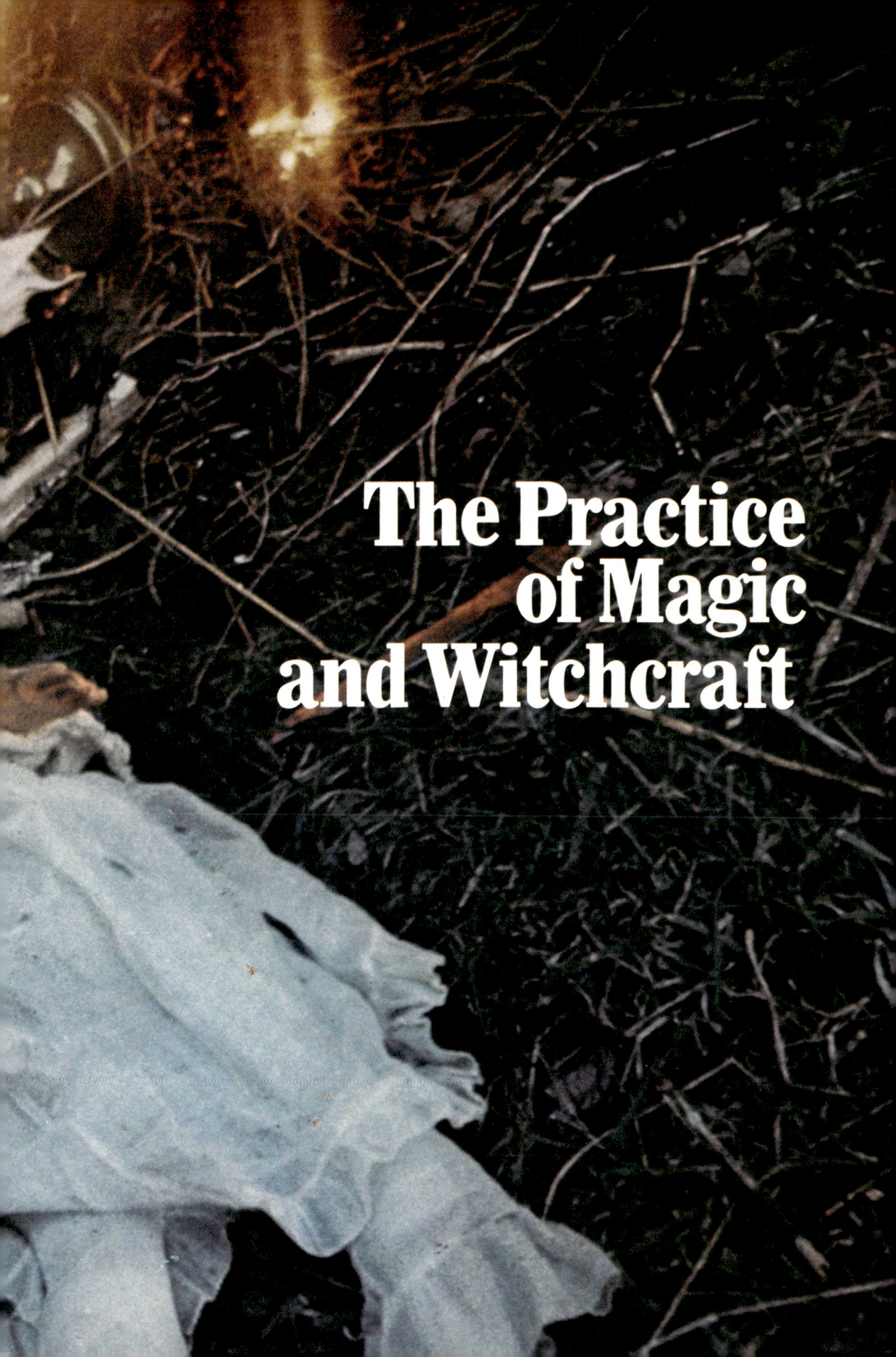

The Practice
of Magic
and Witchcraft

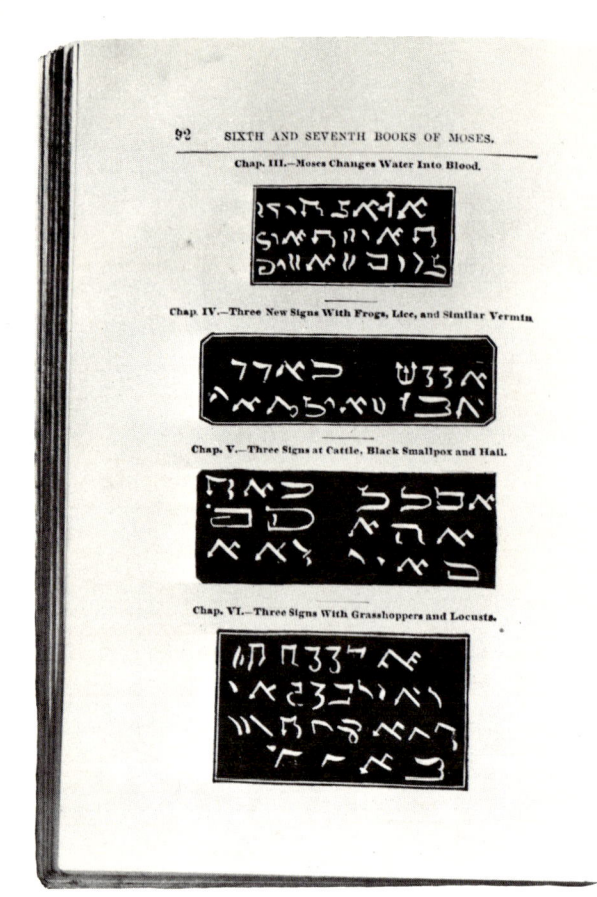

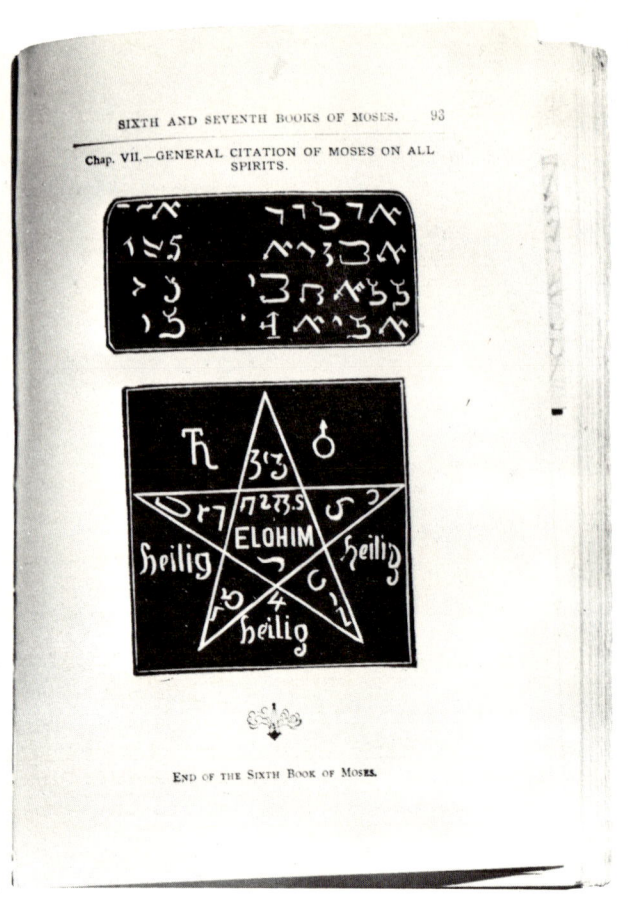

Previous page *injuring by proxy: a form of imitative magic* Above *words of power* Facing page *magical symbols* (above), *and religious daubing* (below) *in Katmandu* Below *the demon Behemoth*

The practice of magic has been defined as harnessing, or co-operating with, invisible powers, consciously using them to influence events on earth. And magic itself is described as a vast, planet-wide, timeless and invisible storehouse of knowledge.

To tap this knowledge, magic-workers all over the world make use of certain themes, types of behaviour and ways of preparing for magic. Words, colours, scents, herbs and numbers are among the most consistent elements.

Colours have significance in both folklore and magic. Red is associated with fire, blood, physical energy, anger and war. Indeed Mars, the planet of war, is described as the 'fiery' planet by astronomers. Green is the colour of growth, vegetation, the forces of life pushing through the earth into manifestation. The significances vary from culture to culture, but on inspection they often turn out to be not as different as they first seemed. As a simple example, black in Western cultures is usually the colour of mourning. But in China the colour is white. Two ways of looking at the same thing: black to Western man represents the body going into darkness; white to the Chinese

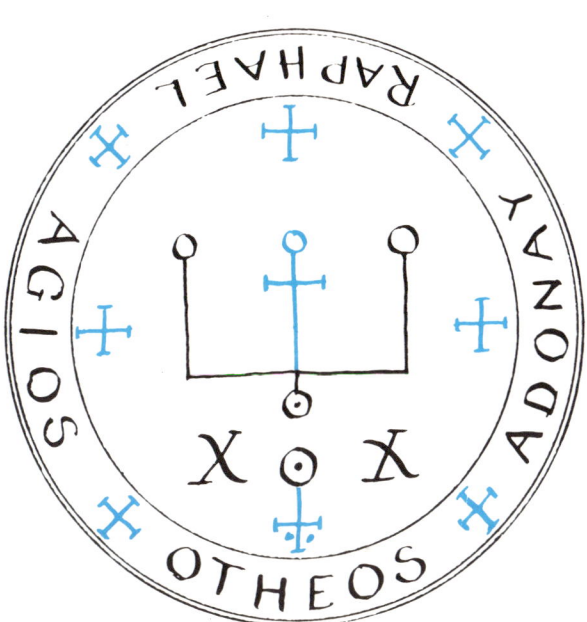

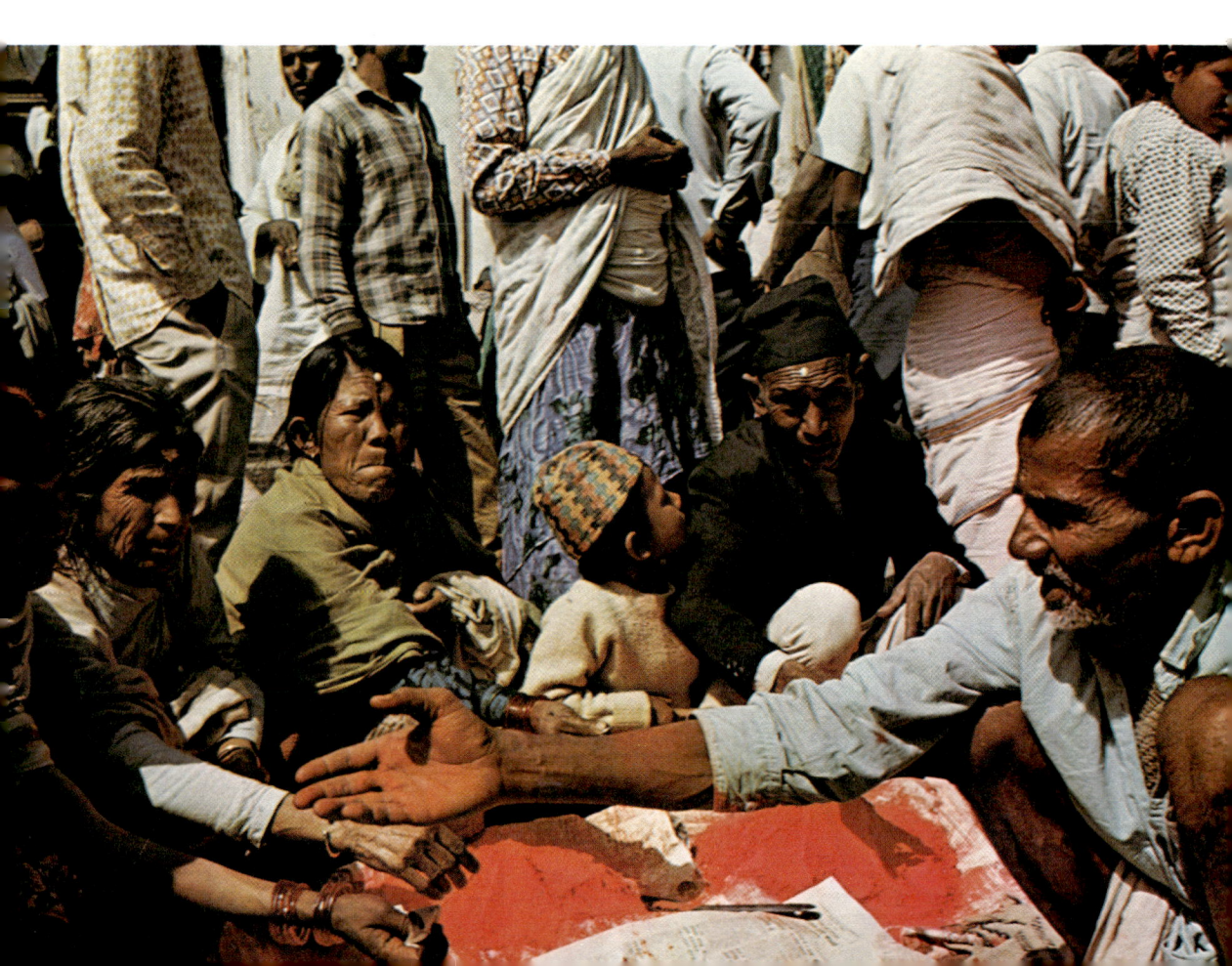

GABRIEL — RAPHAEL

Many different objects are used in magic-making. In some cases they are thought to be inherently powerful, in others the magician charges them with magical force Facing page *skeletons, snakes and a crucifix* (above) *are among the paraphernalia used by primitive witches* Below *decorated Easter eggs in Hungary; according to British tradition witches fly through the air or sail the seas in unbroken egg shells*

suggests the soul escaping into 'flight'.

Words and numbers also have great significance in magic. To 'name' something is to have power over it, and certain magics involve writing down the name of the person to be affected, and then treating the 'name' as if it were the person :- immersing it in water, perhaps, for drowning, or setting fire to it, with appropriate ceremonies, for a conflagration.

One of the most famous of magical names is ABRACADABRA. It has been used so widely in magic that it has passed into the stage magician's repertoire. Daniel Defoe, in his *Journal of the Plague Year*, written in 1722, tells how people tried to ward off the plague by its use.

The earliest instructions on how to use the word ABRACADABRA come from a poem on medicine written by a Roman doctor in the 3rd century AD. In order to ward off fevers, he said, the word had to be written down in an inverted triangle:

```
A B R A C A D A B R A
 A B R A C A D A B R
  A B R A C A D A B
   A B R A C A D A
    A B R A C A D
     A B R A C A
      A B R A C
       A B R A
        A B R
         A B
          A
```

The paper on which the word was written should be tied round the patient's neck, worn for nine days, and then thrown backwards over the shoulder into a stream running eastwards. As the word shrinks away to nothing, so will the fever.

'Words of power' – the names of gods and spirits – are similarly frequently used in European magic; by using the name of a supernatural being, his power is automatically tapped. But the name must be pronounced correctly, and declaimed or chanted in such a way that vibrations suitable for carrying the energy of the god or spirit are created. A magician would inscribe the names of God in the rim of a magic circle, to prevent the forces of evil from breaking into it. Indeed, so powerful is God that magicians used his biblical names and titles for their incantations.

All numbers have meanings and associations. 'One' is a holy and lucky number in many magical systems because the magician, as the religious person, knows that all things are essentially one, underlying and unifying all existence. One is said to be good, and two, the first number to break away from one, is traditionally the number of evil. In Christian numerology it is said to belong to the Devil.

Nine is considered to be the highest of all, the last and highest of the numbers before ten, which is essentially a repetition of one, but on a higher level. A human child is carried in its mother's womb for nine months, Troy was besieged for nine years before Ulysses started his wanderings (which also took nine years); the names of God number nine hundred and ninety nine (the thousandth cannot be uttered, presumably because this is the final initiation to the total and highest one). Like other numbers of completeness, notably three and seven, nine is particularly powerful in magic. A magic circle, in witchcraft, should be nine feet in diameter. Many spells involve nine operations, often in series of three.

Natural things, such as herbs and plants, also play a part in magic and have properties and associations which are important because they can be magically activated. Dill is an ingredient in many spells, and myrtle and rose may be burnt during magical rituals dedicated to Venus.

Other examples are salt and water. Both of these are symbols of life, and are used in ceremonies of initiation into witch covens. The red-and-white spotted mushroom, *ammonita muscaria* is traditionally associated with fairies – traditional (and modern) illustrations always show them sitting on this kind of mushroom and no other. It is said to be a hallucinogen (which is like a drug, that gives one hallucinations).

Much magic is also done by the use of amulets and talismans. The words are used interchangeably by some

Top *the magical reputation of* Ammonita muscaria *probably arises from its hallucinogenic properties: Mexican sculpture*
Above *mandrakes were used as amulets: faience mandrake fruits – Egyptian*
Right *corn is associated with life – Swedish figure*
Facing page *a high priestess wearing ritual robes*

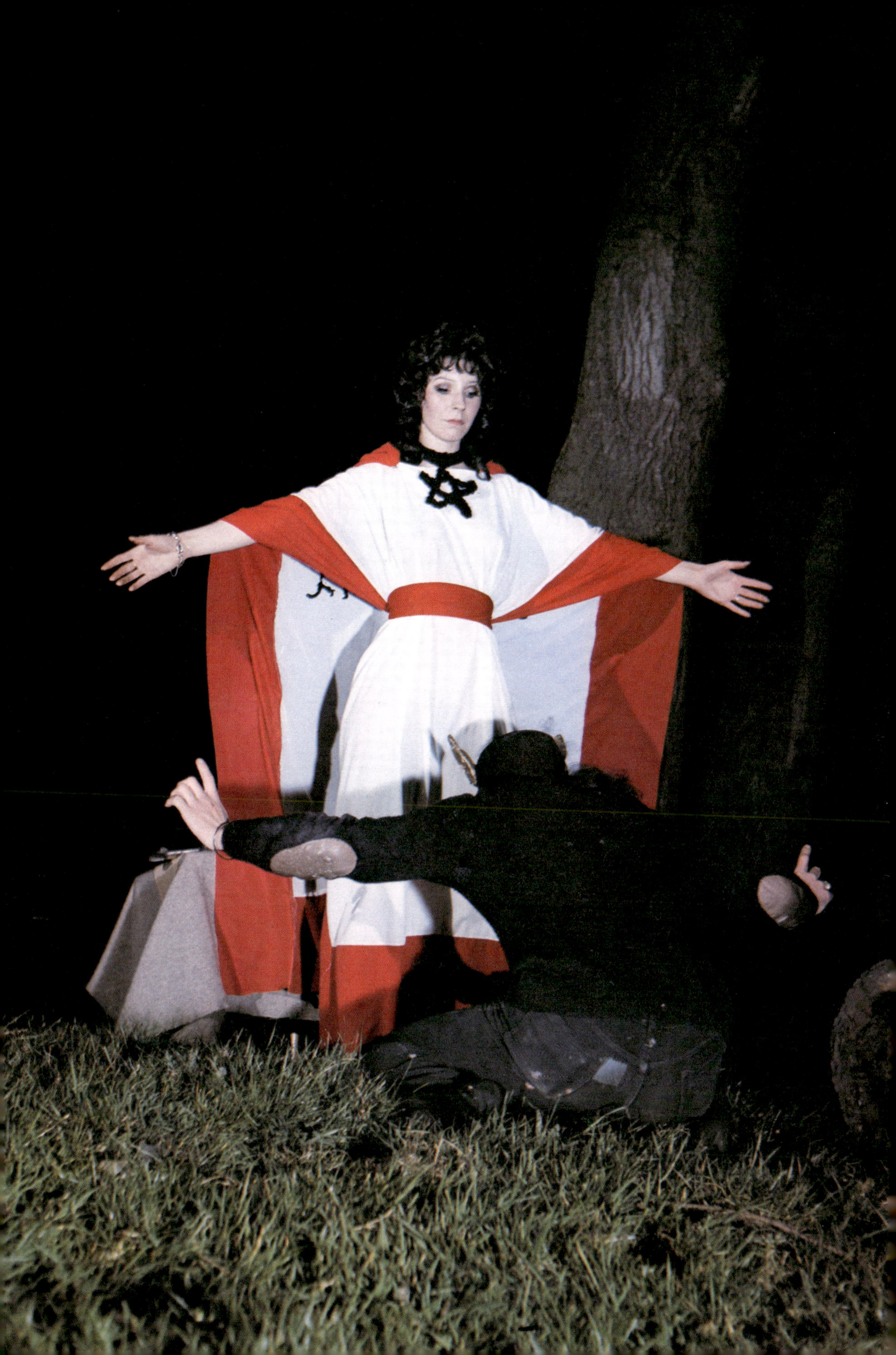

The red-and-white spotted mushroom is traditionally associated with fairies, who are shown sitting on a mushroom of this kind in old and modern illustrations: Puck and the fairies, illustration of a scene from A Midsummer Night's Dream

authorities. But it is usually accepted that an amulet tends to be a natural object whose innate power is used passively for protection. A talisman is more often a man-made object whose power is used actively to bring good forces into play on the wearer's behalf.

The mandrake root, which for centuries has been said to have powerful magical properties is an example of an amulet. It was heralded as an aphrodisiac, a narcotic, and an easer of pregnancies. Modern chemical research has to some extent confirmed this, for the roots have powerful sedative and stupefying effects. But for magicians even its physical appearance becomes part of its power. The roots are seen as representing male and female bodies, partly because of their forked shape. And so the mandrake came to be used as an amulet and was fastened to soldiers' shields or around the necks of babies to protect them from evil.

The ancient Chinese sometimes carried peach stones as amulets, while in India amulet necklaces are made from special berries. Another example of a natural amulet is the rabbit's foot charm; ten million of these are sold in the United States every year, as are four million four-leafed clovers.

Although a hand-made talisman may contain some element of natural magic, this is usually so only if the materials used in its making are already magically powerful. Otherwise the talisman is not innately magical, and must be *charged* with magic like a battery. The charging may be managed quite simply, as in the case of talismans that are decorative containers for scraps of paper that bear a powerful magic name or names. An example is the Jewish *mezuzah*, a protective talisman fastened at the door, which contains a small roll of parchment bearing a divine name or Talmudic text. The power of the divinity, or of the writings, charges the talisman with the power to protect the dwelling.

The variety of talismanic forms is immense and includes sophisticated and beautiful artifacts like the *ankh* of ancient Egypt, or that civilization's many representations of the sacred scarab beetle. Magic rings are often used as talismans, as are various inscribed pendants such as the superb carved jade pendants of the Maori, the *hei-tiki*. Less splendid to look at are the

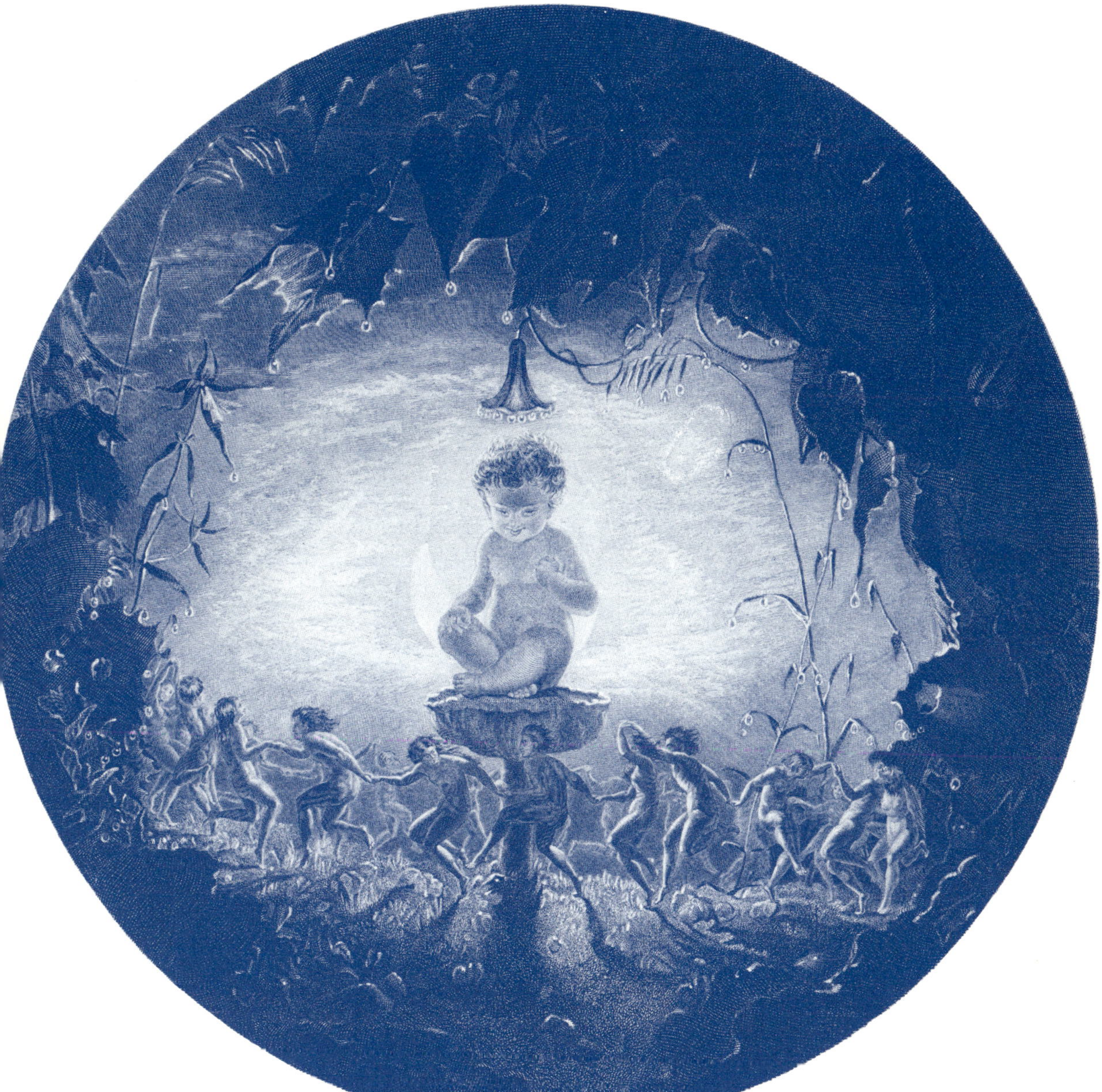

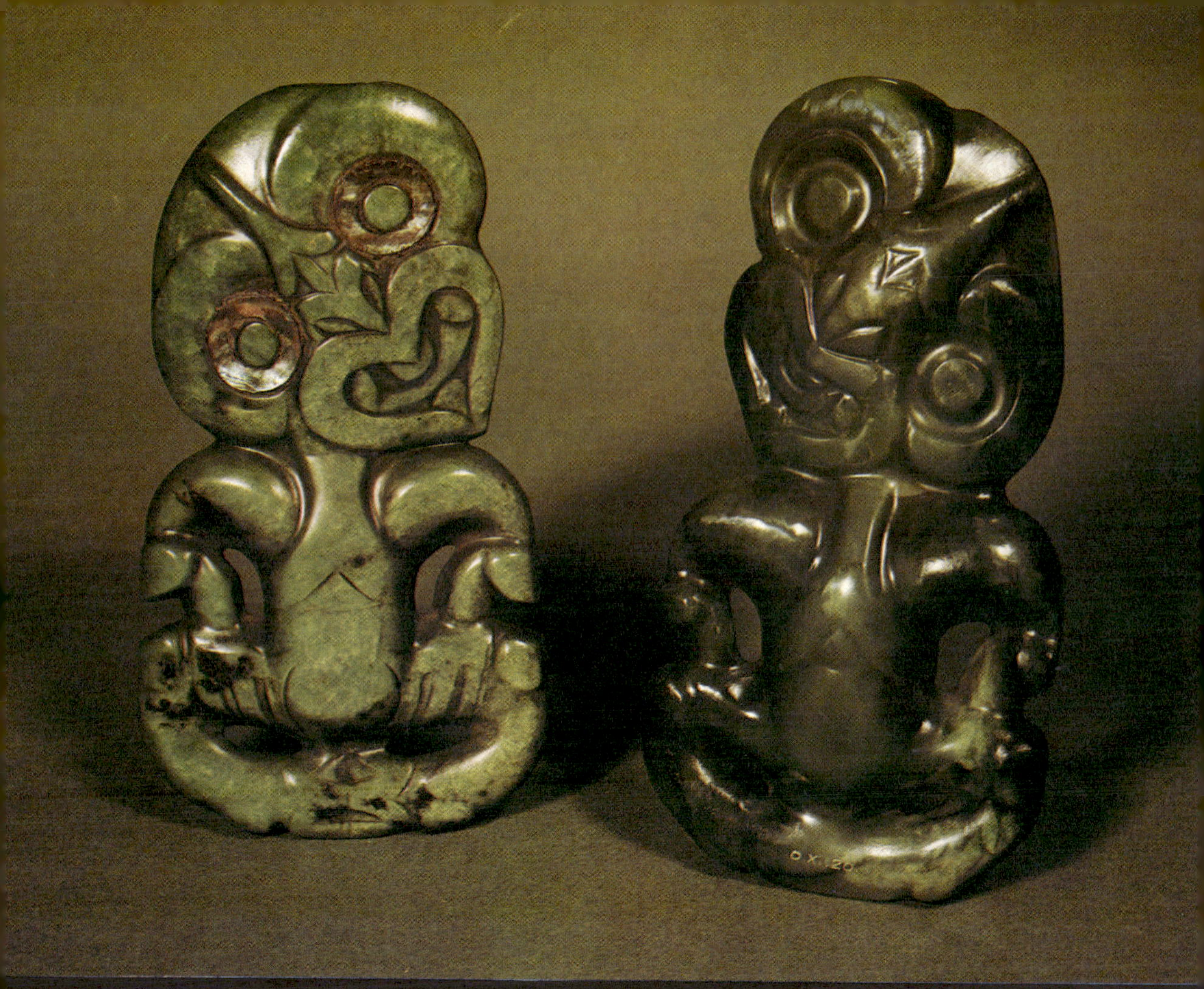

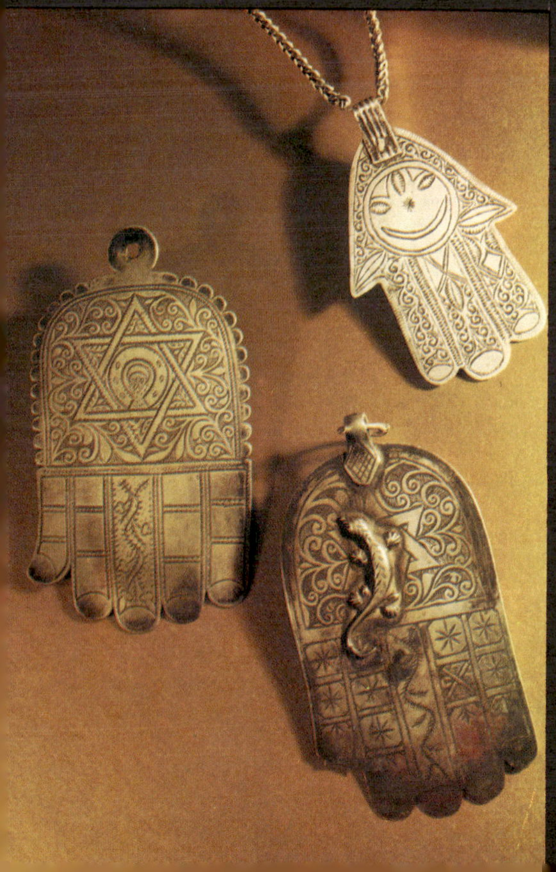

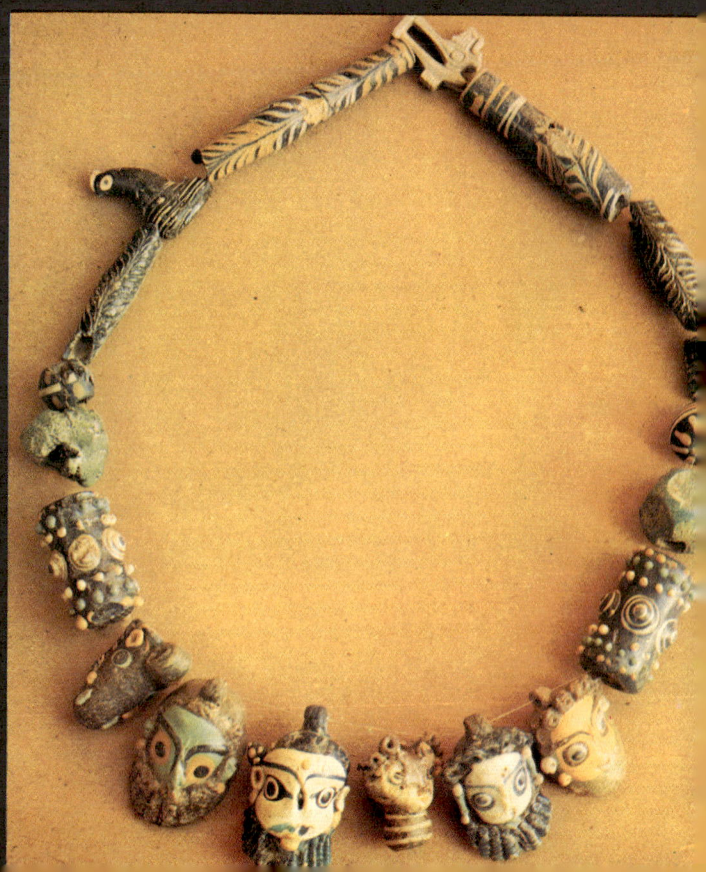

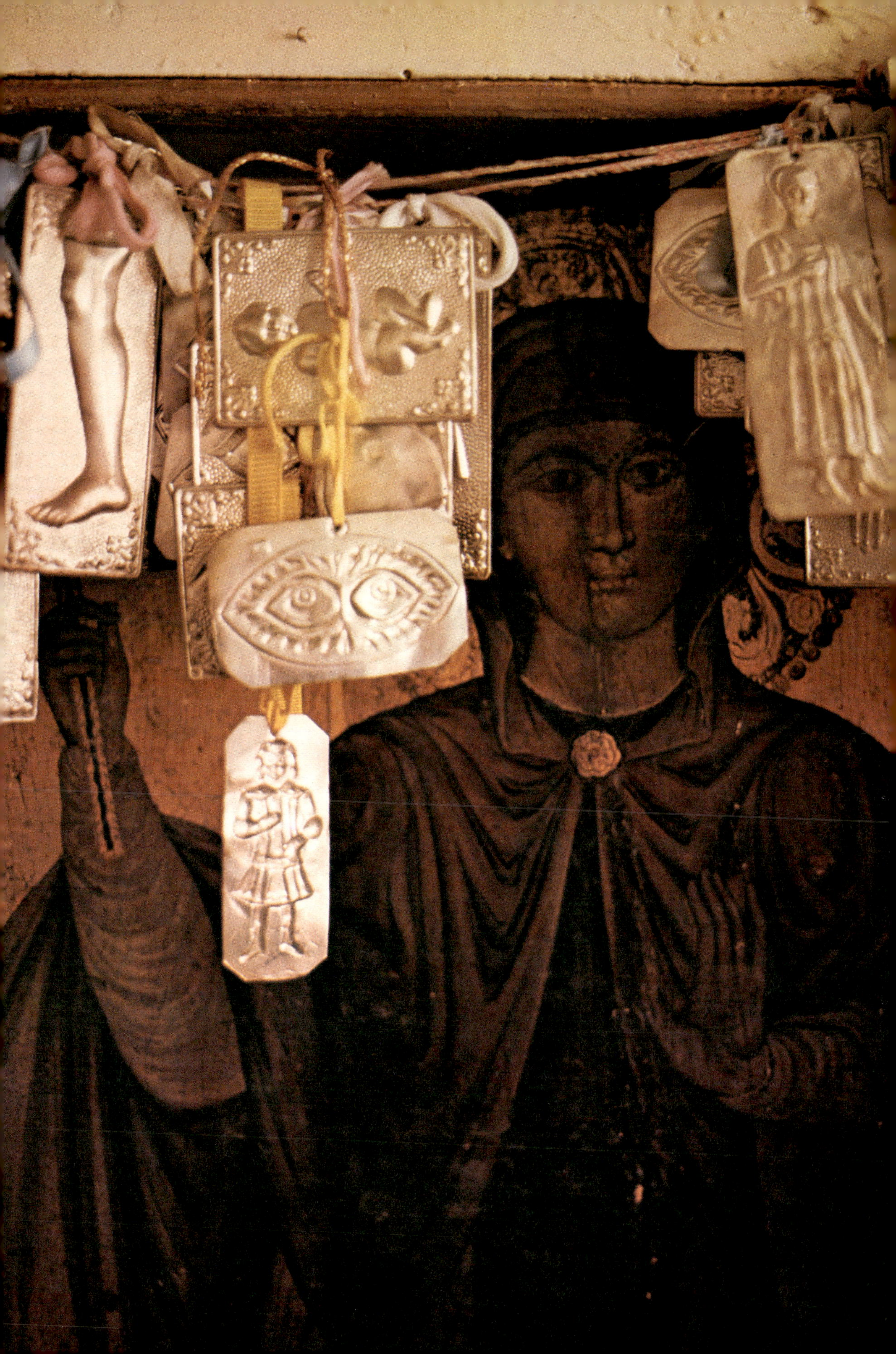

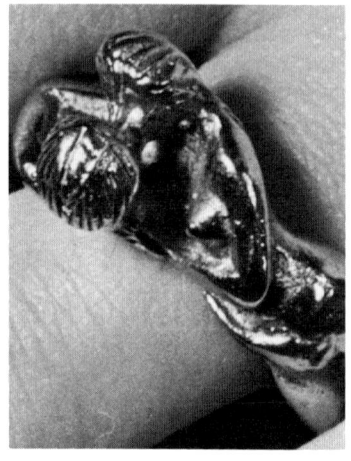

Previous pages *talismans are man-made objects charged with magical powers that attract good influences to the owner or wearer. Jade* hei-tikis *from New Zealand* (above left) *and* (below, far left) *North African 'hands of Fatima'. Necklace from a 4th century Sardinian tomb* (below centre); *the faces ward off evil spirits. Votive offerings* (right) *in a Cretan church*
Symbolic jewelry worn by modern Alexandrian witches: Top *high priestess's amber-and-jet necklace, and rose-ankh pendant* Above *witch's ring; two lovers in gold*

'conjure' magic bundles from America's deep south. Ringing the changes on magical traditions handed down from African slaves, the southern Negroes had an immense range of 'gris-gris' or 'voodoo' magic, which usually involved an assortment of curious materials tied together in a red cloth. Materials might include chicken feathers, bat's blood, ashes, bones, graveyard dirt, and pebbles. The bundles could be active and specific magics, to cure illness, wreak harm, induce love or whatever else was desired.

The magical charging process that activates talismans is exemplified in the ritual connected with a famous British talisman, the 'Lee Penny'. This is a medieval silver coin with a red stone set into it, which has belonged to a Scottish family since the 14th century. The coin was a healing talisman, and performed its magic when it was dipped into water and swirled round three times.

Jewels are credited with great magical powers. In some cases they may be used purely as amulets for protection: diamonds, for example, have been thought to repel poisons, witchcraft, madness and the terrors of the night. But diamonds, and other stones, have occult powers that are more than purely protective. A topaz, if taken in wine, was said to relieve asthma; worn on the left hand it could banish melancholy. Crystal, which was said to induce sleep and pleasant dreams, also had the power of producing visions; a belief that is perpetuated in the crystal balls used by clairvoyants and fortune-tellers.

The occult properties of jewels play an important part in ritual magic. Pearls, for example, are often worn during ceremonies invoking lunar forces because of their iridescent qualities.

Creating a Magical Atmosphere
In magic-making, the powers inherent in the various objects used by the magician would cause his mind powerfully to associate through them with the forces to which they were linked. In this way, he would penetrate into the world in which the forces operated. The associations, in fact, could 'spring' the mind from its rational cage.

David Conway, author of *Magic: an Occult Primer*, explains that a cosmic force is contacted by visualizing its traditional form and that '...... every object within range of the adept's senses has a symbolic connection with the idea behind the ceremony. This symbolism may not always be apparent, but you may be assured that having evolved over hundreds, nay thousands, of years, it is already well known to those deeper levels of your mind that are in communion with the collective unconscious... Form, sound, colour, and movement, all are pressed into the service of magic, as also is incense – which through the sense of smell can appeal to whatever part of the subconscious that it is wished to arouse.'

Music and dance are also important to magic-making. Notes are said to have certain 'vibrations' which reach out into the invisible world and alert the forces with which they are associated, and the belief in the supernatural power of the chant, or rather, in the power of a certain intonation while chanting, is deep, ancient and widespread. Its eerie effect can be heard even today in the religious chant of monks, and it is not dissimilar to the sound made by snake-charmers in North Africa, or by Black Forest herdsmen who murmur an ancient chant into the ears of their animals when they lead them to market.

All over the world there are cries which 'heat' soldiers going into battle, and others which banish demons, or shatter objects. It has been said that the chant derives its virtue not only from the images or ideas in the words, but also from the physical and psychological effects of tones and rhythms.

A rhythmic three-stepped dance is often described in documents on witchcraft; and the whirling dance performed by witches who, hand-in-hand, move ever more swiftly in a circle during their rituals, is an integral part of their ceremonial. They believe that the dance enables them to draw down to themselves a fount of occult power. Traditional movements of arms, head and fingers are used as magical gesture: cursing may involve the first and fourth finger being pointed at the victim; a pointed forefinger or a forefinger along the staff of the magic wand, disperses demons.

Positioning the arms to form a cross with the body, descriptive of suffering and death, is found not only in Christian symbology. It is in the Egyptian tradition too, usually associated with the god Osiris.

Following pages *music and dancing are important ingredients in magic-making. Occultists believe that notes have vibrations which reach out into the invisible world to alert the forces which the magician wishes to contact. Dancing is also widely regarded as a means of reaching out to the unknown* (left above) *an Australian aborigine sounds the didgeridoo* (left below) *the horn dance of Abbots Bromley, Staffordshire, is thought to have its origins in the ritual dances of Stone Age man* (above centre) *a festive dance performed by North American Indians; dancing in a circle is a potent magical exercise* (right) *Indian folk dancers* (below right) *the whirling dance of the Mevlevi dervishes; moving swiftly in a circle draws down occult power*

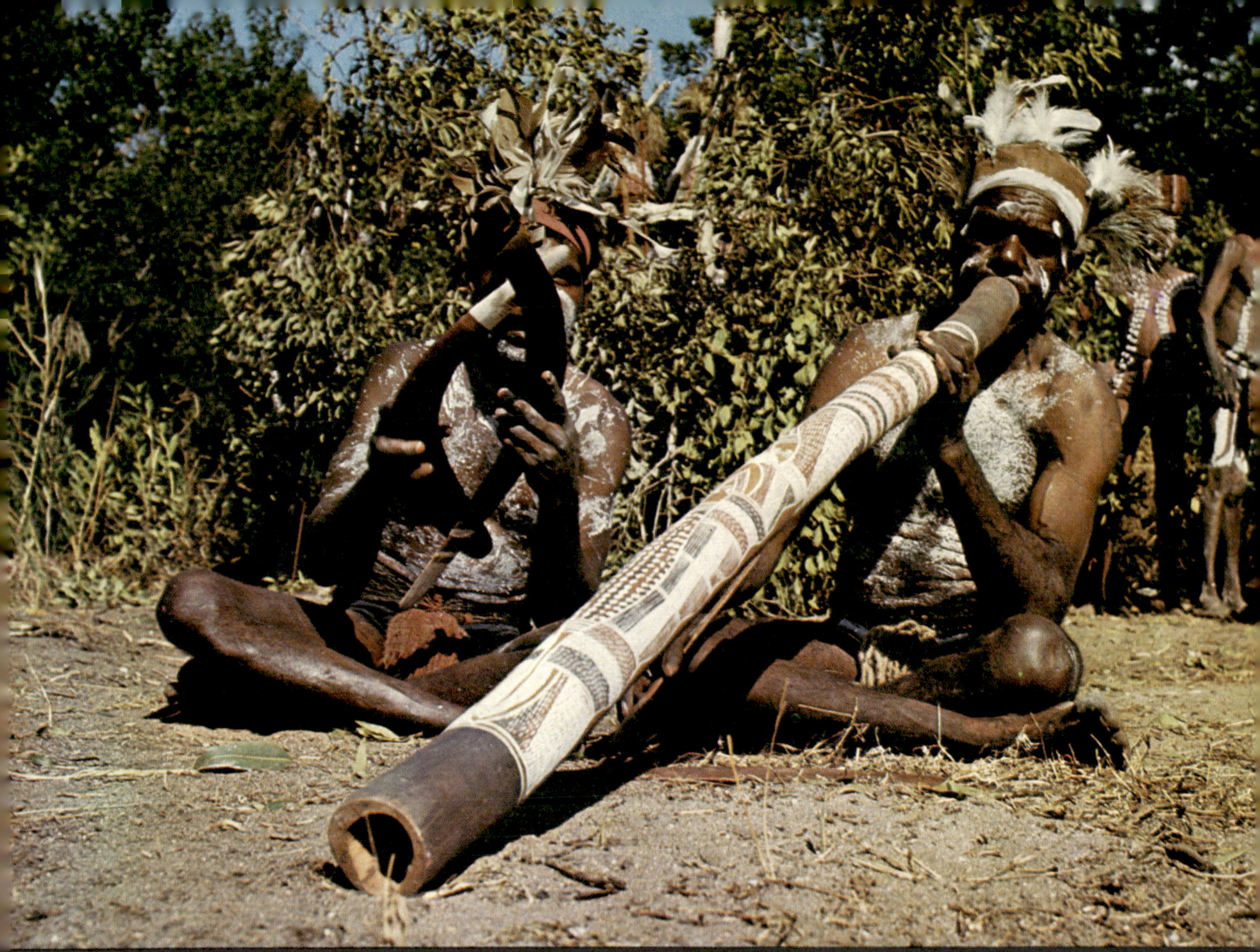

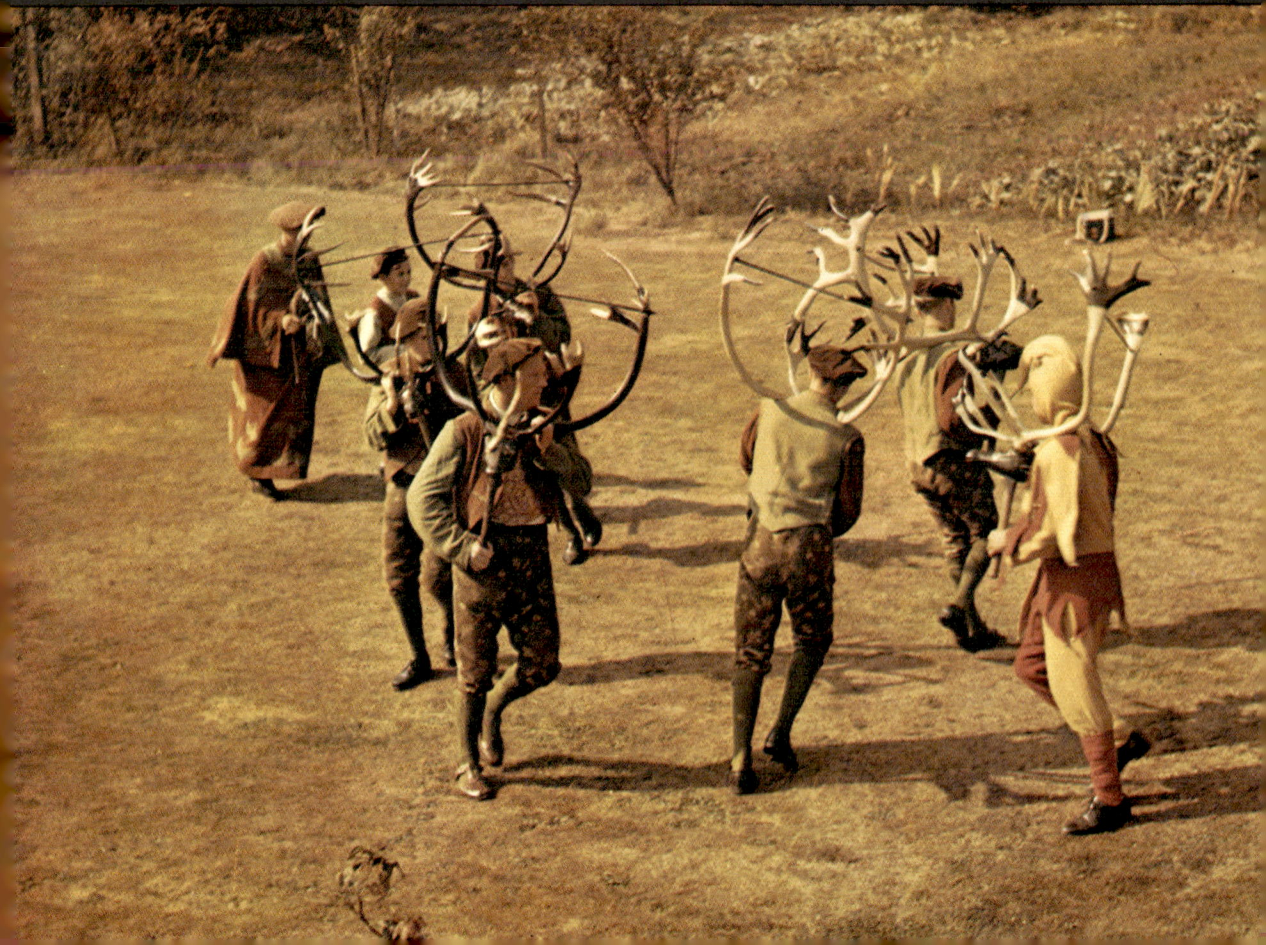

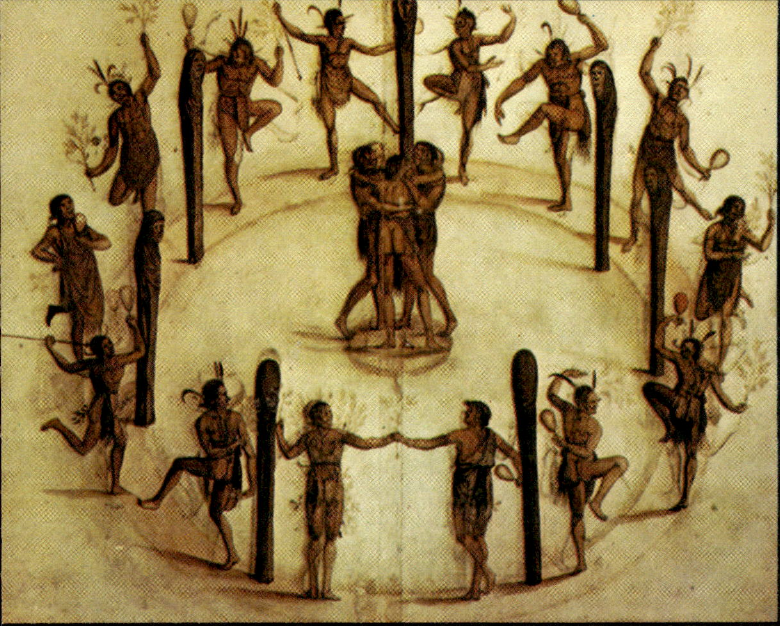
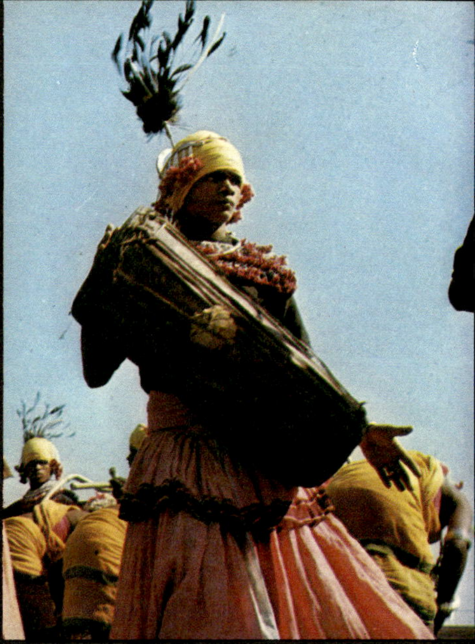
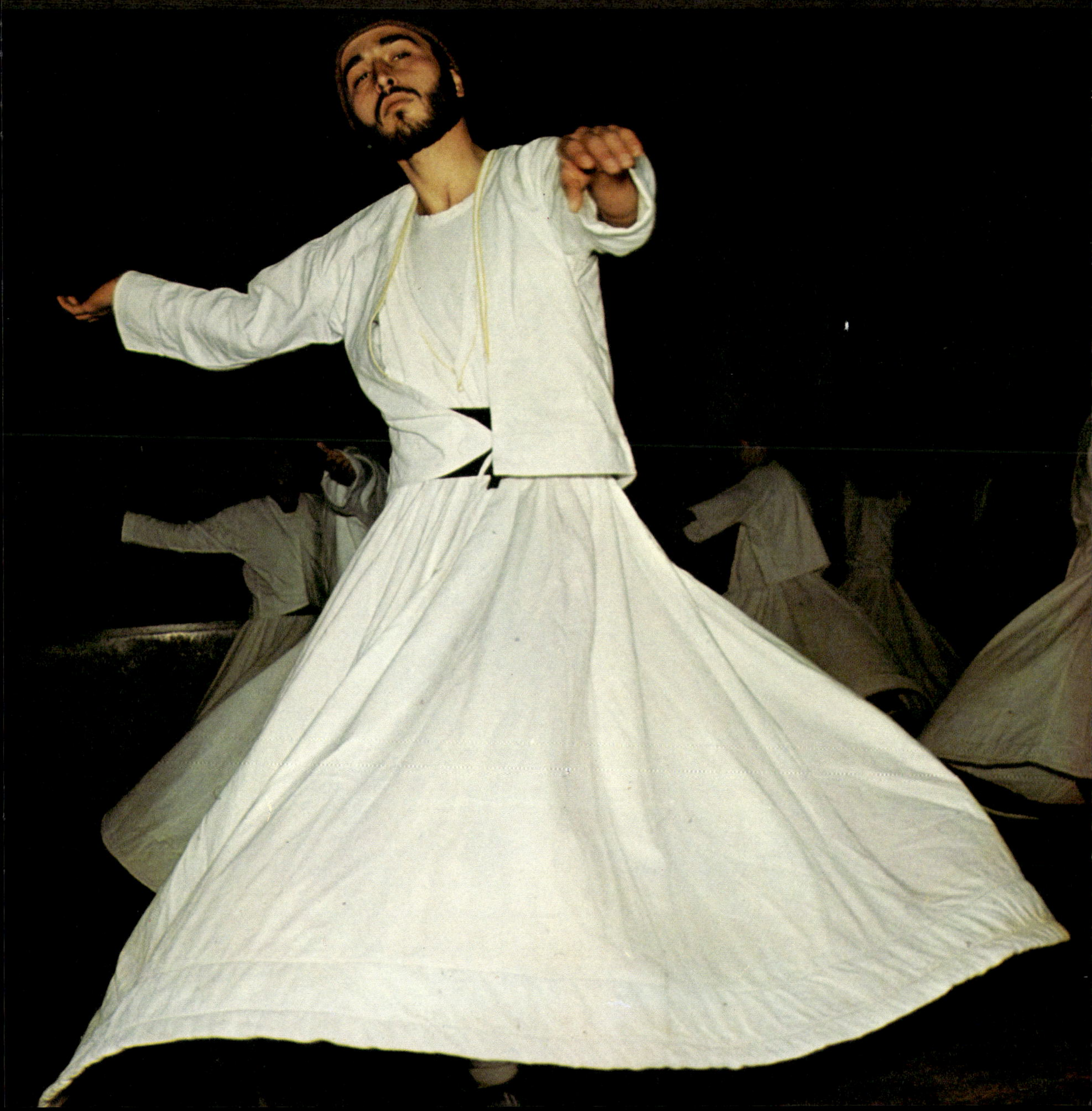

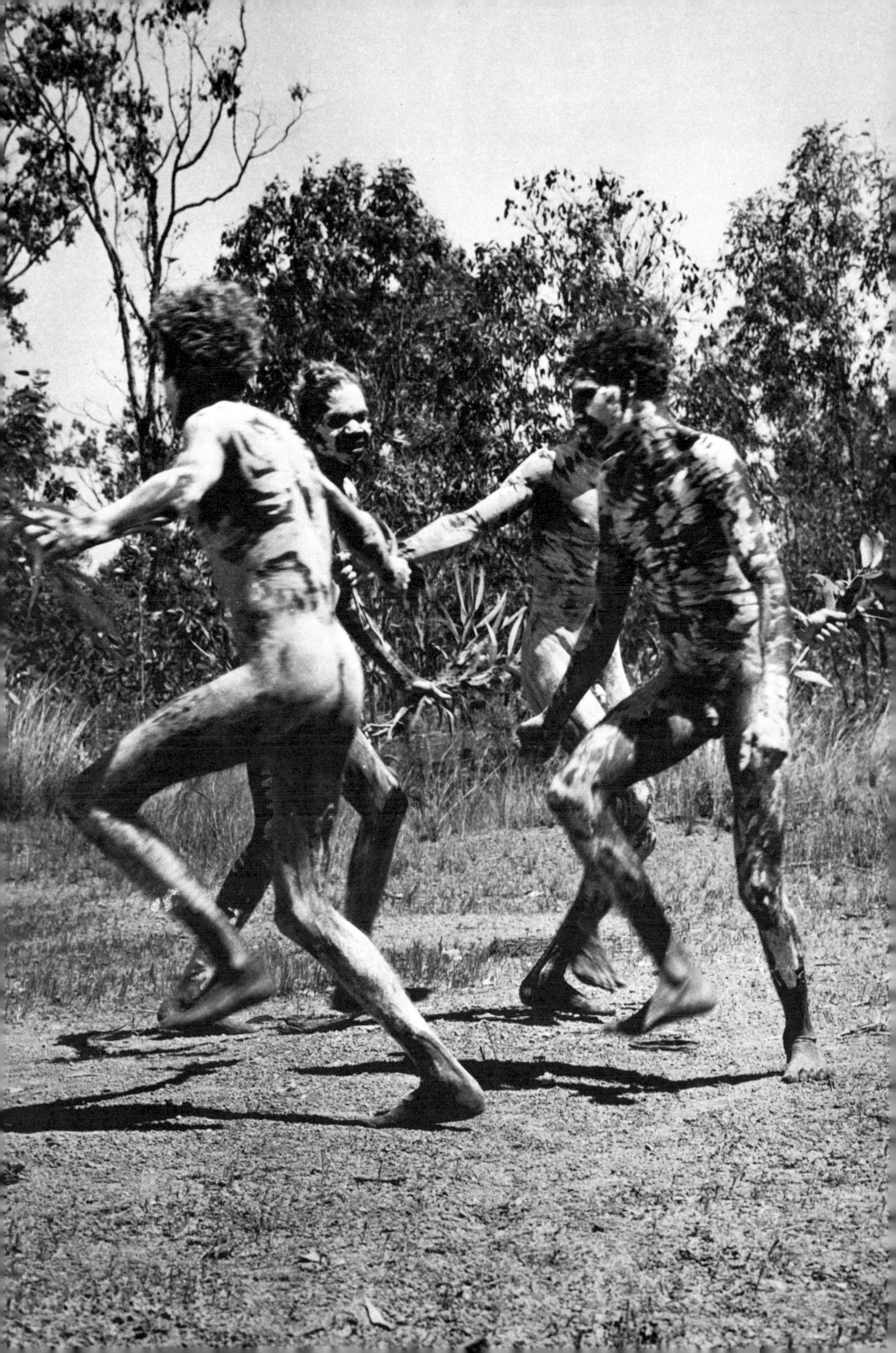

Stones and cave-paintings from Neolithic times reveal a range of magical gestures. There is, for example, in Brittany, an ancient monumental stone. One of its carvings shows a god with upstretched arms supporting a goddess whose arms are crossed and whose hands are held up in a gesture which has been described, by at least one anthropologist, as 'the union of true hearts'. At the top is a pre-Christian figure, its arms extended on an equal-armed cross.

Many of Egypt's pyramids and tomb paintings show these magical gestures, and postures of ritual significance. So do familiar dances around the world. The ritual dances of India, in which the palm is the calm centre of the individual and the fingers the five senses in action round it are an example. The upraised hand of the Buddha has been said to symbolize the centre of the universe in the palm, and the pillars of the extremities of the world in the upraised fingers. These are also the extremities of man's individual universe – the five senses.

Sexuality is another element in magic-making; in a ritual context, the energy involved can be directed to a 'magical' level, and the normal connotation of sexuality, although often evidently there, no longer

Ritual dances may be based on the movements of birds or animals Left *Aborigines perform a 'corroboree' based on the movements of the Australian crane; their faces and bodies are painted with white ochre. The crane, a harbinger of spring, was associated with warmth and fertility; its elaborate courtship dance was thought to be a form of magical ceremonial, and was imitated in many parts of the world*
Above *an African religious leader plays the* mbira, *which can be seen inside the gourd*

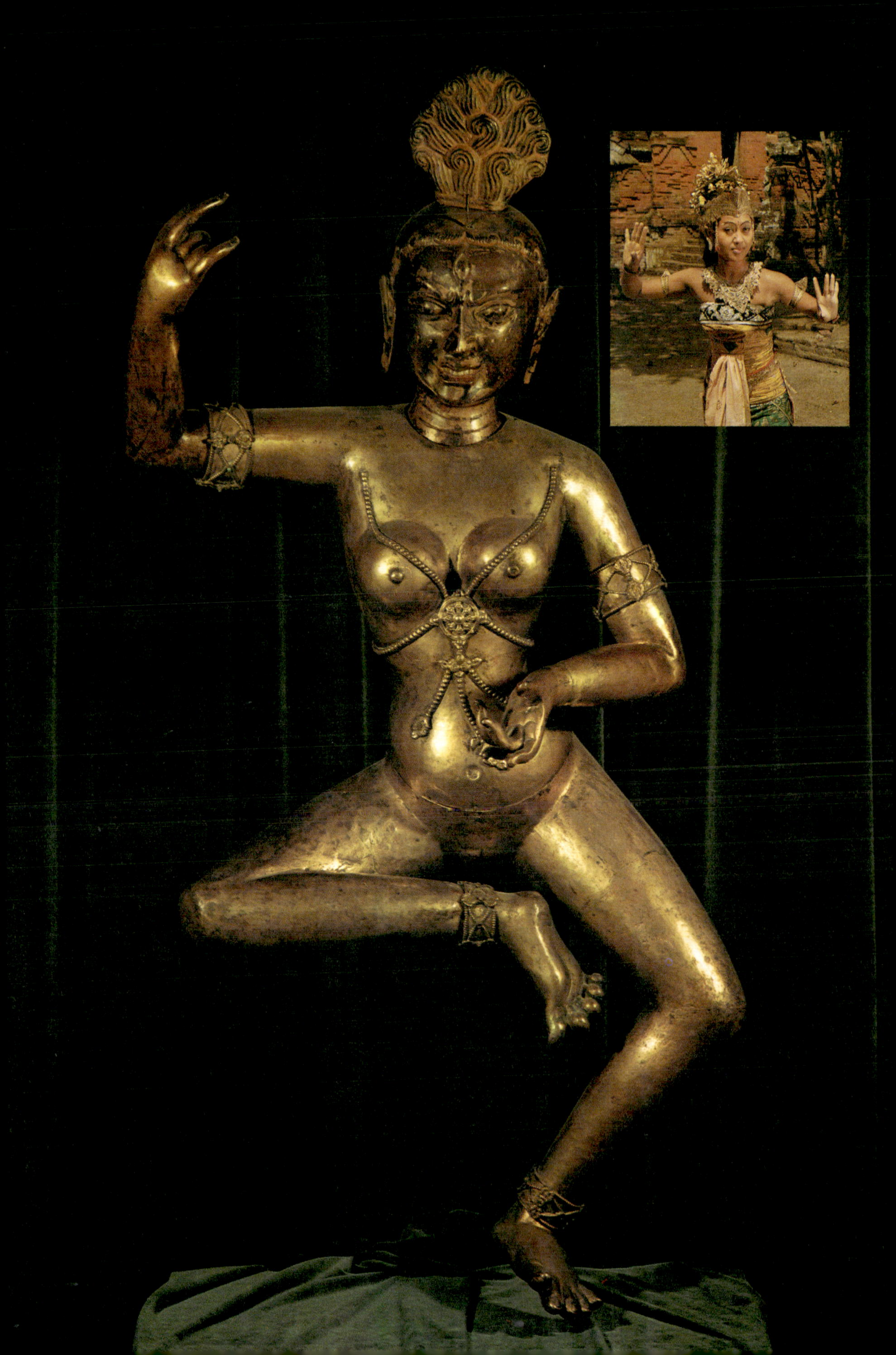

applies. The use of this energy has given rise to the many stories of orgies and sexual caperings in magical ceremonies. The rumour was reinforced, of course, by many groups who preferred the sexual element in magical activities for its own sake. Even in the 20th century, Aleister Crowley used up and discarded one woman after another in his attempts to use their sexual energies to 'fire' him into the state he wished to attain.

Magical Processes
These, then, are some of the basic elements assembled in magical operations. When combined correctly they will focus the forces from whom advice may be sought; or the powers of these forces may be drawn directly through the magician's body. The spells he uses are combinations of symbols, colours, and 'steps' in the procedure. They are written down like recipes in ancient magical textbooks – grimoires – which are, in fact, very like recipe books. They describe the ingredients to be used, and the method. Like recipes, they are boring nonsense to anyone who is not a cook.

It could be said, with a fair amount of accuracy, that the magician does indeed 'cook up' his magic. As the scientist may apply heat to chemicals in order to change their characteristics, make them separate out, or fuse, so the magician combines his ingredients, using a 'subjective' method of heating with himself as the crucible. Indeed, the Elema tribe of eastern New Guinea actually use a word meaning heat to describe the 'fire' of the magician.

Similarly, among the Mailu, also of New Guinea, the sorcerer chews pepper leaves or wild ginger root in order to acquire 'heat' or 'power'.

Once the operation is begun, the processes of magic involve certain physical manifestations which are more or less the same all over the world, whether in a Western living-room set aside for magic, a Haitian temple, a witches' coven, or a shaman's cave. They often include possession, hysteria, ecstasy, and trance. The best-known descriptions of possession come from voodoo in Haiti, and modern anthropologists have told clearly of the ceremonies in which, even today, the gods of the island possess and 'ride' their worshippers.

But whether possession takes place during a voodoo

Magically effective gestures are known throughout the world, and many ritual dances emphasize their importance Left *statue of an oriental dancing divinity, and Balinese dancer* (inset). *In India the palm of the hand symbolizes the calm centre of the individual and the fingers are the five senses*

Invoking spirits results in physical manifestations that include possession, hysteria, ecstasy and trance. In Voodoo, a religion in which worshippers gather together to call down the gods, the ceremony starts with members of the congregation dancing on a floor marked with magical symbols

ceremony or elsewhere, the phenomenon is very much the same. The god in voodoo, or the invoked entity in magic, 'takes over' the worshipper. Sometimes, while the spirit is gaining 'entry', the possessed person will thrash about wildly; he may stagger, roll his eyes, and lose his balance. When the initial crisis is over – and the entry may take anything from a few moments to a much longer period depending on how experienced the invoker is – the personality of the entity or god becomes apparent in the host body. The person who invoked the force may change his voice, his accent, his posture, his temperament. The possession may last for minutes or hours – and it is during this period that any magical operation will be done.

The process is similar among primitive communities like the Azande of Africa. There the singing and dancing of the witchdoctors produce hysteria both in themselves and their audience, and they behave very much as if they are possessed, performing tremendous physical feats, uttering strange cries, and becoming subject to hallucinations.

It has been suggested that Western man is also subject to possession by demons and other forces; and that nymphomania may be a form of possession.

The state of trance in which the magician falls unconscious, is another result of contacting unseen forces. It is thought to be a process roughly similar to possession, but the activity is 'inside', and not acted out.

Magicians of the Past

One of the most eminent of all the magicians of the past is Paracelsus. A Swiss alchemist and physician who lived in the first half of the 16th century, Paracelsus is credited with having performed many astonishing and miraculous cures. He always insisted that these cures were not entirely due to his medicines, believing that the health of the body was linked to the well-being of the soul housed in it. He also believed that man was inseparable from the line of the universe. Paracelsus is often described as the father of modern medicine. His death is commemorated on September 24, and healing operations which invoke his assistance are performed on that day.

Another of the famous magician-figures of the West was Cornelius Agrippa, who died in 1535. His contemporaries regarded him as being undisciplined, unstable and erratically brilliant; the fate of many magicians who do not always know how to conceal

Voodoo Dancers strive to attain a semi-conscious state in which the gods will speak to them, or take them over. A possessed person may thrash wildly about, stagger, and lose his balance while the god is gaining entry. This also happens in European magic when someone is taken over by a spirit

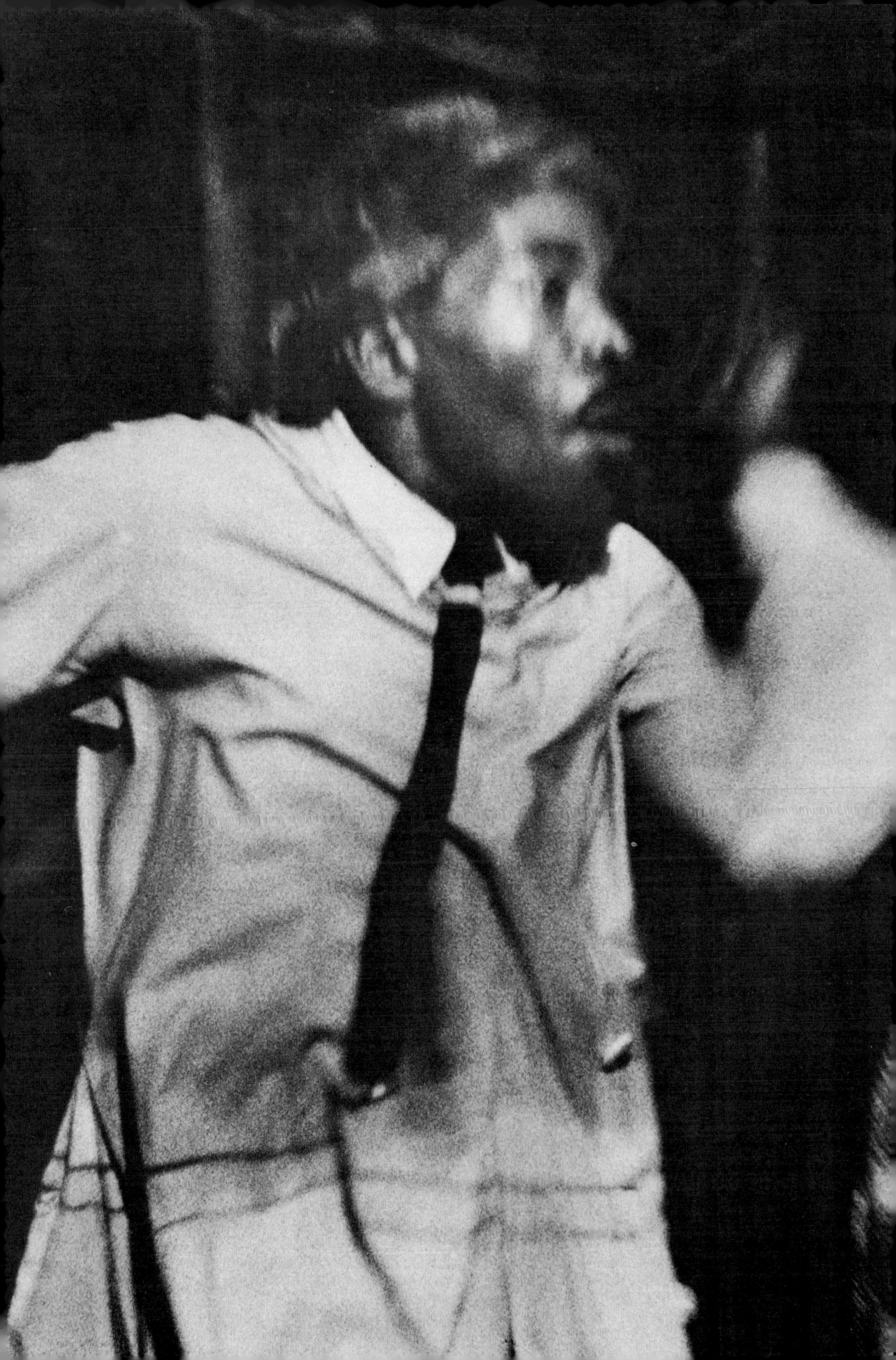

their behaviour or scale it down to conform with local conventions. Agrippa lived by his wits. At different times in his life he was occult scholar, alchemist, faith healer, demonologist, court astrologer, theologian, lawyer, historian, financial adviser, doctor, town orator, and secret political agent. He mixed with royalty and was imprisoned for debt; worked both for the Pope and the German Emperor; and wandered restlessly round Europe. The details of his life are unknown, but even before his death he was considered a master magician.

One of many stories told about Agrippa was of how he went out one day, leaving the key of a secret room in the house with his wife. She foolishly lent it to his lodger, a student, who went into the room and found a huge book of spells which he began to read. After a while he looked up and found a demon standing in front of him, asking why it had been summoned. He gaped at it in horror, and the demon strangled him.

Agrippa returned and, fearing a charge of murder, made the demon restore the student to life for a few

Left *possessed by spirits, a priest dances rhythmically round the ring formed by his followers*
Above *Haitian 'trial by fire'; taken over by a god, the priest is able to handle fire yet remain unmarked*

The ability to communicate with the spirit world while in a trance is a characteristic of mediums and many priests
Above *a Zar priestess in Ethiopia; she expels evil spirits, called* zars, *from members of her flock when in a trance state*
Right *a Brazilian youth prepares to become a medium; his initiator wears special robes based on those of an Indian chief*

hours. The young man was seen walking down the street, but when the demon's magic wore off he collapsed and died.

Another magician was Count Cagliostro, born in Palermo, in Sicily, in 1743. Like Agrippa, he was a flamboyant and mysterious figure. He claimed to be a master of every branch of magic. One of his more famous exploits was the magical manufacture of a huge and brilliant diamond, which he offered to the French Cardinal, Louis de Rohan. He came to London and attracted a large following because of his ability to forecast the winning numbers in lotteries. He ran into trouble with the authorities, not surprisingly, in spite of his fame as a seer, scholar and magician, and was imprisoned many times, in many countries. So great was his fame, however, among the people of Paris, that in 1786 when he was released from the Bastille, a crowd of 10,000 is said to have turned out to cheer him.

A more modern magician who attracted much attention in Europe was a 19th century Frenchman who

Above *Paracelsus, a Swiss alchemist and physician who lived during the first half of the 16th century, is also said to have been a magician who performed many miraculous cures*

assumed the name of Eliphas Levi. Levi began his career by training for the priesthood, but later abandoned theology for magic. His reputation spread fast, and he collected a wide circle of disciples. Levi was mainly a theorist, but he records an episode, late in his magical career, when he attempted to conjure up a spirit – Apollonius of Tyana. When he succeeded he fell down in a faint of terror. Levi describes this episode with great simplicity, in a style quite different to the extravagance of much of his earlier writing.

The Witch's Path to Magical Power
Witches are constantly associated with magic, probably because they are the most familiar of all the groups using magic – and always have been through the centuries. They were usually easily accessible to ordinary people. Living in villages, they were available for consultation, and for harnessing non-human powers in order to make crops grow, cure diseases, ensure good harvests, harm rivals, and bring good luck to friends. They have therefore been more visible than magicians, occultists, and other more anonymous groups dealing in magical matters.

Witches have existed since the start of human history. There is the Witch of Endor in the Bible, an aged, knowing soothsayer who conjured up Samuel. And witches appear in the folktales of almost every society in the world. Sometimes they are old, wise women; often they inspire fear. Ocasionally a witch takes on the form of a beautiful enchantress to snare the unsuspecting.

But the common picture of the witch is the beak-nosed hag of medieval woodcarvings and Victorian childrens' books, riding broomsticks, casting demonic spells, muttering over cauldrons, and dancing naked in the moonlight. Traditionally witches have always made a pact with the Devil in order to gain their powers. In return, they do his bidding whenever called upon and whatever it may be.

A 17th century Italian demonologist, Francesco-Maria Guazzo described an involved ritual for entering into such a pact. He listed 11 separate stages:

1   A spoken denial of the Christian faith.
2   Rebaptism in the Devil's name when the novice gains a new name, discarding his Christian one.

Top *Count Cagliostro was said to have used magic to make a magnificent diamond*
Above *Eliphas Levi, a 19th century magician*
Right *the master magician Cornelius Agrippa*

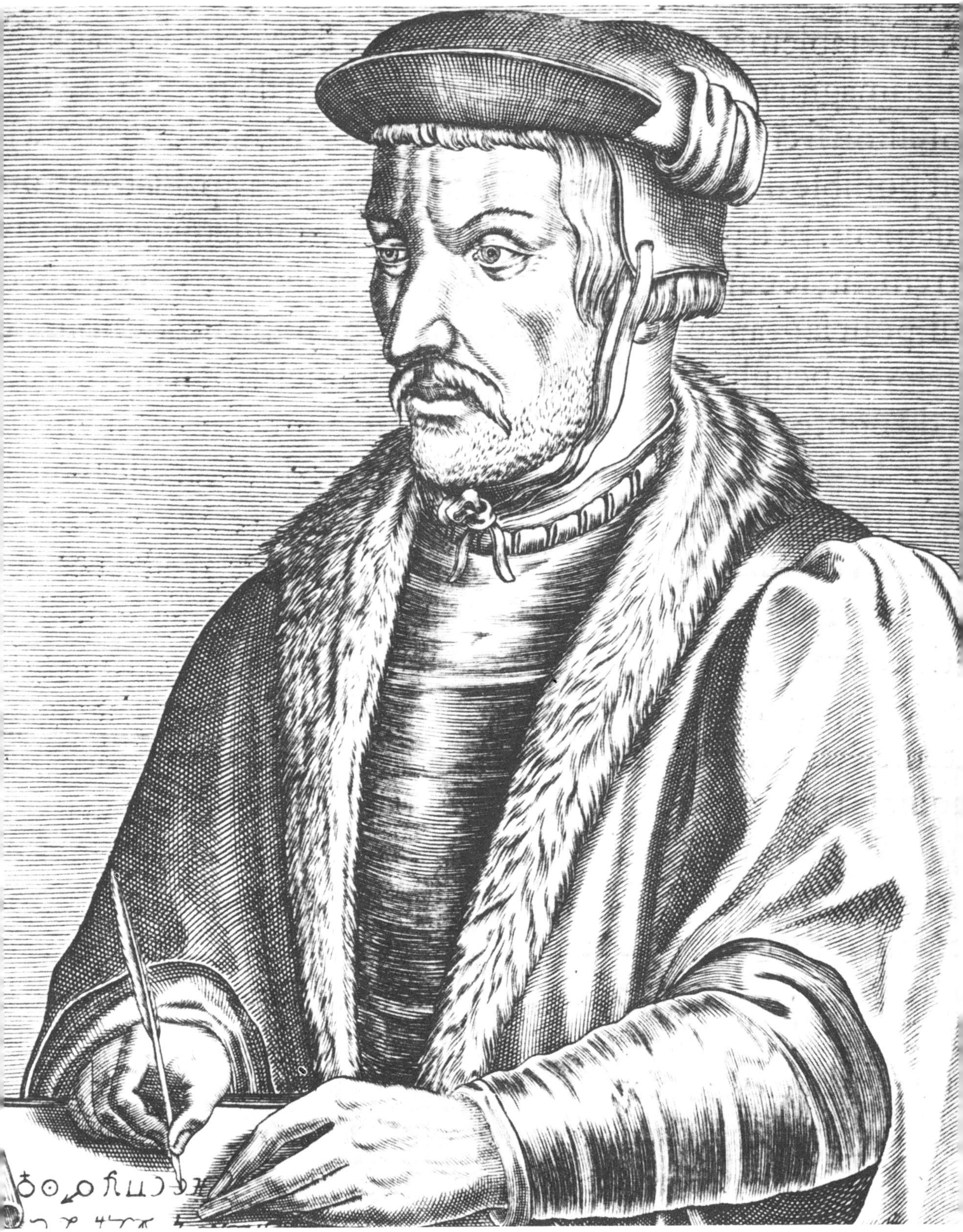

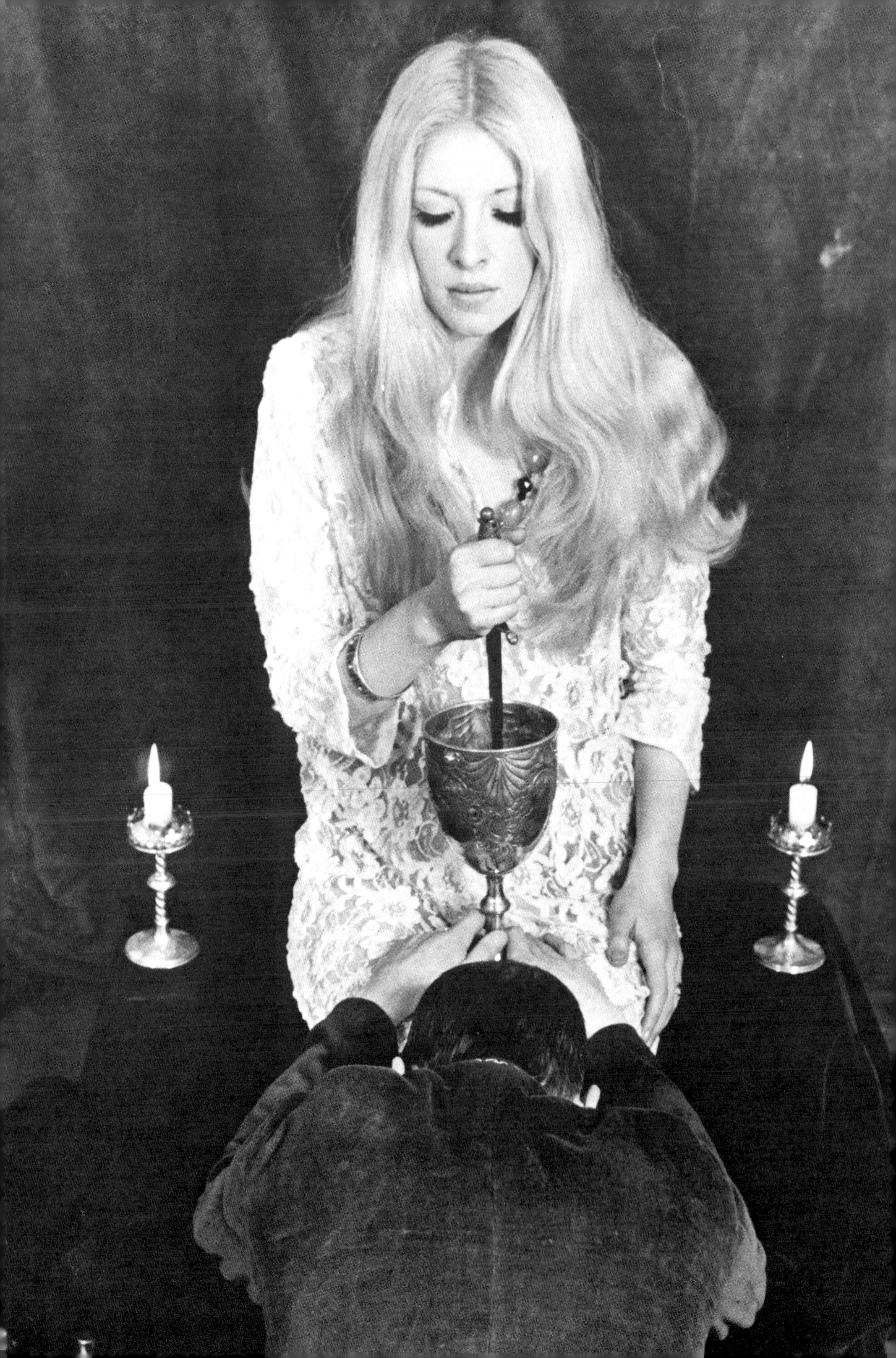

3   Symbolic removal of the baptismal chrism (conservated oil) by the Devil's touch.
4   Denial of the godparents and gaining new sponsors.
5   The gift of a piece of clothing to the Devil, as a token of submission.
6   An oath of allegiance to the Devil, while standing in a magic circle and thereby divorced from any of the world's ordinary influences.
7   Inclusion of the initiate's name in the 'Book of Death'.
8   A promise to sacrifice children to the Devil.
9   A promise to pay annual tribute in the form of gifts of black objects, etc. to the Devil.
10 The marking of the initiate with one of the Devil's marks.
11 Vows of special service, including keeping the secrets of the sabbat and the destruction of holy relics.

A female initiate was also usually required to have sexual intercourse with the Devil. Other pacts called for an obscene kiss in the cleft of the Devil's buttocks.

The Devil himself was thought to be sexless and able to take the form of either a man or woman depending on who was to be seduced into his service. A girl who had become pregnant would often confess that the Devil was the father. Not that the confession

Witches are constantly associated with magical power, possibly because they are the most familiar of the groups that use magic
Left *the high priest and high priestess of a modern witch coven consecrate wine*
Above left *witchcraft is still alive and feared in many parts of Africa; a Kenyan witchdoctor cuts a client's palm to protect him from evil spirits*
Above *a witch riding to a sabbat; 15th century woodcut*

Witches have existed throughout history. Many were old, wise women who had the ability to cure sickness, but most witches were thought to have sold themselves to the Devil Above *a wise woman in Scandinavia* Right *and above right the Devil was often said to possess his subjects, making them rant and curse and vomit strange objects; during the 17th century nuns in a convent at Loudun, France, claimed they were tormented by demons at the bidding of a priest, Urbain Grandier – scene from* The Devils Right *a traditional witch riding a broomstick*

helped her. Far from getting her out of her difficulties, she was more likely to be burned as a witch as a result of it.

The Devil often 'possessed' his subjects, as the spirits of Voodoo and other religions possess theirs. He would make his entry and then, according to eye-witnesses, the victim's face and body would go into startling contortions, taking on a cunning, devilish look. The victim would rant and curse, vomit strange objects, and become uncontrollably violent.

Many explanations have been offered as to why witches were generally thought to be women. In the 16th century many writers thought it was because they were more credulous and impressionable than men, and could therefore be more easily tempted by Satan. Others felt that Satan was male and preferred women as his helpers – a possible distortion of the role sexual feelings play in magic and witchcraft.

Later authorities considered demonic possession a form of sexual hysteria that occurs only in women. (*Hystera* is the Greek word for uterus). Others, including anthropologists, suggest that the supposedly irrational tendencies of women made them susceptible to occult or quasi-religious beliefs. They adduced this from the considerable evidence that shamans of primitive tribes and groups in Siberia and the Arctic and central Asian regions were largely female.

Shamans cured sicknesses and directed communal ceremonies and sacrifices. They escorted the souls of the dead to the next world, and were said to have the power to leave their bodies at will. A similar form of magic, of which many witches are said to be capable, is shape-shifting – the ability to change shape at will and assume the form of virtually any object, a stone, an animal, or another recognizable human.

Although much witch activity can now be seen as merely the odd habits of the eccentric, old and lonely, there is little doubt that some people known as witches or magicians were able to cause disease or death, and to make love potions or poisons. These were often, no doubt, produced by people who genuinely 'knew something'. In many cases, what they would have known were the properties of drugs and herbs. Their love potions may well have been made of ingredients which modern pharmacologists now know

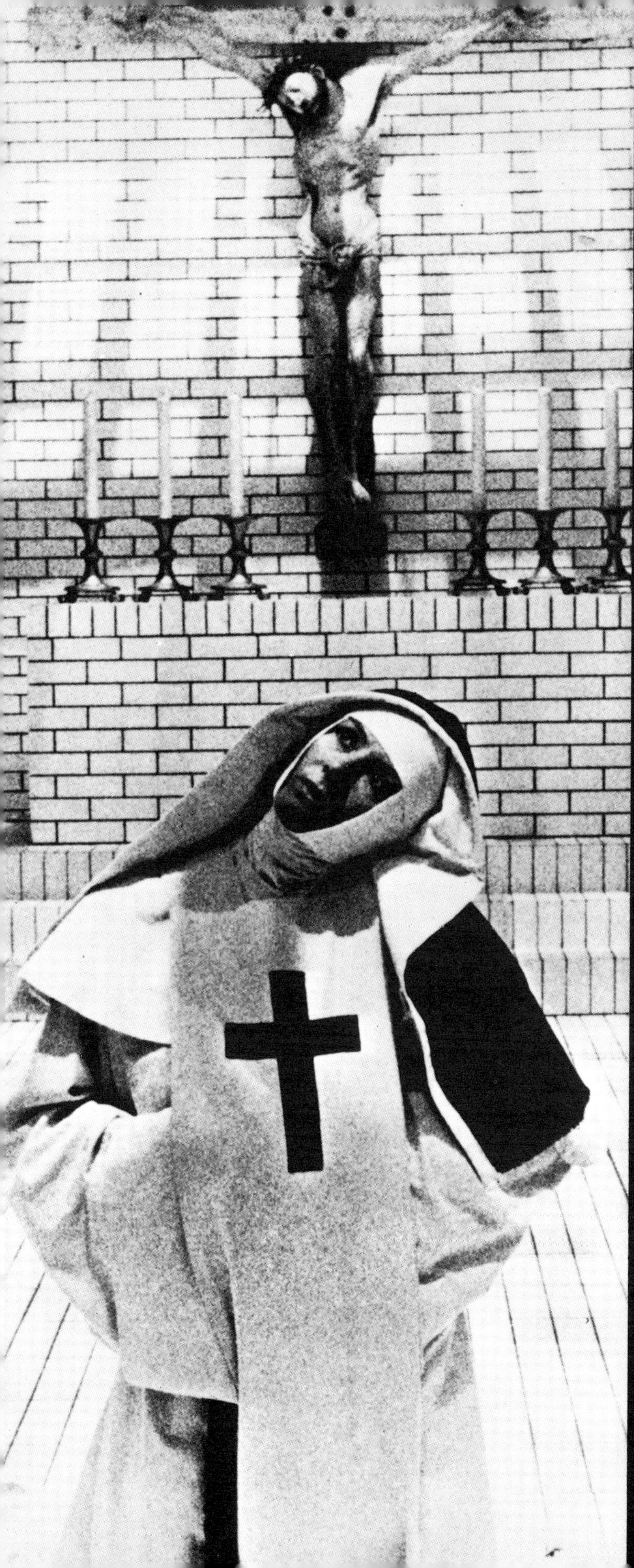
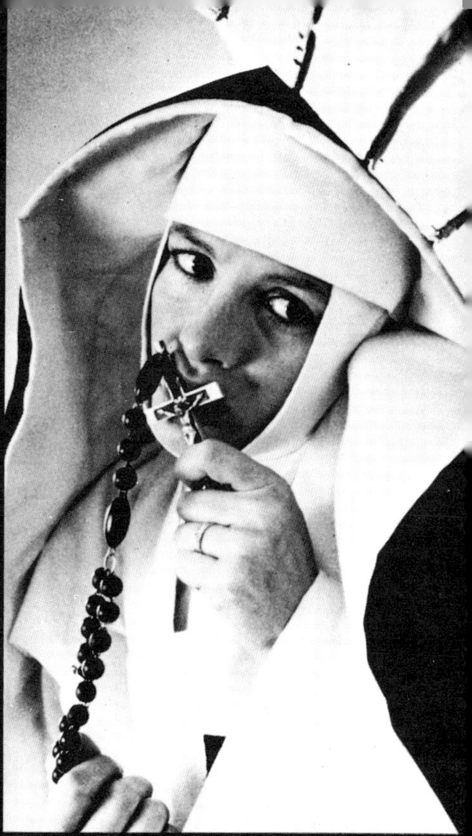
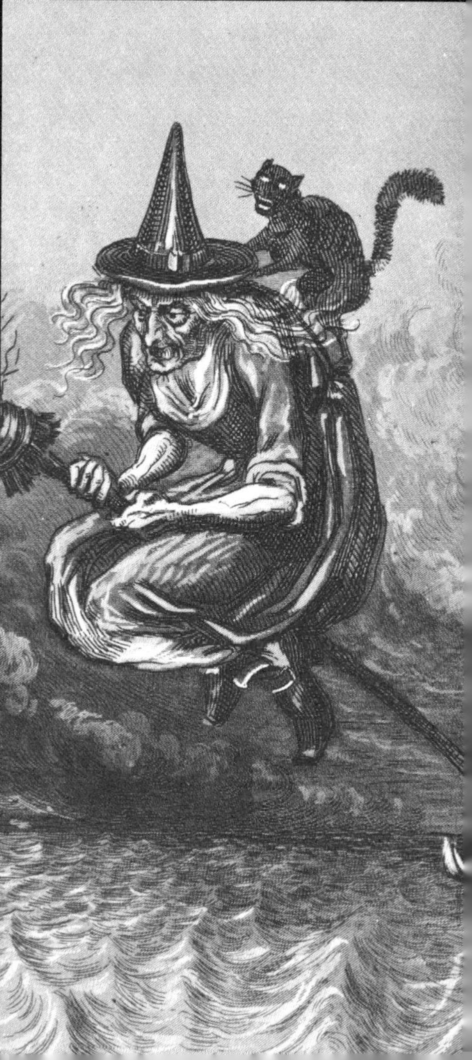

would most be effective. And death potions would most certainly work if natural slow poisons were used.

Knowledge of herbalism could also have produced many of the sensations of 'flying' that European witches consistently referred to in their confessions. They told of how they anointed themselves with 'flying ointment' – presumably made from one of a number of powerful hallucinogenic drugs that most certainly have produced this effect. Some of the formulae given for this ointment include belladonna, aconite and other hallucinogens, which would certainly take the witches on 'a trip'.

Magical Principles

To be successful in their magic-making, witches of all types, whether in Europe or among more primitive societies, depend basically on sympathetic magic.

It relies on two magical principles.

The first is that objects that have been in contact continue to affect each other, even at a distance, after contact has been severed. For a spell or a magical cure to be effective, the magic-worker must obtain part of the body, or something belonging to, the person who is to be bewitched. In Melanesia, for example, most magic is of this type. The witchdoctor

Below left *the Devil, half-goat and half-man, presides over a sabbat – 18th century French illustration. Witches gathered at sabbats to pay homage to their master, report on their activities, and welcome new recruits*
Below *yet another shape assumed by the Devil*

Witches with some of their paraphernalia, including the figure of a man with a pin sticking into it. This kind of imitative magic may seduce or kill. It is based on the belief that the pin piercing the image will either 'pierce' the heart of the person who is represented with love, or kill him, depending on the intention behind the act – painting by Austin Osman Spare

will perform his rites and spells over the nail-parings, excreta, or hair of the person to be 'treated' by him.

The second magical principle holds that like produces like, that mimicry will produce a mimicking effect. It is known as imitative magic, and its influence is very much alive even in apparently everyday 20th century situations.

For instance, many people react to danger by keeping still and closing their eyes. They pretend they are not there so that danger will not be able to strike. This is an unconscious appeal to imitative magic. Spectators watching runners at an athletics meetings may strain and tense themselves in the hope of magically inspiring the runner with energy – another appeal to imitative magic.

This type of magic also makes use of representations of the objects or people that are to be affected. The use of wax, clay or lead dolls to kill or injure the person the doll represents is well known in all cultures. Records of this practice survive from Egypt and Mesopotamia, from India, Greece and Rome. More recently, a Morrocan financier was reported to have stuck pins into the photographs of business rivals.

There are many other examples of imitative magic, from the belief that sexual intercourse between men and women will promote the growth of crops, to the Christian gesture of blessing in which two fingers are closed so that the thumb and two fingers still open represent the Trinity.

Excommunication, the Christian ritual by which the Church cast a sinner into outer darkness, also incorporated the magical principle of mimickry in a solemn ceremony consisting of three acts: a bell was tolled as for a dead man; the book from which the curse of excommunication was read was closed, and all candles were extinguished, symbolizing the offender's removal from the sight of God.

Imitative magic is also behind a form of love magic which depends for its efficacy on the appearance, shape, symbolism or qualities of the object used in the spell. Owing to their fecundity, fish have always been regarded as aphrodisiacs, as has the partridge, which is commonly thought to be lascivious. And the sexual organs of numerous animals have been eaten by lovers hoping to perpetuate or restore their own

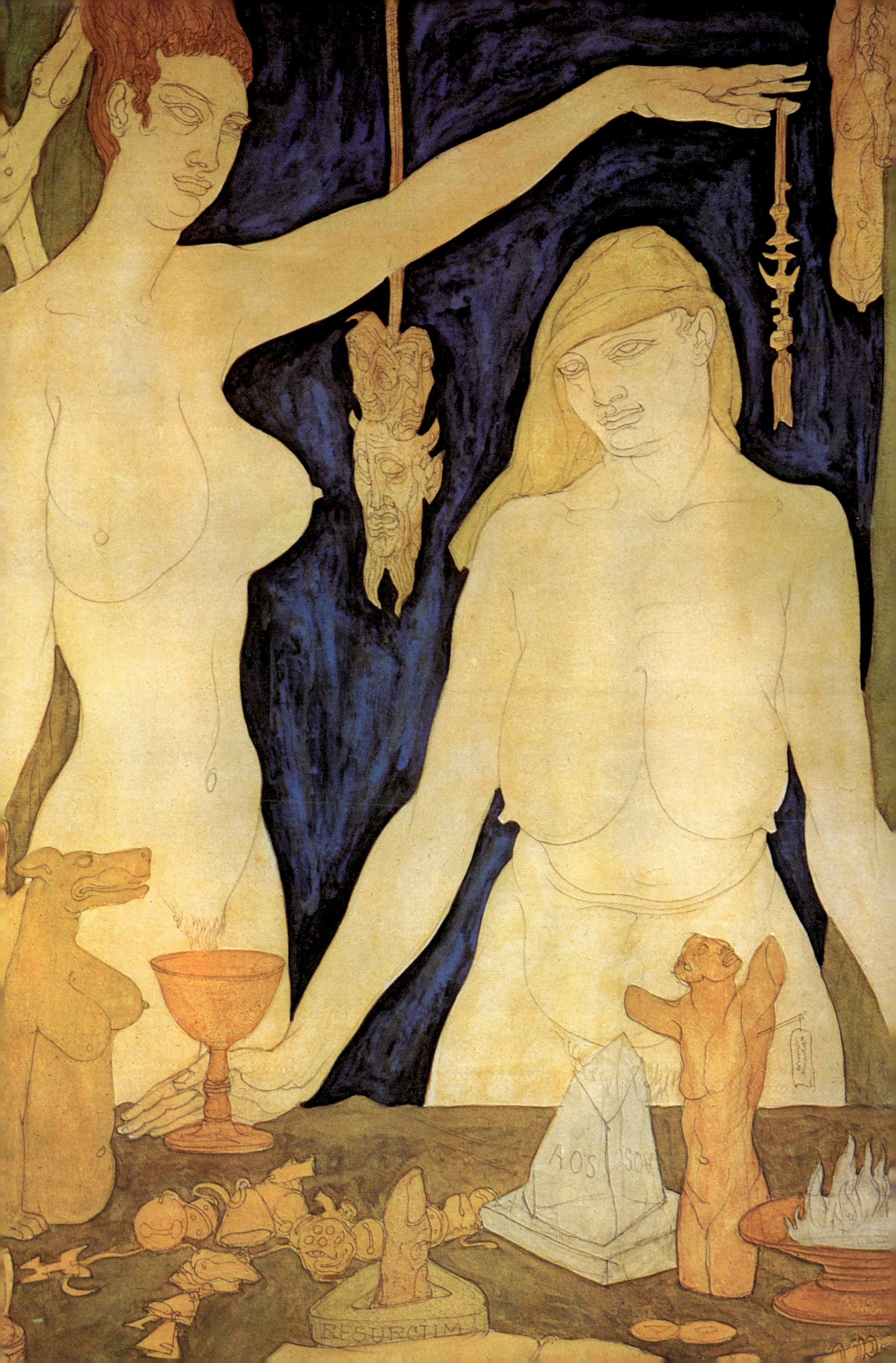
AOS
SOU
RESURGAM

energies in that sphere.

One method of making a girl fall in love with a man was to make an image of them from ground stone mixed with gum. The two images were then put facing each other into a vase containing seven twigs. The vase was buried in the hearth, a fire lit, and a piece of ice put in the fire. When the ice had melted, the vase was taken out again. The fire melting the ice was said to be love melting the hearts of man and girl.

The two principles of sympathetic magic, the 'law of contact' and the belief that 'like produces like', are in fact often combined in magic-making. The best-known example is the cursing or ill-wishing procedure when a lock of the victim's hair is added to the wax doll made in his image.

The Effects of Magic

Natural objects, numbers, names, jewels, can all be used either for their inherent qualities, or symbolically in magic-making. Ceremony, ritual, dance, song, and gesture all play their part in tapping the storehouse of knowledge that is magic. And the magical effect can be either white or black, because magic itself is neutral. It is coloured by the intention of the operator.

Modern, beneficent witches, for instance, use wax dolls to bring good to the people they represent, claiming that this particular use of imitative magic is not the exclusive province of black magicians and witches.

The knowledge of the strength and potentialities of magic has been shared by witches (and other magic-workers) for centuries. And the instruments used by modern witches are basically the same as those used by their predecessors for hundreds of years. There is the athame, the magical sword that each member makes for himself or herself. There is the horned copper helmet, representing *the Horned One* who was probably thought to be the Devil in past centuries. There is the word 'coven' itself, and the symbol of the broom.

The use of objects either similar to, or very like, these, can be traced back to a 9th century group of dervishes

Far left *mimicry is deeply engrained in human nature; soldiers under training, for instance, imitate the actions and emotions of battle Because dolls are miniature representations of human beings they figure largely in imitative magic* Below, far left *a doll version of the initiation of a Yoruba saint and* (below left) *an example of harming by proxy, using a doll* Below *dolls used* by North American Indian medicine-men

Following pages *witches consistently claimed to be able to fly, and it is thought that hallucinogenic drugs may have been included in the 'flying ointment' with which they anointed themselves – painting by Goya*

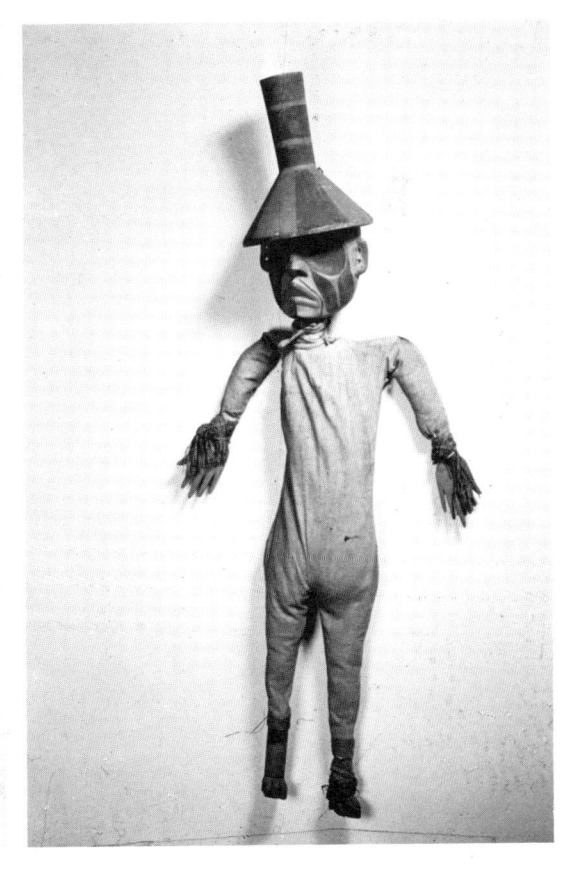

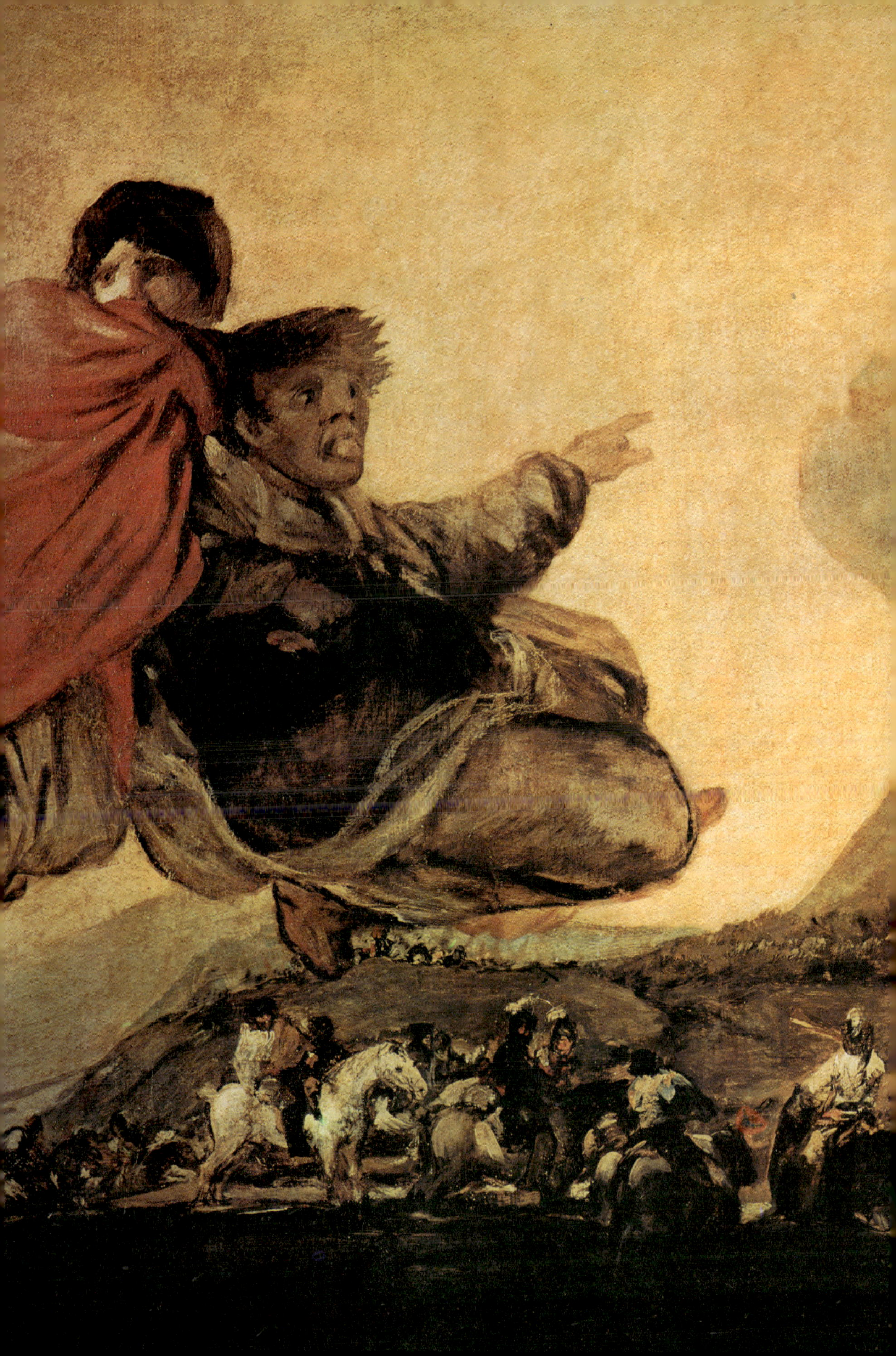

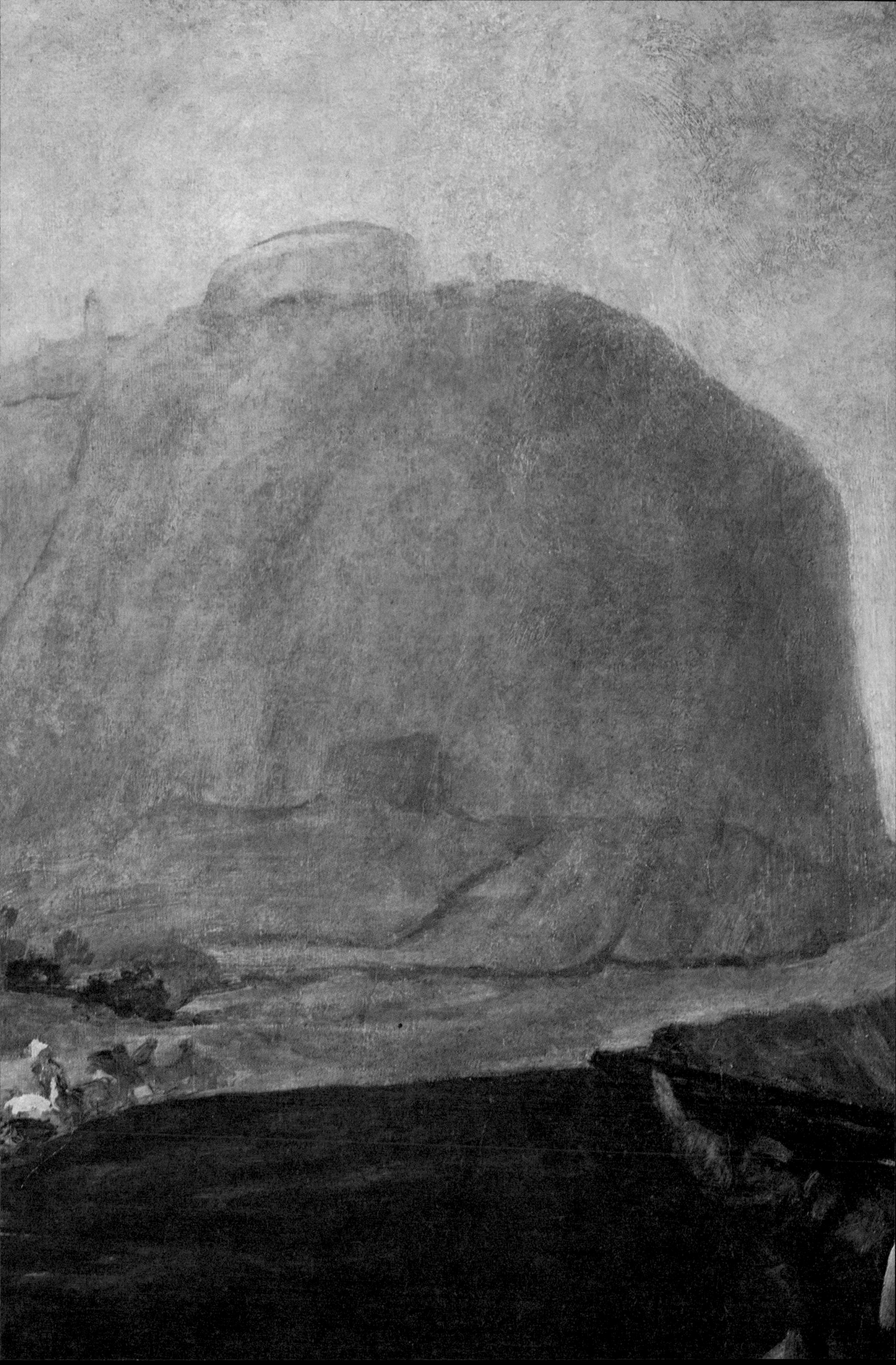

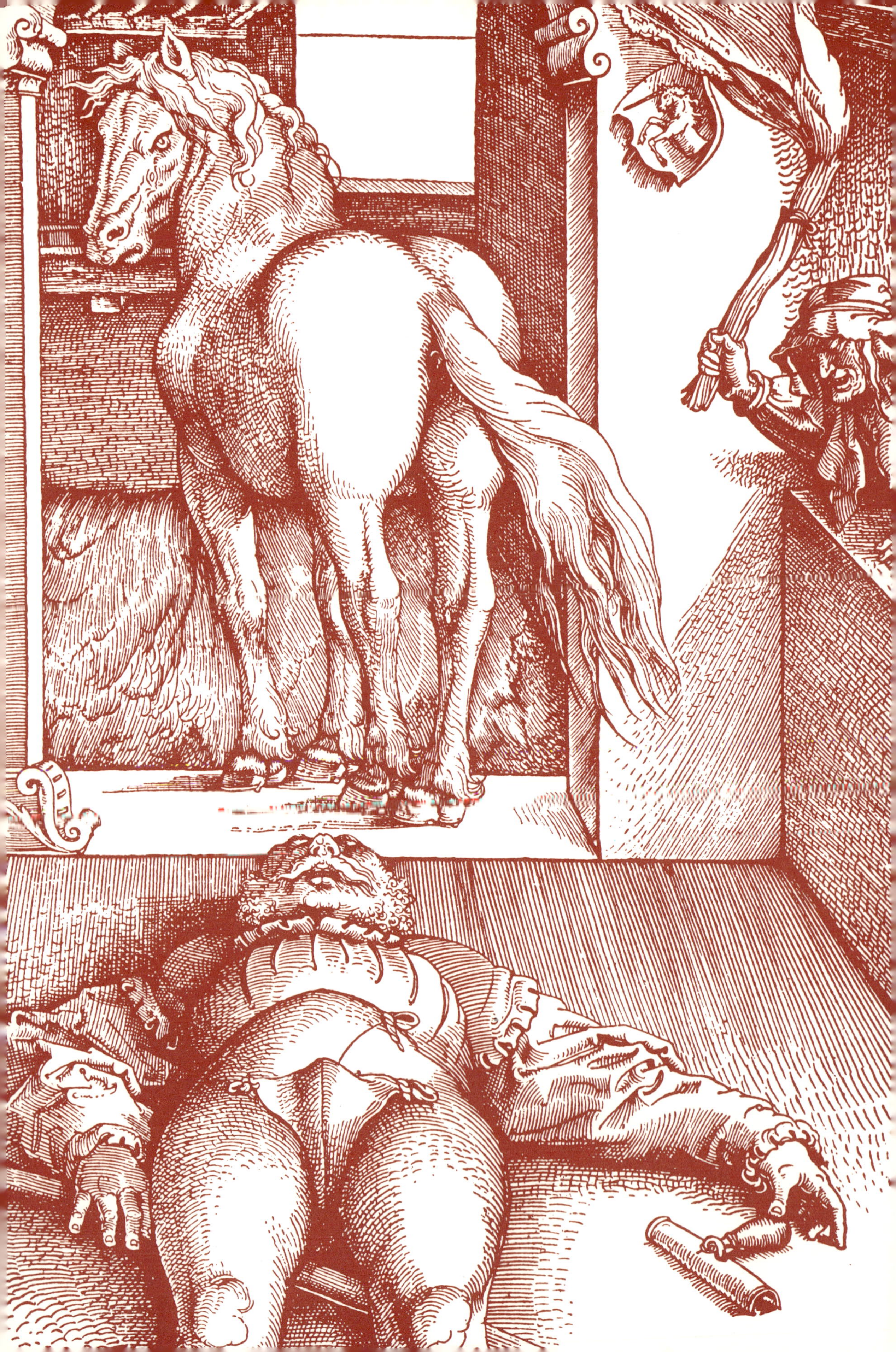

in Arabia, whose practices have much in common with traditional witchcraft customs in the West. These practices have been described by the celebrated author, Idries Shah in his book entitled *the Sufis*.

The horned helmet, and also the persistent re-presentation of Satan in the form of a goat, are reflected in the candle set between two horns which was the emblem of this 9th century group of mystics, and in the fact that the founder came from the powerful Aniza or 'goat' tribe. Athame is a fair representation of the sound of the Arab word *ad-dhame*, which literally means blood-letter, and was the name of the ritual knife of these groups or covens which numbered 13. They danced in a *kafan* (literally, winding-sheet and probably the derivation of coven), at a meeting known as *az-zabat* (literally 'powerful occasion', and close both in sound and meaning to sabbat). And even their cry of 'Eko, eko azarak...' is very close in sound to the cry of modern witches.

Casting spells: the bewitched groom by Lucas Cranach (left); Titania entranced by Bottom (top); Tristram drinking a love potion (above) – illustration by Aubrey Beardsley

Magic is a neutral force or power that can be used for good or evil, depending on the intention of the operator
Above *a modern witch leaps over a cauldron, a symbol of life and plenty, during a fertility enhancing ritual; most modern witchcraft is benefi cent and its great festivals are geared to the seasons*
Right *the more sinister aspect of witchcraft; a horned figure dominates the ceremony*
Facing page *an elemental spirit — painting by Austin Osman Spare*

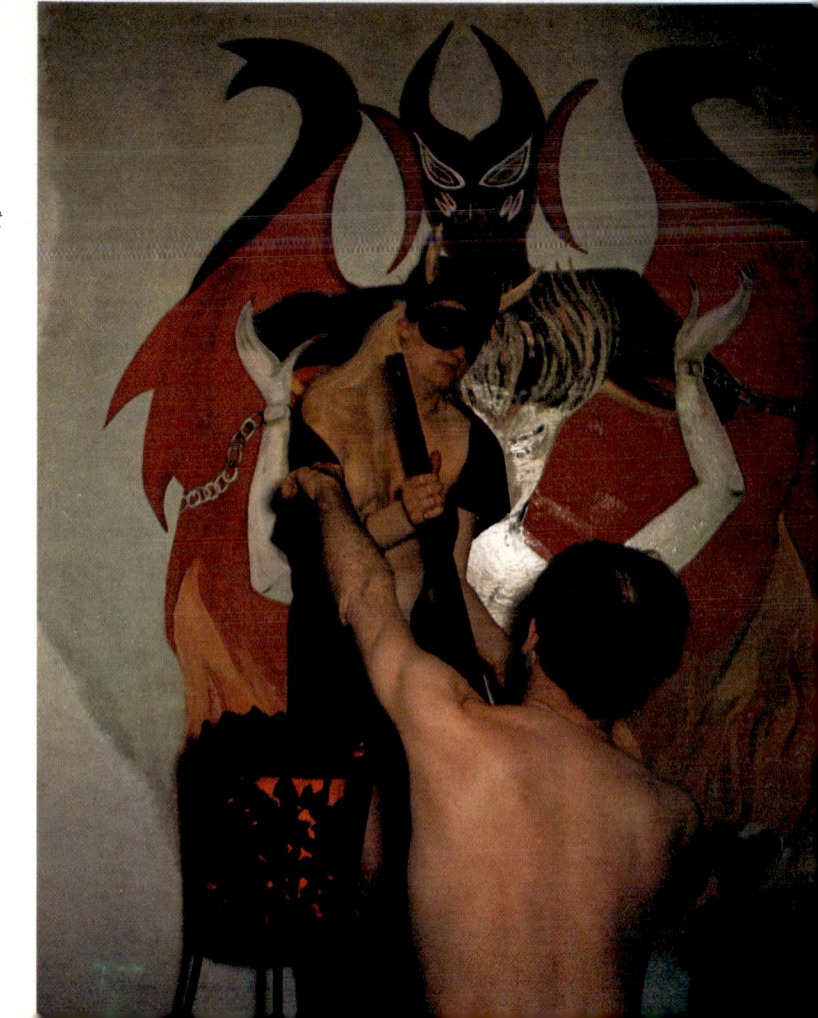

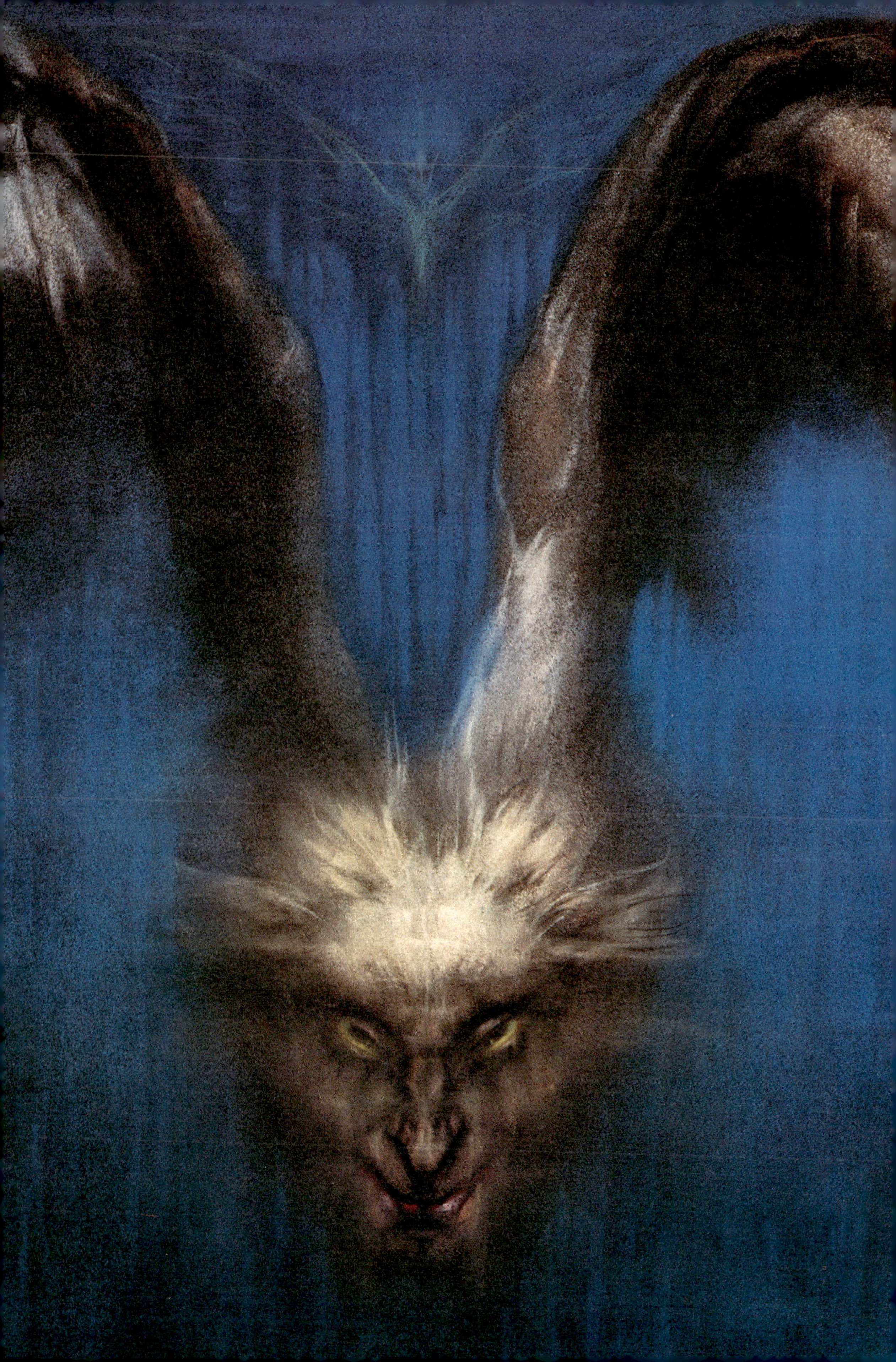

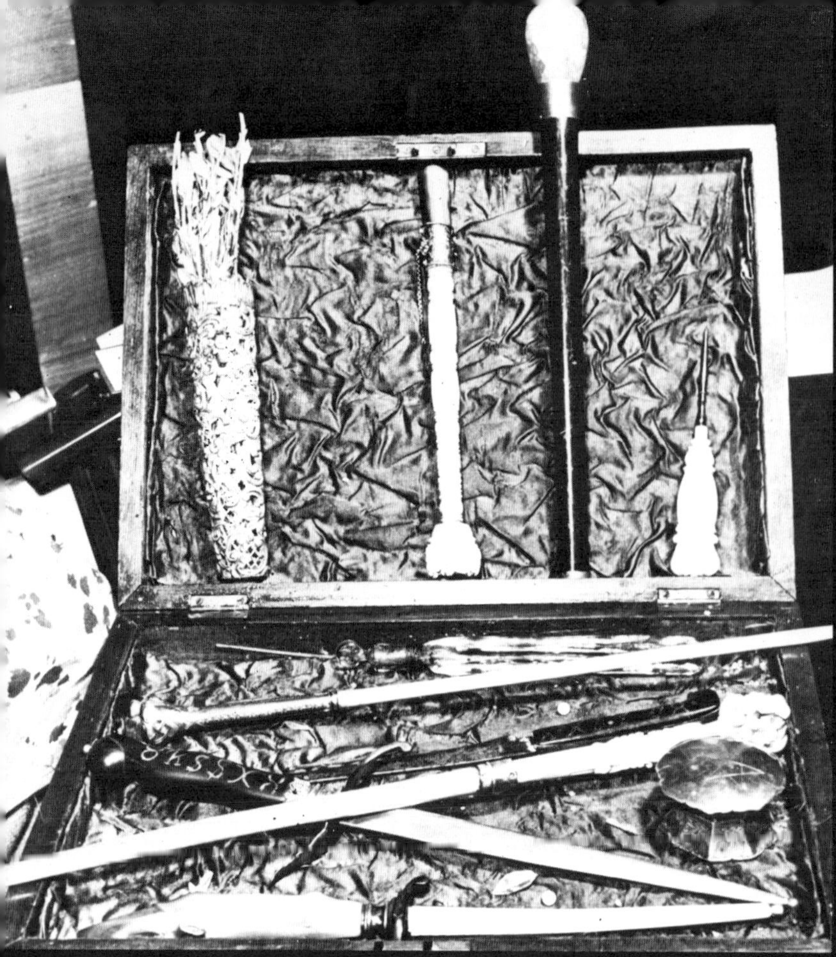
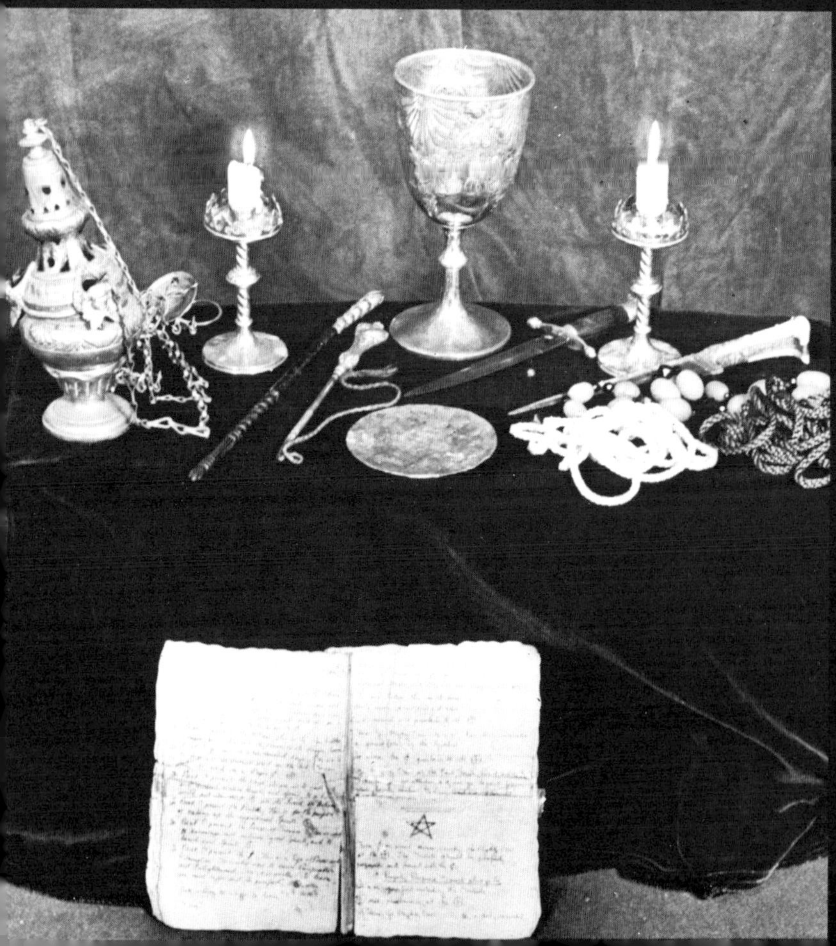
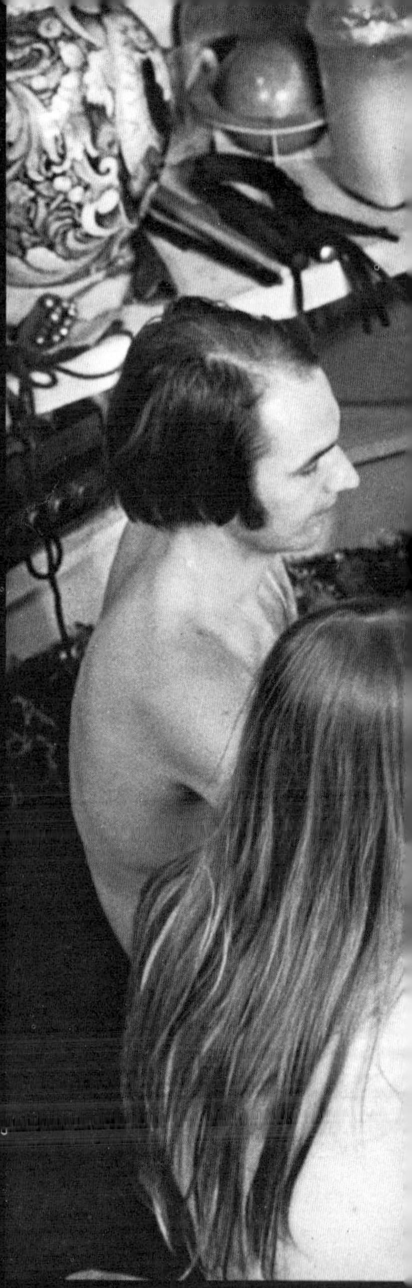
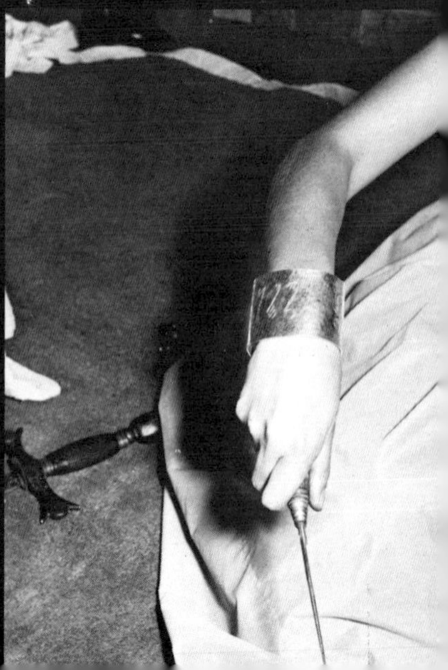

In conclusion it is certainly safe to say that these facts support the belief that the practice of magic is a world-wide and unbroken tradition, and that its resources are tapped by practitioners who use tools as universal and unchanged as magic itself.

Instruments and methods used by modern witches are much the same as those of their predecessors
Far left *magical paraphernalia used by witches* Left *a witch holds her athame or ritual knife* Above *cord magic, a means of concentrating and uniting a coven's willpower in order to work spells*

The Forces of Nature

The belief that everything in Nature has an inner life, either inherently or because it is the home of a god or spirit, is at the basis of mythology and religion all over the world. There is scarcely any natural object, or living creature, that has not been worshipped, respected, or feared, because of its supernatural power.

Although the spread of modern technology and scientific knowledge has rationalized these beliefs to a large extent, their echoes remain in folklore and superstition. The natural world still hides a wealth of magical meaning.

Some magics, such as the curative properties of certain trees, plants, flowers and herbs, were based in scientific fact. Foxgloves, whose leaves were used to treat heart disease, are an example. They contain digitalis, a derivative of which is used in the modern treatment of heart ailments. But the magic remedies were not often harmful and usually ineffective.

The following pages list just a few of the multitude of magical powers that have been attributed to various aspects of Nature, and hint at the supernatural significance of some familiar objects.

Trees

Eerie and sinister, the wildwood of legend is now just an evocative echo of the days when much of the earth's surface was covered by dense, impenetrable forest. But to many people trees themselves are still thought to retain their magical powers, recalling the ancient belief that they were the homes of spirits.

Oak: Sacred tree of the Druids, Scandinavians, Greeks and Romans. Gives protection against witchcraft. Decoctions of oak bark heal throat diseases and are used to dress sores.

Yew: Traditionally the graveyard tree of death, but also a symbol of fertility. A girl who places a sprig of yew, picked from a churchyard, under her pillow will dream of her future husband. Because of its longevity, the yew symbolizes life after death.

Elder: In American tradition, burning an elder stick on Christmas Eve will reveal all witches, sorcerers and practitioners of evil in the neighbourhood.

Ash: Gives protection against snakes — and witches; cures warts.

Hawthorn: Surrounded by Christian tradition, said to groan and sigh on Good Friday. A symbol of fertility, often used to decorate maypoles.

Birch: One of the traditional materials used for making the brooms ridden by witches.

Rowan or Mountain Ash: Protects against the Devil; wearing a rowan sprig will ward off witchcraft.

Apple: Associated with healing and fertility. A tree which becomes malformed presages its owner's death.

Willow: Symbol of grief and forsaken love, but also used in love magic to conjure up the appearance of a girl's future husband.

Fir: Symbol of constancy and fertility. A partly burned branch protects the bearer against lightning.

Hawthorn trees, and (inset) *a rainbow magically linking heaven and earth*

Plants & Flowers

Plants, flowers and berries were among man's earliest sources of food and therefore were soon credited with life-giving properties and with strong magical powers. In many cases there is an obvious association between beauty and supernatural power, but some more humble plants are equally effective.

Rose: Symbol of beauty and love, but also associated with death: its petals are strewn on graves. It is said that a girl who wears a rosebud, plucked on Midsummer Day and kept fresh, to church on Christmas Day, will meet her future husband.

Fern: Carrying the seed of the fern is supposed to make the bearer invisible. At one time, anyone caught gathering fern seed was suspected of witchcraft.

Geranium: Protects against snakes, in Massachussets. Used by certain North American Indians to cure dysentery and cholera.

Poppy: Symbolizes sleep, and death; often believed to spring from the blood of warriors killed in battle. Because it turns away love, it was used in love potions as an anaphrodisiac.

Lotus: A recurring theme in Eastern symbolism; the emblem of fertility and of creation.

Marigold: Protects against witchcraft. To sew marigold seeds in earth taken from a loved one's footprints is to ensure faithfulness.

Clover: Provides protection against witchcraft and evil, because its three leaves symbolize the Trinity. The luck-bringing qualities of the four-leafed clover may derive from its similarity to the shape of the Cross.

Peony: Said to be of divine origin, it wards off evil spirits and storms. Cures many diseases, including epilepsy.

Aloes: Used in magical compounds, especially for ceremonies associated with Jupiter.

Forget-Me-Not: Cures the bites of serpents and mad dogs. Used in poultices made to cure sore eyes.

Herbs

Herbs were important ingredients in the pharmacopoeias of past physicians. Their medicinal qualities, and the resultant belief that they could mean the difference between life and death, is one of the reasons why they are said to have magical powers.

Basil: The herb of the Devil, but also a means of protection against witches. Although it is said to breed scorpions, it will draw the poison out of an insect sting or snake-bite.

Parsley: Grows best where the wife is in charge of the household. According to legend, it takes a long time to germinate because it must first travel seven times to the Devil and back.

Dill: In some regions it is abhorrent to witches, in others it is an ingredient of their brews.

Lemon balm: A woman who wears a sprig around her neck will be beloved and happy. Placed on a wound, it staunches the flow of blood.

Lovage: In a love potion it inspires everlasting devotion. It relieves stomach-aches, and clears the skin of freckles.

Fennel: In the keyhole of a bedroom door it ensures that nothing unpleasant will disturb the occupant's sleep.

Garlic: Protects against witches, vampires and the Evil Eye. Placed in the ground it drives away moles.

Rosemary: Wards off diseases and black magic; symbol of fidelity and remembrance. It flourishes where the wife rules the household.

Sage: Confers long life on its bearer. Its flourishing – or withering – also reflects the state of its owner's business.

Bay: A bay tree is a defence against evil and the powers of darkness, and also a protection against storms.

Mandrake: A painkiller and sleep-inducer, ingredient of witches' brews used in clairvoyance and imitative magic. Its forked roots resemble a human body, and because of its fearful shriek when it is uprooted, it must be dug up by a dog and not pulled by humans.

Top left *herbs were grown for medicinal and magical purposes: illustration from 14th century herbal*
Far left *a Derbyshire well 'dressed' with flowers*
Left *uprooting a mandrake – 16th century drawing*

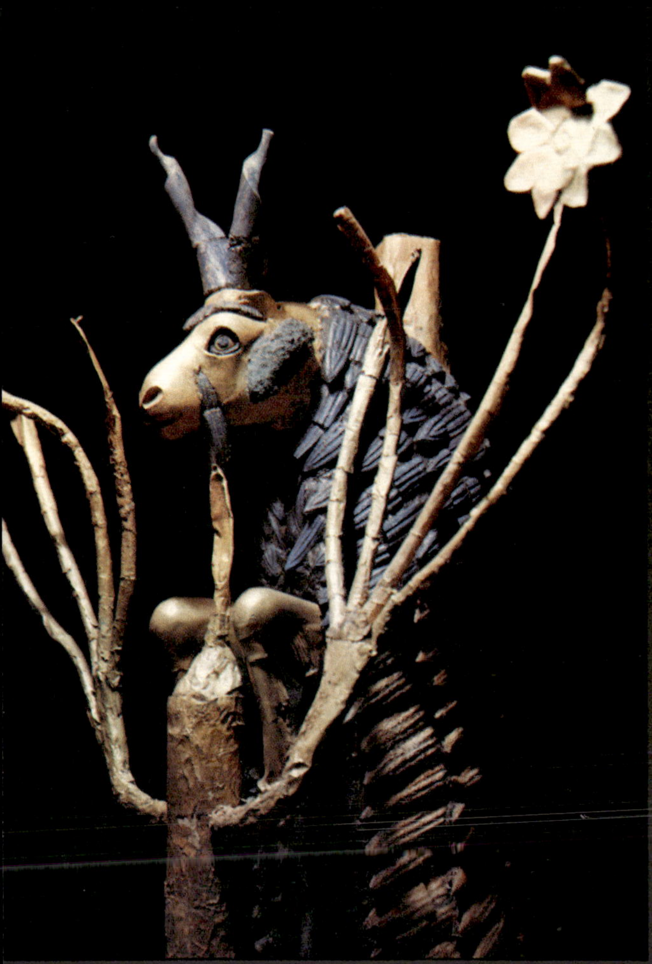

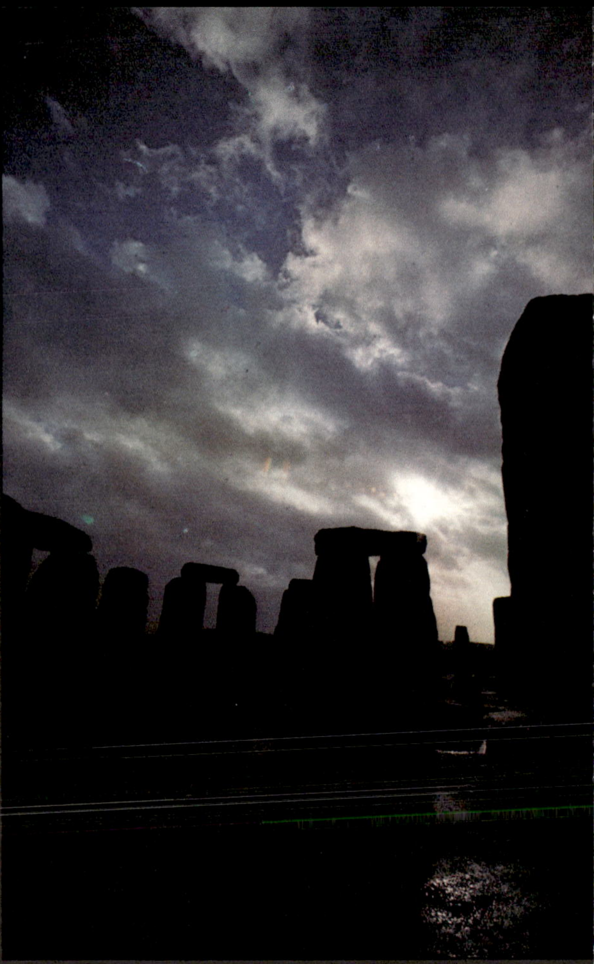

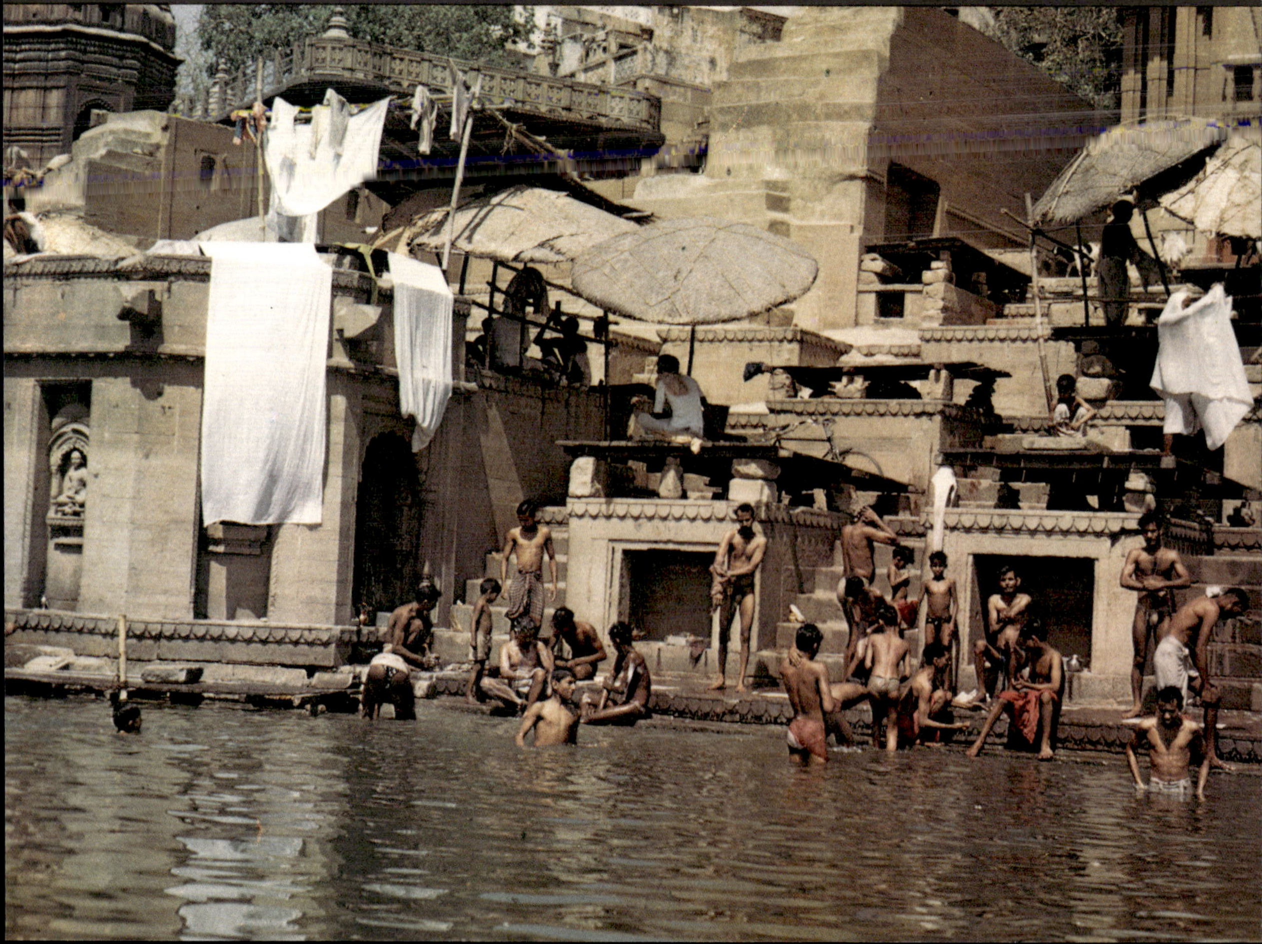

Far left *Sumerian ram in a thicket; made from gold and lapis lazuli* Left *Stonehenge, a sacred and holy place* Below left *bathing in the Ganges, India's divine river*

Stones & Water

The physical qualities of stones, their solidity, weight and inherent strength, inspired belief in their magical efficacy. Water, a basic necessity of life, is regarded as being essentially sacred. Both these natural substances, in their varied forms, enshrine a multitude of magical powers.

Stone of Scone: Part of the coronation throne of Britain's sovereign. It has been identified with the legendary coronation stone of the kings of Ireland, which was said to shriek when the heir to the throne stepped on it.

Fountains: Sources of fertility, youth and rejuvenation, and sometimes of wisdom.

Mirror stones: Highly polished stones, used in divination. According to the Indians of South America, the face of death is reflected if someone doomed to die soon looks into one of these stones.

Wells: Abodes of ancient spirits and deities, many will grant wishes, or heal the sick.

Stones with holes: Used in weather magic: drought can be caused by repeatedly passing a burning brand through the hole. Passing through holes in certain boulders will make barren women fertile.

Rivers: The source of life, rivers also symbolize the inevitability of death. Many, like the Nile, are bearers of fertility; others, such as the Ganges, are inherently divine.

Standing stones: Groups of rocks or boulders, similar in appearance; often believed to be human beings turned to stone.

Lakes: Often the homes of monsters, enchantresses, and other supernatural beings.

Stones in circles: Magically extremely powerful, because of the protective power of the circle. Witches celebrate their sabbats in some stone circles. Others, such as Stonehenge which is associated with the sun-worship of the Druids, are sacred and holy places.

Jewels

Rare, beautiful, and seemingly fired with inner life, jewels are credited with strong supernatural powers. Like precious metals they are used in magical ceremonies. Able to heal and protect, many imbue their wearers with the qualities they symbolize.

Pearl: Symbol of purity and virginity, its lustre dims if its owner falls ill, disappears completely if he or she dies.

Amber: Worn while casting enchantments, it is associated with sensual appeal. A charm against witchcraft in Italy, the Chinese believe it to be the soul of a tiger, transformed after death.

Amethyst: The jewel of the high priest, used in magical rituals performed to achieve power. It can protect against drunkenness, and controls passions and evil thoughts.

Diamond: Used in magical ritual it makes the magician indomitable. A symbol of male creative energy. Certain diamonds, such as the Hope diamond, are associated with ill-luck.

Emerald: The jewel of romantic love, and of Venus. It relieves eyestrain, staunches bleeding, and cures gastric upsets. An emerald will liquefy the eyes of snakes who look at it.

Carnelian: Used in healing magic by Australian medicine-men, it counteracts the effects of sorcery, and drives away nightmares and evil spirits.

Ruby: Associated with blood, violence and destruction, also with the administration of justice. The star ruby is used to conjure up, and control, spirits of all kinds – good and bad.

Sapphire: Symbol of femininity, imbued with magical power.

Gold: Used in the highest and most important magical ceremonies, it symbolizes riches, wisdom, life, and perfection. It protects against disease and drowning.

Silver: Destroys evil; in many areas witches, sorcerers and evil spirits can be vanquished only by a silver bullet.

Animals

Sharing man's basic needs, and familiar figures in his environment, animals were nevertheless regarded as mysterious creatures, and endowed with supernatural powers. Worshipped as gods, they have also been credited with perceptions that extend beyond the everyday world.

Cat: The familiar of witches, in medieval times a black cat was widely believed to be the Devil himself. Welcomed as luck-bringers by sailors and actors, generally unlucky if met out-of-doors.

Dogs: Faithful friends of man, but sometimes terrifying spectres when they sweep through the countryside as packs of demon dogs, threatening death or misfortune to anyone who sees them.

Snake: The tempter of the Old Testament, who caused Adam and Eve to be expelled from the Garden of Eden, the snake is generally a symbol of evil. A live adder on the doorstep is an omen of death, but the skins and other parts of snakes are used in folk medicine.

Bat: A symbol of death in many parts of the world, said to possess occult powers. The Devil is widely believed to assume its form.

Frog: An ingredient of magical brews, the frog is one of the shapes that witches are said to assume.

Horse: Sometimes the familiar of witches, at other times a human being transformed by witchcraft. Particularly susceptible to the Evil Eye, they wear horse brasses as protective devices.

Pig: A weather prophet, able to see or smell the wind. In the United States hogs are said to know when a tornado is approaching. They are vulnerable to the Evil Eye, and demon pigs are common in folklore.

Goat: One of the forms assumed by the Devil at sabbats, but also a symbol of fertility, given as bride gifts.

Bear: A symbol of fertility. Its grease is said to cure baldness, and riding on a bear's back will cure whooping cough. Bears' teeth are used in charms against toothache.

Above *Zodiac signs reflect the qualities of the animals associated with them – 17th century illustration* Below *snake charmers;*

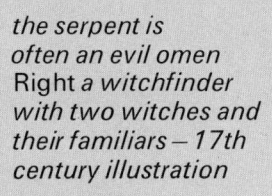

the serpent is often an evil omen
Right *a witchfinder with two witches and their familiars — 17th century illustration*

Birds & Fish

Birds were thought to be in touch with the spirits and gods who live in the sky, and the supernatural knowledge they gained enable them to forecast the future. Like birds, fish inhabit a mysterious environment, hostile to man; they have always been credited with magical powers.

Cock: Sacrificed in black magic ceremonies; it exorcizes evil, and frightens away devils.
Dove: A symbol of love and fertility, used in divination and love charms.
Herring: Eaten raw, it will enable a man to conjure up the shade of his future wife.
Cuckoo: A prophetic bird, able to foretell how a long a person will live, or remain unmarried. Seeing and hearing a cuckoo is a good omen for a marriage.
Owl: The bird of wisdom, but also frequently associated with evil and misfortune. Sometimes the familiar of witches.
Crow or raven: Associated with disaster and death. It foretells storms, and according to tradition the disappearance of the ravens from the Tower of London will presage the downfall of Britain.
Kraken: A legendary sea-creature of enormous size; possibly a survivor of giant prehistoric cuttlefish.
Stork: Bearer of babies to human households, it weeps human tears if it is wounded. A stork's nest will protect a house from fire.
Peacock: Attacker of serpents, its raucous calls forecast the coming of rain. It cures diseases, and in some places its feathers are used to ward off evil; in others the 'eyes' in the tail represent the Evil Eye.

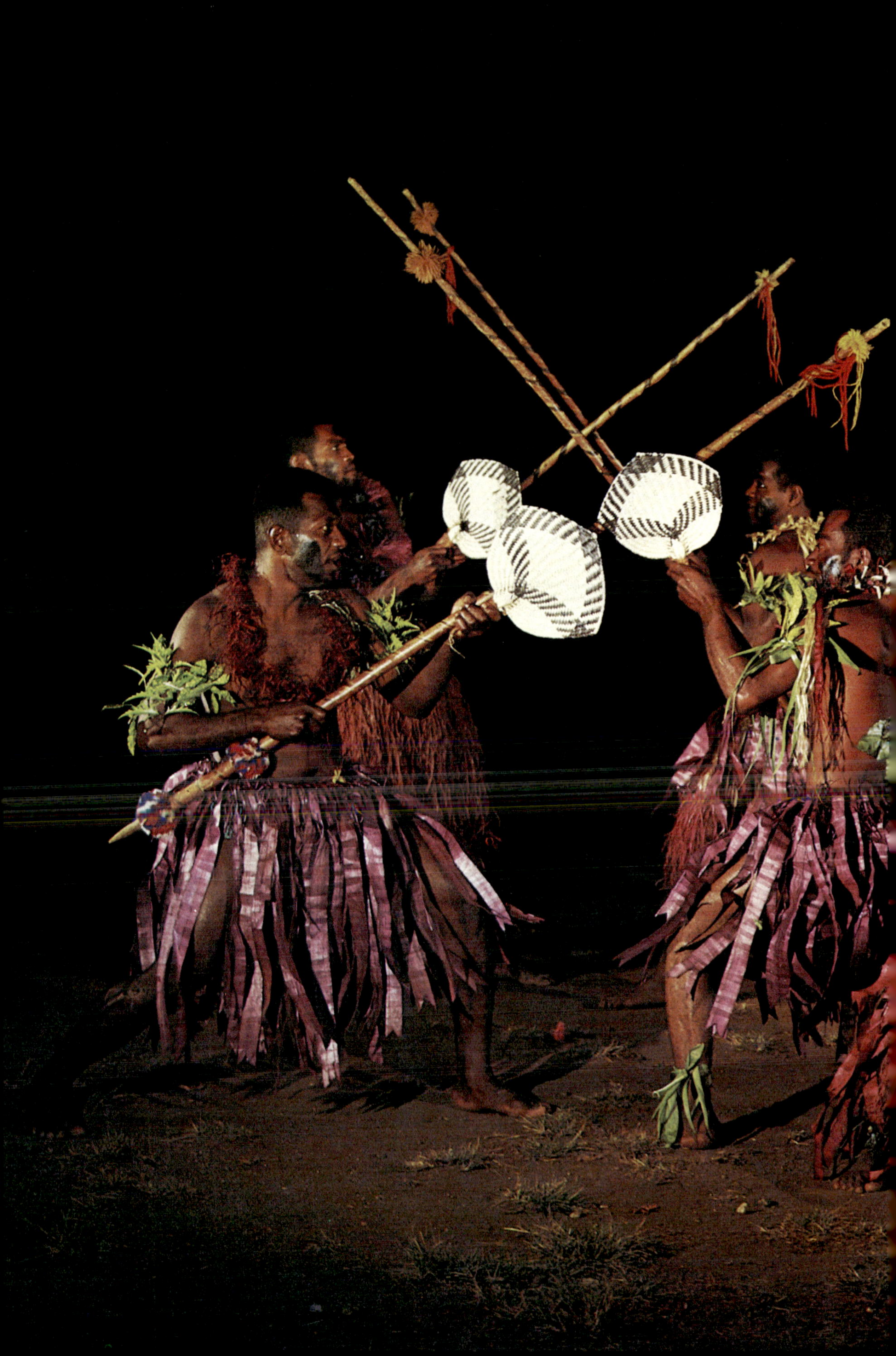

Ritual and Ceremony

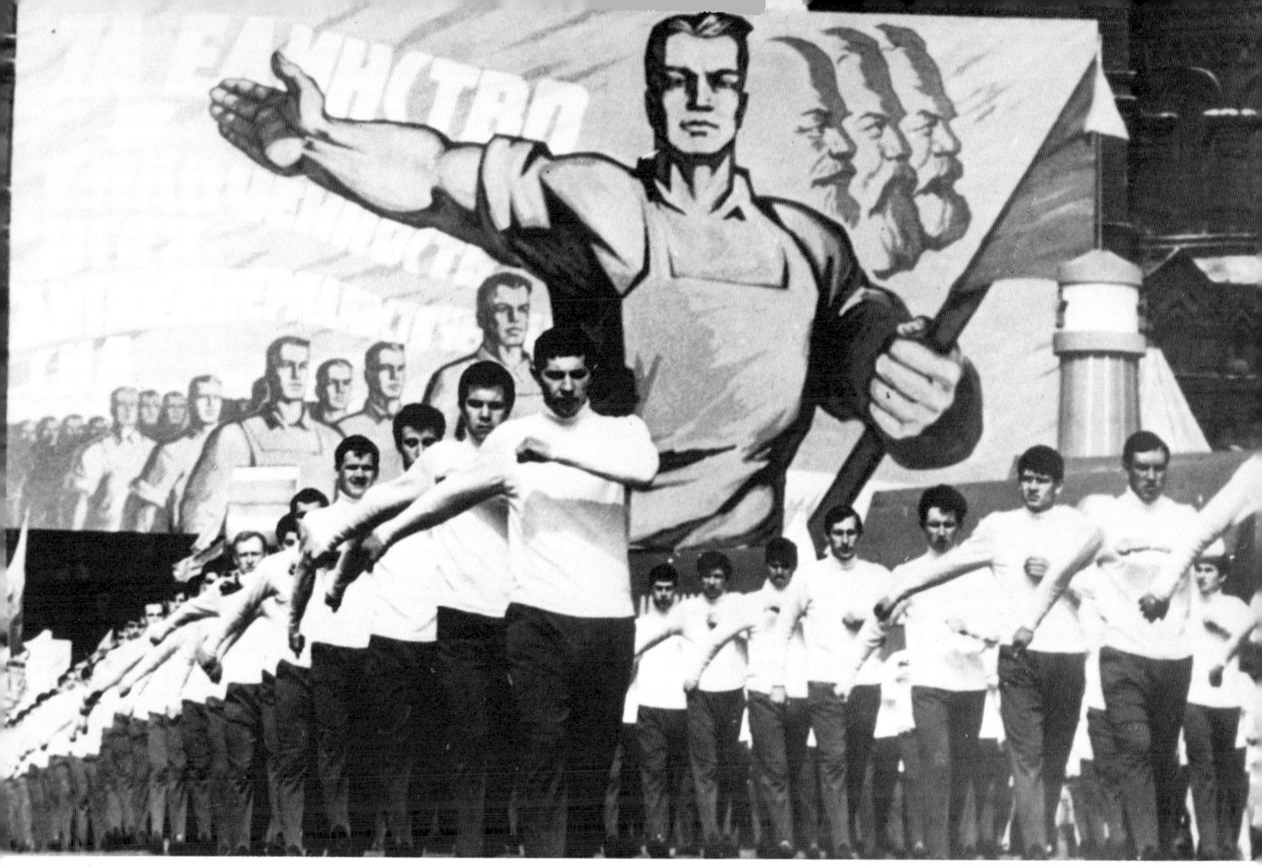

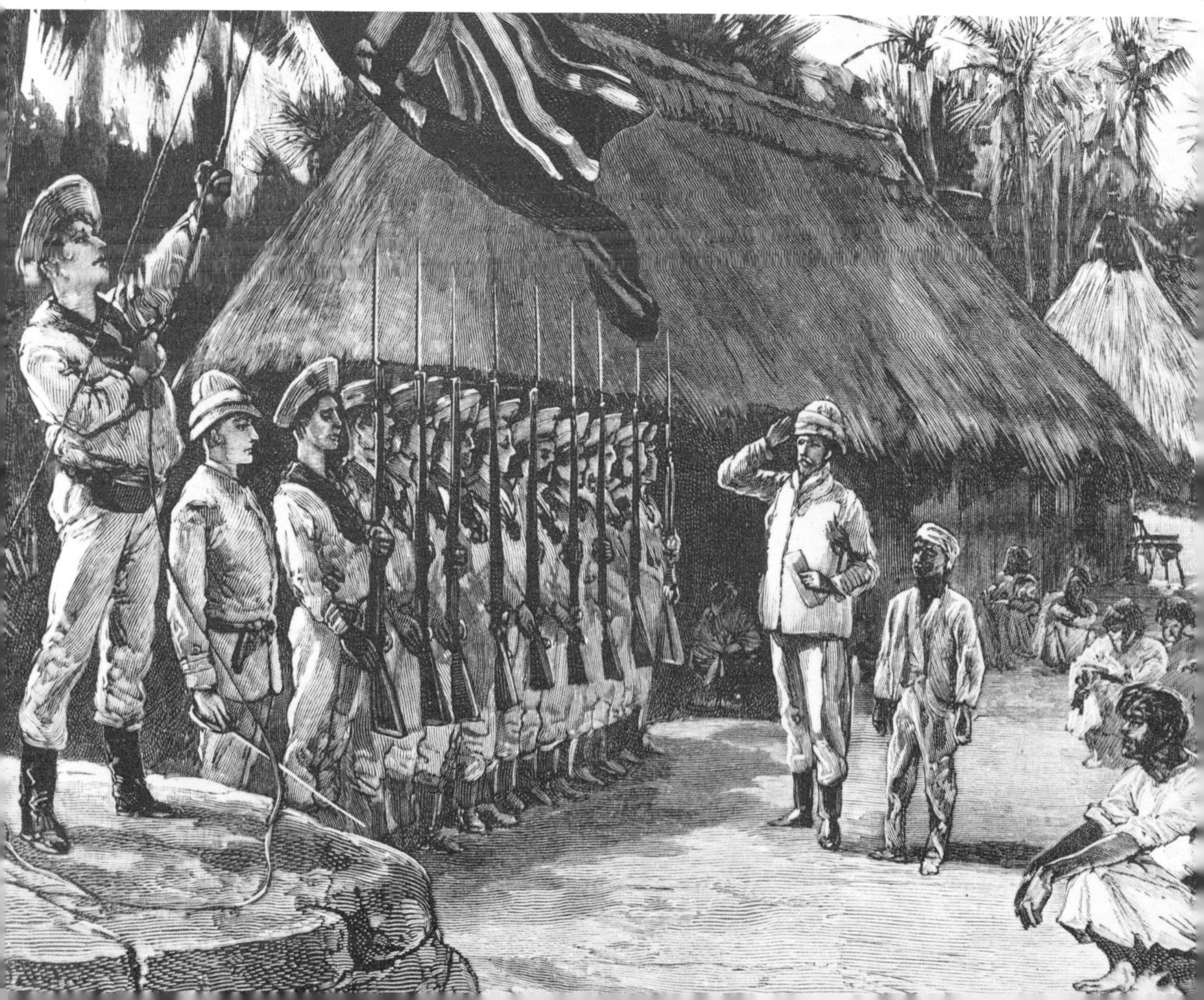

Ritual can be defined as the performance of a set of actions or words in order to obtain some real or imagined result. Sometimes anthropologists refer to the mating activities of certain animals as 'ritualistic', and, in the sense that the actions are formal and instinct plays a part in the process, the description is accurate. But human ritual is more difficult to define.

The anthropologist Max Gluckman divides the human process of ritual into three categories. Ceremonial, which may be used to describe actions involving symbolic statements of social status; examples are a Coronation Day procession, or the May Day parade in Russia. Ceremoniousness is that which describes ceremonial when the practitioners have no idea of occult powers being involved – for instance the practice of standing to attention when the national anthem is played. And finally, ritual can mean ceremonial in which ideas of occult power are present. Into this last category fall the simple initiation ceremonies of primitive peoples, the complex procedure of a solemn High Mass, and a wide range of activity between the two extremes.

Everyone has experienced ceremoniousness in day-to-day life. A classic example is the formal rite of afternoon tea, the very making of tea itself being subject to solemn and rigid procedures. Many a hostess would feel a deep unease if forced to disregard her tea-making rules. Similarly, many workmen insist on setting their tools out in careful order before beginning a job. Here, ceremoniousness begins to merge with superstition in that the carpenter 'wouldn't feel right' if his chisels were not placed side by side – even though he may have begun to lay them out in this way as an apprentice for purely practical purposes. A precise example of ceremoniousness merging with ritual is to be seen in the modern Royal Navy, when an officer formally salutes the quarterdeck on boarding a ship. The quarterdeck is the domain of the ship's commander and if the officer were saluting the commander's authority, his action would be an example of ceremoniousness. Technically speaking, however, he is not doing this. In pre-Reformation days, a crucifix always hung on the quarterdeck and was saluted as an act of propitiation and worship. The modern officer will still salute the place where the crucifix was before turning formally to greet his

Ritual in its various forms is important to all human societies Previous page *the ceremonial dress worn by these Fijian warriors, and the formality of their actions, defines their role as soldiers*

Above left *sportsmen marching in a May Day parade in Moscow also affirm their social status* Below left *raising the British flag; saluting the flag is a formal gesture with no obviously supernatural associations*

Following pages *dance of Arab tribesmen* (above left) *and the procession of the 'chief' in Dahomey* (below left). *In ceremonial rituals participants realize that occult powers are involved: the Patriarch of Jerusalem conducts a service* (below centre). *The importance of ritual is frequently emphasized by special robes or costumes: American Indian ceremonial figure* (right)

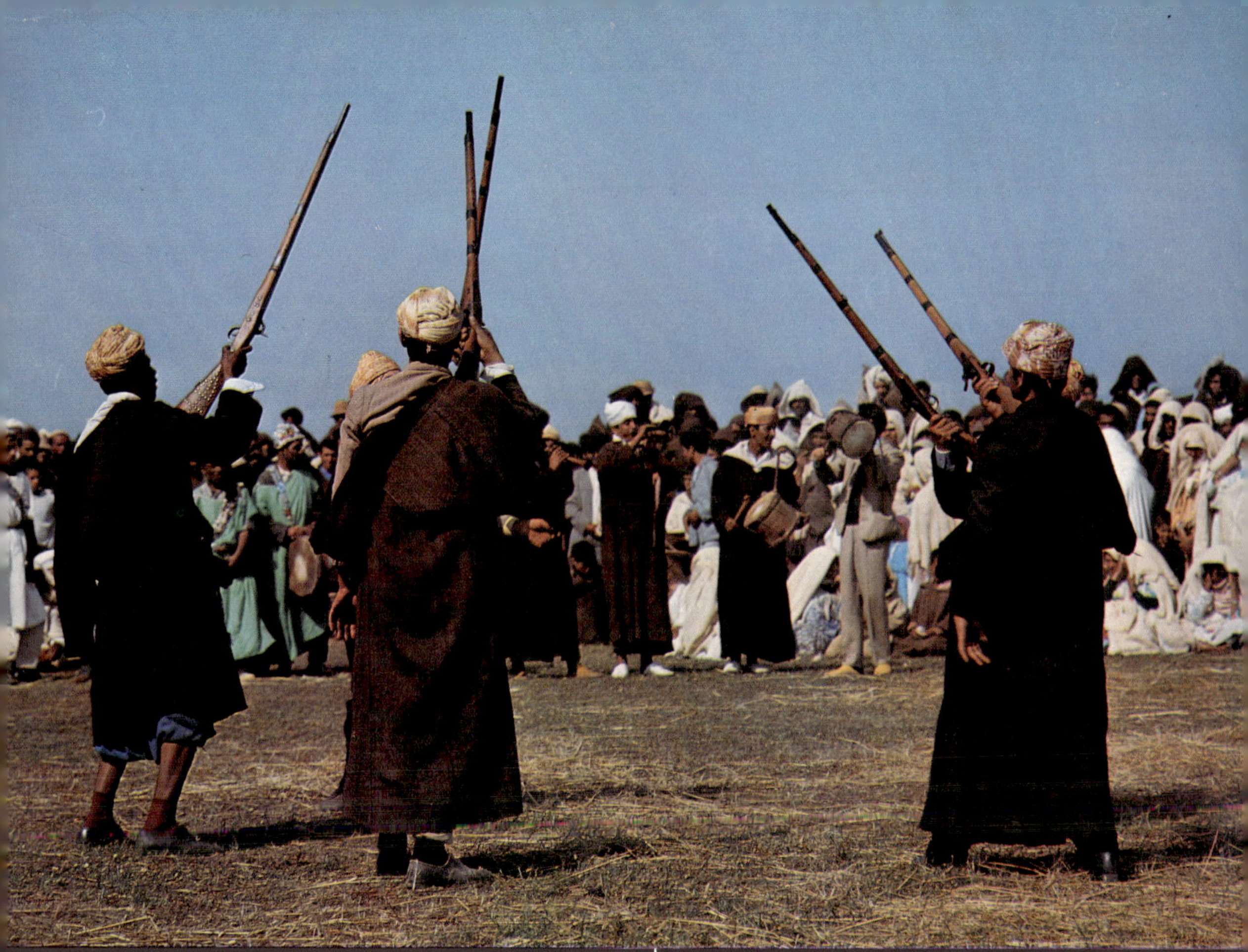

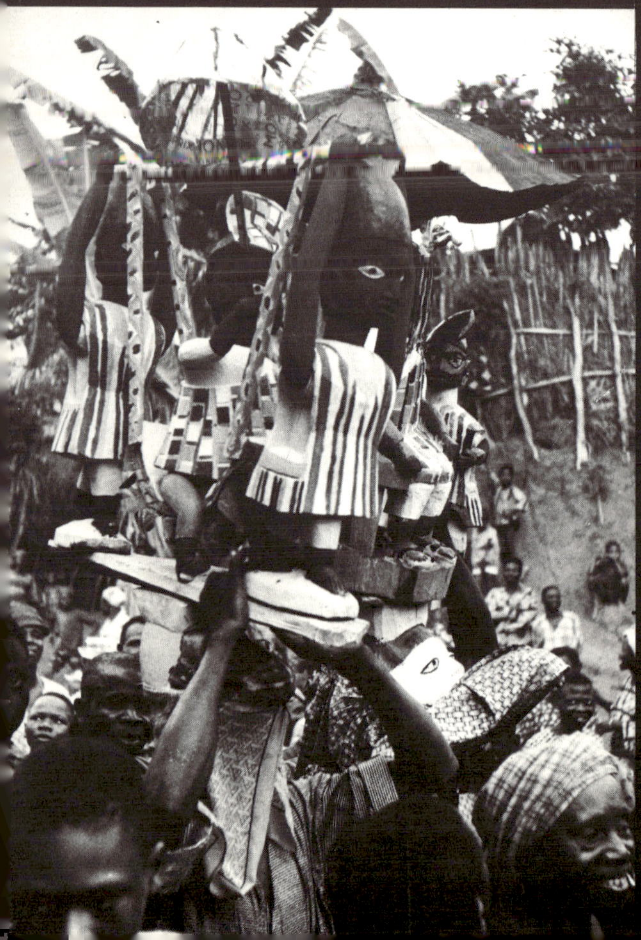

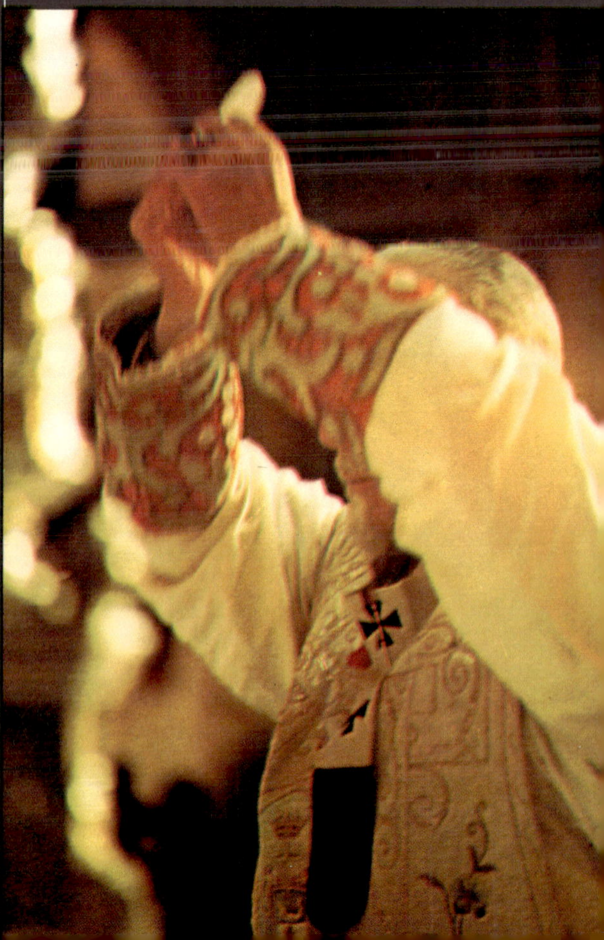

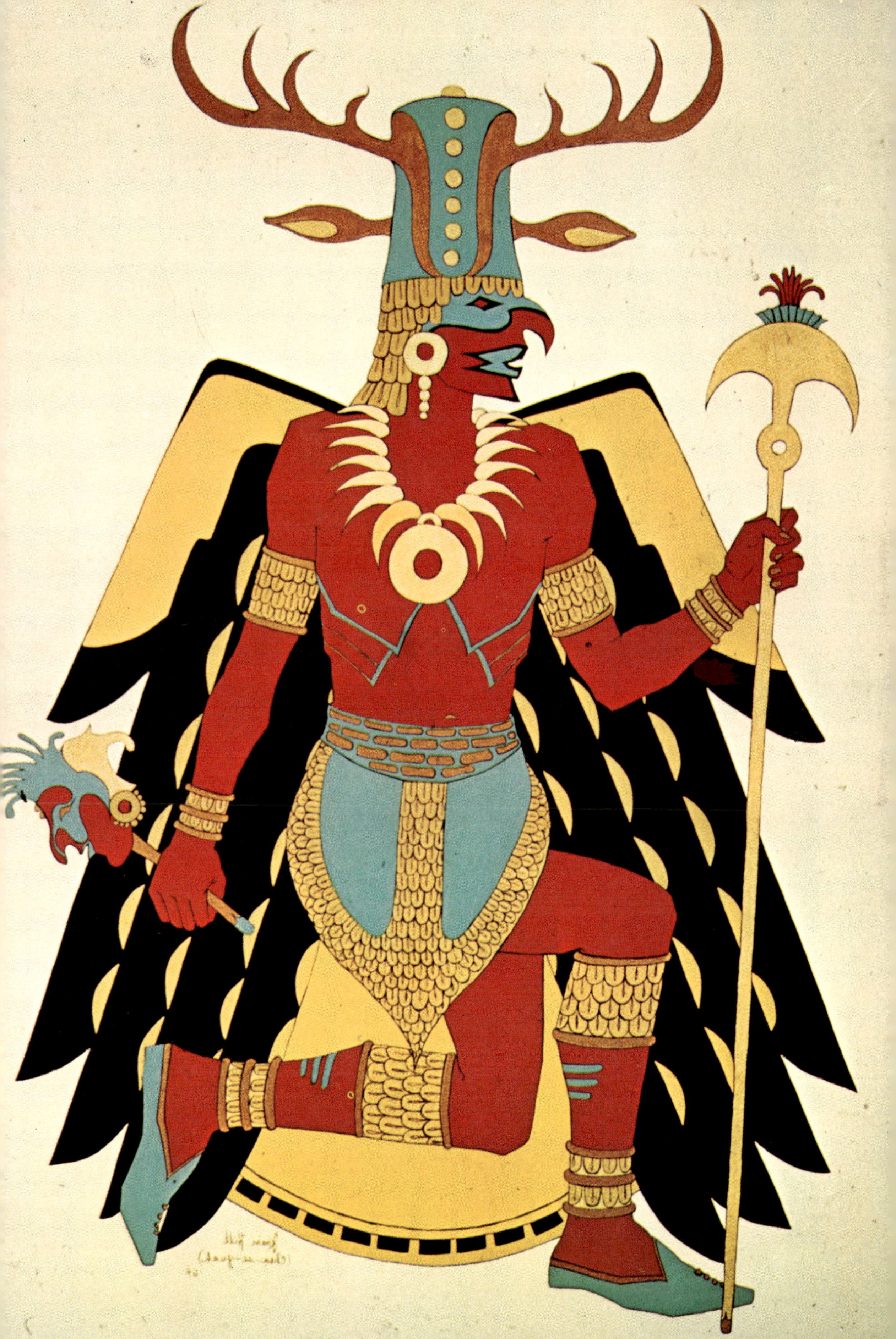

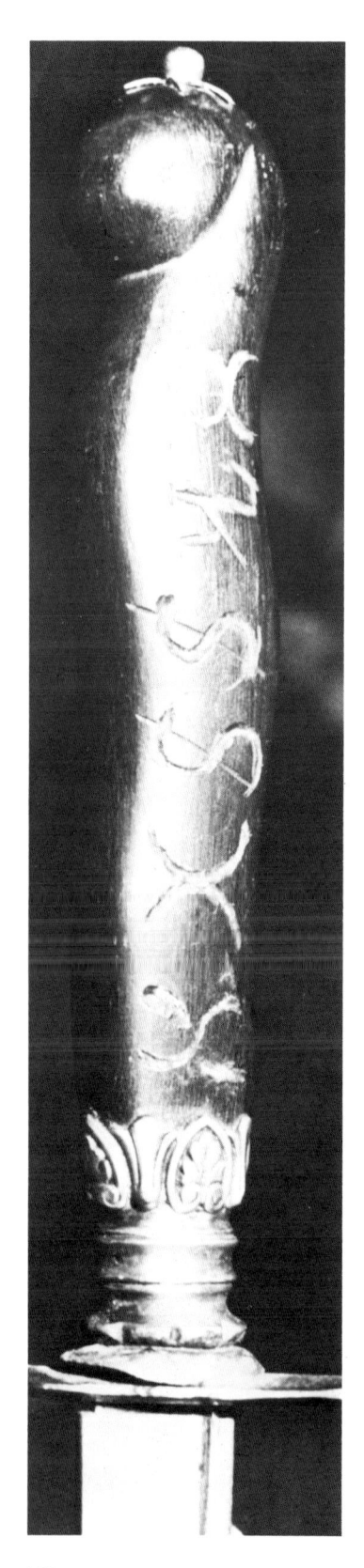

superiors, thus involving himself in a ritual.

Ritual plays as big a part in life today as it ever did. Every Sunday, Christians participate in the ritual of churchgoing. And whether it is a simple non-conformist service or High Anglican liturgy they believe that through these rites they are contacting God on a personal plane for the purpose of worship and supplication. The same basic motives, of course, apply to all religions, whatever form their ritual takes. In fact, the same methods, if not motives, are used by the ritual magician, white or black.

Catholicism, with its rich use of symbolism and its deep understanding of the psychology of ritual, has a close kinship with high magic. The principal reason is that medieval magicians and alchemists were usually Catholics (or Jews, in which case they had a similar background of ceremony and symbolism) and drew their power from the same sources as did more orthodox worshippers. As the 19th century French magus Eliphas Levi pointed out, no one can sincerely believe in the power of the Black Mass if he does not believe in the White Mass.

Both Catholics and magicians use ritual to the same end; the channelling of occult force in a sacrament or a spell. And in both cases it is the power that matters, rather than the method used for concentrating that power. The outward and visible sign, whether cross or pentacle, is merely the focusing point which enables the worshipper to come into psychic contact with the force that is the animating life of that symbol. And the sharper the focus, the better the result.

To achieve this focus, the magician and the priest appeal to all five senses: the smell of incense or opium; the taste of wine or blood; the feel of the chalice or the sword; the chanting of liturgy or incantation; and the sight of altar, candles, robes and vestments, and all the other paraphernalia of the rite in question. In examining a magician's ritual in detail, it is best to look to psychology rather than history for an explanation of the tools he uses and the ways in which he uses them to summon – and control – the forces of the occult.

Grimoires, the medieval magician's textbooks, give numerous instructions for making magical implements as well as for their use. Most of these instructions pile difficulty upon difficulty, and only the truly dedicated student will persevere to the end. For instance, one grimoire gives the formula for making the knife used in most ceremonies. First the magician must make a cleaver, inscribe it with symbols and words of power, and dedicate it. With this cleaver he must cut, at a single blow, a piece of ram's horn to make the handle for his knife. He must carve appropriate symbols on the cut horn, and dedicate it. He then turns to the knife blade. This must be shaped at midnight, in one forging, and must be cooled in mole's blood. The mole is blind and therefore unable to 'see' the magical secrets of the process. Finally, the blade itself must be dedicated, inscribed and fitted to the handle with suitable ceremony. The fact that each of these processes should be carried out at propitious astrological times, not a moment too late or too soon, gives some idea of the complexity of the 'black arts'.

Ideally, the magician should himself make each of the items of equipment, though to possess an implement made and used by a dead magus is equally advantageous. In both cases, a powerful psychological impulse is exerted on the possessor of the tool; he feels it to be charged with power.

The use of magical symbols based on ancient knowledge is common to many rituals
Left the handle of a magician's wand is inscribed with esoteric signs
Top an Australian aborigine is painted before initiation
Above the Book of Spirits contains symbols representing names of power

124

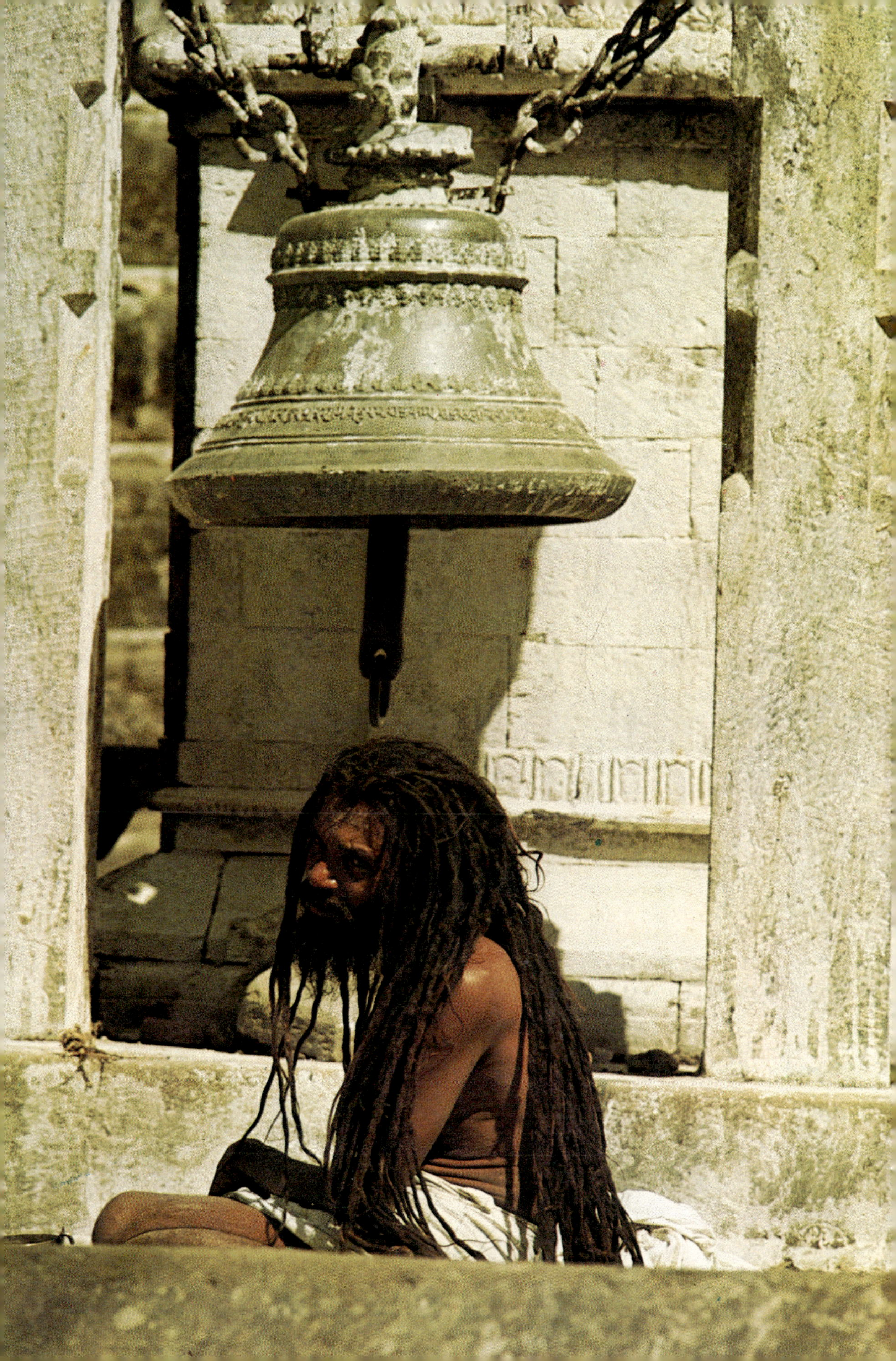

Previous pages *Tibetan exorcising dagger* (left) *and the top of Aleister Crowley's wand* (centre); *making magical implements requires dedication and perseverance. An Indian holy man meditating* (right); *the Western magician must practice abstinence before attempting to raise a spirit from the dead*

Below *an open coffin; a magical circle, to contain the returning spirit, would be drawn around it during a necromantic rite*
Below right *a graveyard scene*

This process of self-hypnosis, of the magician steeping himself in the very atmosphere of the spell he intends to cast, runs through all his activities. The result is that he works himself up into a state in which his incantation, charm or ritual must yield results, even if only subjectively. An example is the necromantic rite.

Summoning the Dead

Necromancy, the art of conjuring up the spirits of the dead, has been an essential part of the magician's art, since the witch of Endor conjured up the spirit of Samuel to warn Saul of disaster. There are numerous other examples in classical literature, and in magical writings such as the *Key of Solomon* and the *Grimoire of Honorius*. Details of the rite vary from operator to operator, but the aim is essentially the same: the magician believes that the dead have arcane knowledge, and can be induced to part with it.

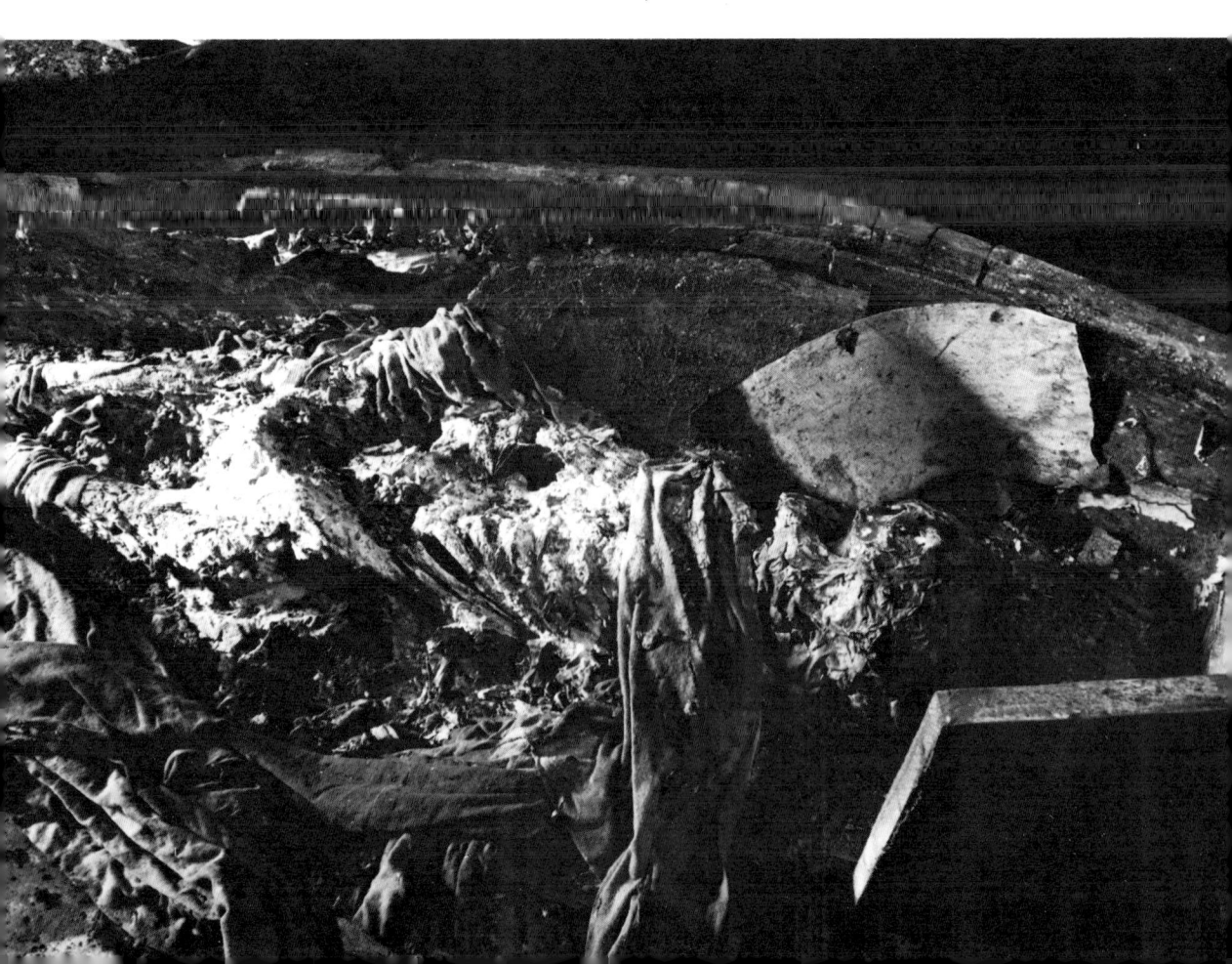

First, the magician must find a body. Having decided on the location of the grave and the body he wishes to use, he retires to his home and cuts himself off from the world for nine full days. Nine is the number of ultimate power in Cabalistic magic.

Once in seclusion, he begins a process of mental suggestion, and concentrates on becoming, as far as possible, the dead person. He dresses in a shroud, sleeps during the day and wakes at night, covers his hair with human ashes and when he eats, sparsely and at midnight, he eats the flesh of dogs and unleavened bread, and drinks unfermented wine. The dog is the animal of Hecate, goddess of death and the underworld; the bread and wine, unleavened and unfermented, and therefore lacking life, are both barren symbols. After his grim midnight meal, the magician recites the burial service, naming himself as the person to be buried. Like many rituals, the necromantic rites use Christian as well as pagan incantations. All occult power is useful, from whatever source it may spring. At no time does the magician permit himself so much as a thought of sex, or any other 'life' force; if such a thought intrudes, his work is spoiled and he must start again. On the ninth night, under cover of darkness,

Above a magic circle has the dual purpose of protecting those inside it from spirits and demons, and of keeping in the magical energy that is summoned during a ceremony; the names of power written in the rim give the circle additional force

Right a witch stands inside a magic circle and dips her athame in a chalice of wine

and accompanied by two acolytes, both of whom have observed the same penances as himself, the magician makes his way to the selected grave. He takes with him, in addition to digging tools, a bowl of incense, salt and water, a sword, six candles, a white-handled knife, and a mallet and sharpened wooden stake.

First there is the laborious and macabre business of opening the grave and removing the lid from the coffin, exposing the body within. Then comes the careful process of drawing two magic circles, one around the open coffin to contain the returning spirit, and one around the magician and his acolytes to protect them from other forces which may be accidentally summoned. The dedication of the circles is a curious mixture of Christian, Cabalist, and pagan thinking. Candles are placed at the head and foot of the coffin, the head of which points to the north. The magician's operating circle is described, with the point of the sword, at the coffin's foot and about three feet away from it. The circle is usually nine feet in diameter. The remaining four candles are placed on the perimeter of the magician's circle, at each point of the compass.

While an acolyte lights the incense in a thurible, or incense burner, the magician mingles the salt and water, symbols of life, and sprinkles some around the coffin circle. As he does so he blesses the ground in the name of Christ and the saints, and prays that these powerful protectors will keep the dead spirit from harming the operator. This done, the coffin circle is suffused with incense, and the magician and acolytes move back into the protective 'operating circle'. This is dedicated in a similar manner to that of the first, but with one difference; the 'great ones' of the four cardinal points of the compass are invoked.

The reason for the order in which this is done is a sombre one to an occultist. In all white magic ceremonies the operator's cardinal point is to the east, the quarter of the rising sun which brings light and warmth. Medieval churches were built facing in this direction so that the morning light would fall on the altar during the dawn Mass. But in the necromantic ceremony the magician, holding his ritual knife in both hands, points upwards, asks the protection of each power in turn, starting with the east, until he comes to the north. Here he pauses, and, taking the thurible

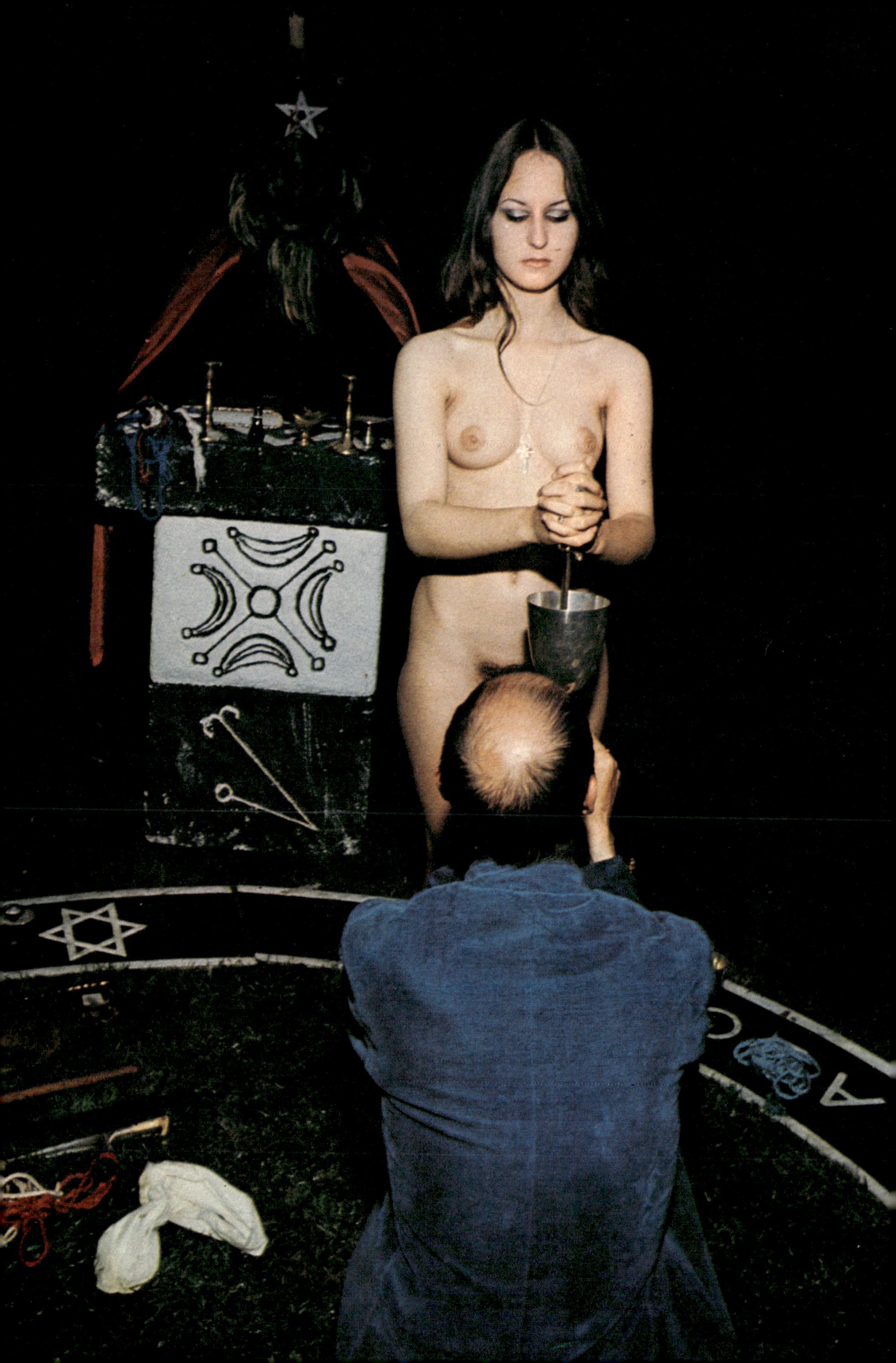

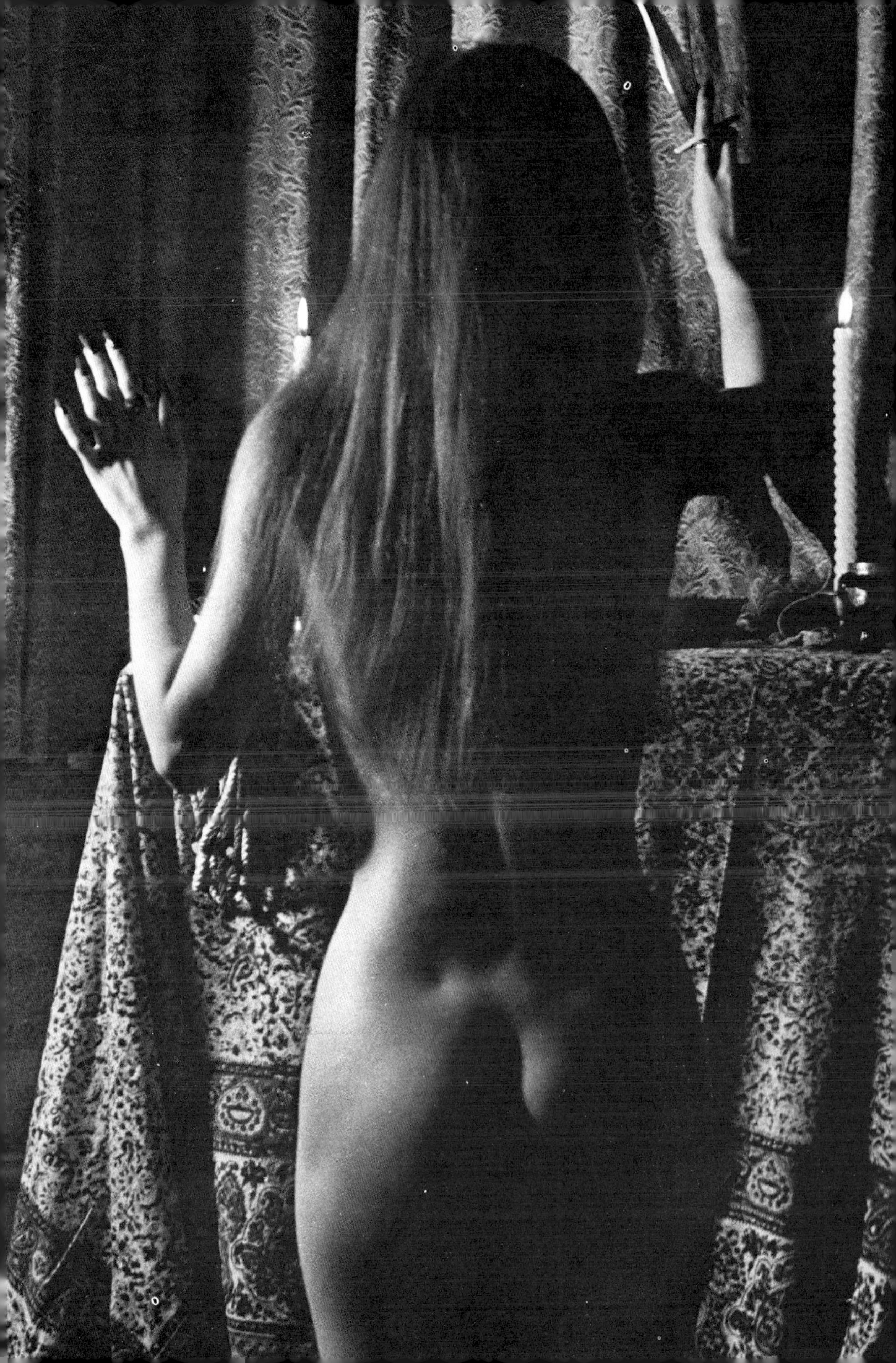

from his acolyte, censes the northern candle 11 times, afterwards touching the northern point with his sword also 11 times.

To a believer, and particularly after having undergone such grisly preparations, this must be a psychologically chilling moment even for the most hardened magus. The north is used as a 'holy point' by only one occult group on earth, the Yezidi of southern Asia – and they are Devil-worshippers. Otherwise, the north is black, the point of greatest darkness, the quarter of Loki, Satan, blood-freezing wind, and death. To the ancient Norsemen Hell was not a cauldron of flame, but a frozen plateau of splintering cold which lay beyond the Northern Lights. To European Christians, the north side of the churchyard was the place reserved for the bodies of suicides; to this day, a little 'Devil's door' through which coffins were carried can be seen on this quarter in old churches.

The 11 puffs of incense, and the 11 taps with the point of the magician's sword, are Cabalistic in origin. They are an invocation of Qliphoth, or evil Sephiroth, the spirit of damnation.

The magician is attempting to summon and command forces such as these as he chants his final incantation. The wording varies from spell to spell but the result is the same. He 'charges and commands' the spirit of the dead person, through the power of Christ and the saints, of Astoreth, Demon of Death and Lord of the Flies, of Loki, Qliphoth and Satan to return to the body from whence it originated. At this point, according to the grimoires, a rush of wind is heard, and a thin, squeaking voice addresses the magician through the mouth of the corpse. Aleister Crowley, in his novel *The Moonchild*, implies that this voice is an objective one, although a ceremonial magician who has tried less ambitious versions of necromancy maintains that it is usually audible only to the magician. Whichever case applies, the magician now asks the 'spirit' his questions, which it is forced to answer truthfully. Finally, in an inversion of the ceremony, he dismisses it to eternal rest using a Christian prayer for the dead. Before leaving he drives the wooden stake through its heart, so that the body can never again be used for magical purposes.

A necromantic rite therefore consists of three parts:

Facing page *a high priestess stands in front of her altar, her athame raised to invoke the Lords of the Watchtowers of the North. To many magicians the North is the point of death, darkness and cold*

...ds of Evil Dæmons   *Powers of Ev...*

Astaroth

Abaddon   *Mammon*

Pub. by Lackington & ...   R. Griffith

preparation, summoning, and dismissal, and, as far as form is concerned it is probably very similar to the undescribed ritual performed by the woman of Endor to raise Samuel. It also resembles most other magical rituals in that in all of them some force or occult power has to be summoned after the necessary preparation, and then dismissed. The spell described above is technically black magic, because evil forces are deliberately invoked. In the eyes of a magus, if the east were used as cardinal point and only Christian or Cabalist forces were called upon, the ceremony would be grey or neutral, provided that the information sought from the spirit was not to be used for deliberately evil ends.

The magician, black, white, or neutral, uses his art in a search for power, and he is ultimately materialistic.

The black magician calls on demons and the powers of darkness to help him to achieve his ends
Facing page *Astaroth, prince of the revengers of evil, Abaddon, and Mammon, the demon of ensnarers and tempters – from* The Magus *(1801) by Francis Barrett*
Above *Andras, the 'Grand Marquis of Hell', who causes arguments and discord.*

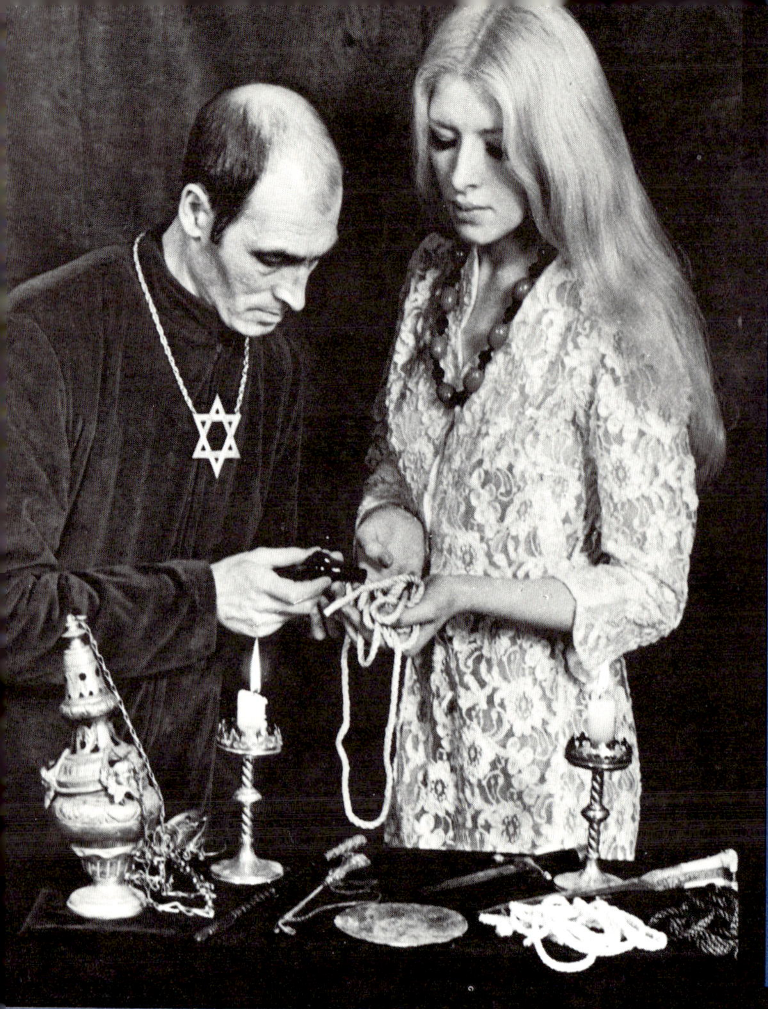

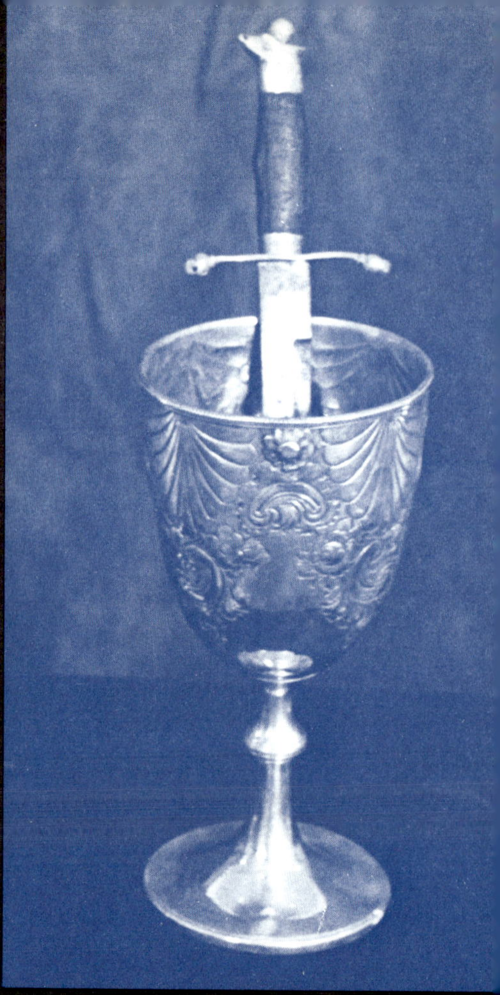

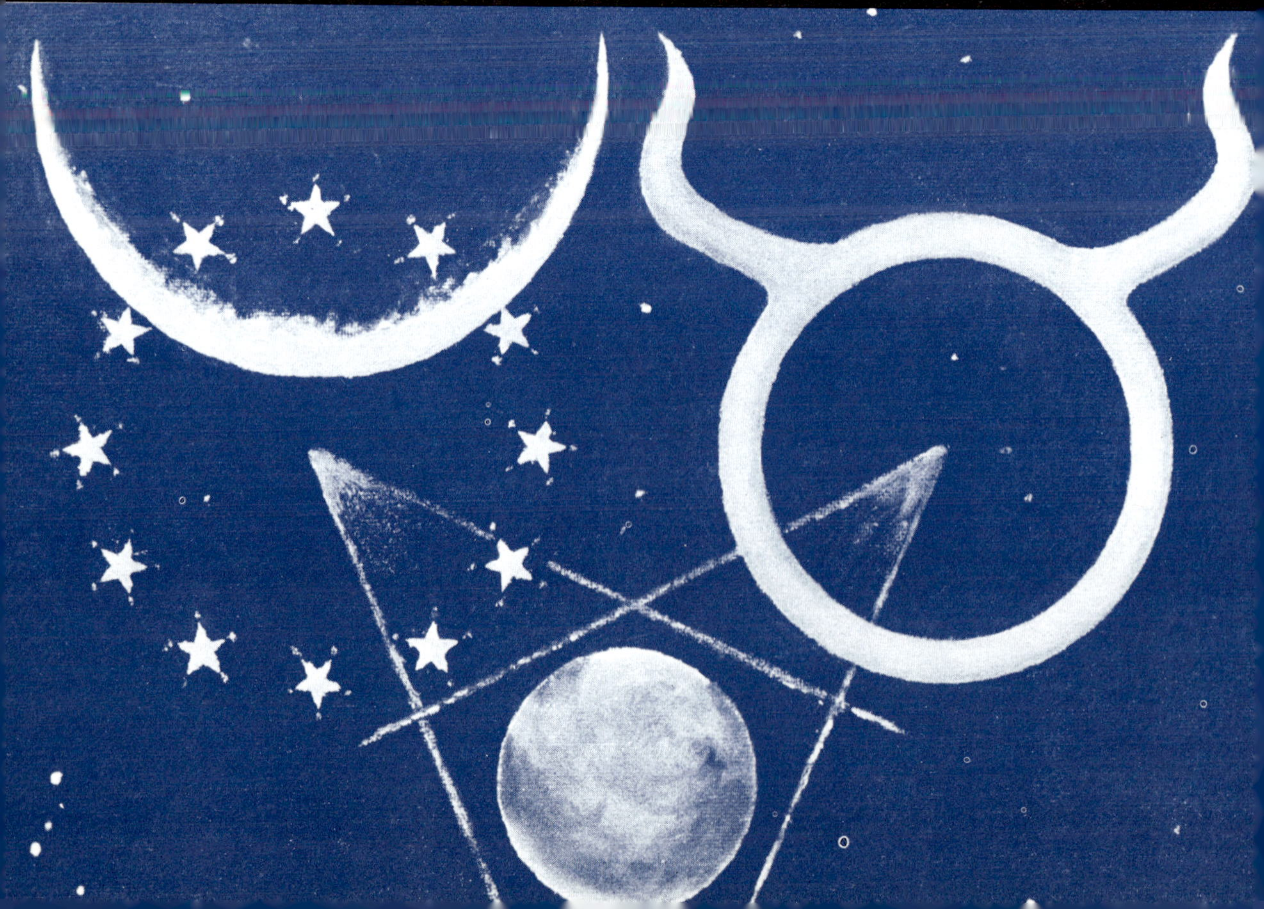

He is constantly attempting to 'eat of the forbidden fruit' and 'be as God'.

Rites of Initiation

The modern witch has no such lofty and perilous aims, but his ritual is on the same basis: preparation, summoning, and dismissal. Although the basis of witchcraft is worship, with magic in second place, the witch too, understands symbolism and the importance of set ritual. The sabbats or major festivals, and esbats, the equivalent of weekly services, are strongly ritualistic in flavour.

Modern witchcraft is a matriarchal cult, the mother goddess being the principal object of worship, with her consort the horned god taking a slightly less important place. The high priestess is therefore the dominating figure in a coven. Although witches are habitually naked during their ceremonies, all of them wear certain items of essential equipment: a necklace, symbolizing eternity and the circle of the seasons; a cord around their waist denoting both their degree within the cult and their symbolic bondage to the goddess and god; and the black-handled knife or athame which is the personal weapon of power given to them on initiation. Like the magician, the witch should ideally make or at least inscribe her own knife.

In addition, the high priestess also wears a garter around her left thigh and a headdress, often of beaten silver, denoting a lunula or crescent moon. The former is a badge of office, and bears a buckle for each coven over which the priestess holds office. She also carries a ceremonial sword with moon symbols on its pommel and cross-piece. This is mainly used for 'opening and closing' the circle, and for initiation.

The initiation of a novice into the coven is probably the most important ceremony within wicca. The novice, naked, is bound around the wrists with a cord and then blindfolded, before being led to the edge of the circle in which the coven operates. On the periphery of the circle he is stopped by a sudden, sharp jab in the chest: the point of the high priestess's sword. 'Are you willing' she asks him by name, 'to make the essay?' The novice replies in the affirmative. The priestess then reads a charge to the initiate, beginning with the words: 'Listen to the words of the Great Mother, who of old was called

Worship is the basis of modern witchcraft, with magic taking second place; but symbolism and ritual play an important part in ceremonies Far left *a high priest and high priestess, Alex and Maxine Sanders, consecrate cords* Left *the chalice, or female element, and athame, or male element; wine is consecrated by dipping the point of the athame into the full chalice* Below *a witches' altarpiece - oil painting by Stewart Farrar. It symbolizes the moon goddess and the horned god, and their influence on the world*

Scenes from the initiation of a novice: blindfolded, she is stopped at the periphery of the altar by the point of a sword (above) *before being led to the altar* (facing page). *When the initiate has been scourged, anointed, and censed she exchanges the sevenfold kiss with her high priest* (top).

among men Artemis, Astarte, Diana...' The charge goes on to demand that the novice be willing 'to will, to dare, to be silent'. At this point the blindfold is removed, and for the first time the novice sees the coven and sets foot inside the circle.

At the centre of the circle stands the altar. This is usually a small, draped table on which are placed a cup of wine, containers for salt and water, a thurible of incense, and a scourge. The initiate kneels before the altar, and is given a 'token' scourging by the priestess. Modern witches usually use scourges made from sewing silk. The priestess then mingles the salt and water, both life symbols, and anoints the initiate on the forehead with the mixture, afterwards censing him with the thurible. The sevenfold kiss, exchanged by priestess and initiate, follows. Each kisses the other on the lips, on the left knee, on the right shoulder, the left shoulder, the right knee, and the lips again in that order. The seventh kiss is on the genitals. This rite is important to the witches, because the order of kissing exactly describes on the body of the initiate the shape of a pentagram, or five-pointed star, the symbol of wicca.

With the initiate unbound and on his feet again, the familiar whirling dance of the witches starts. Hand in hand they hurtle clockwise, in the direction of the sun,

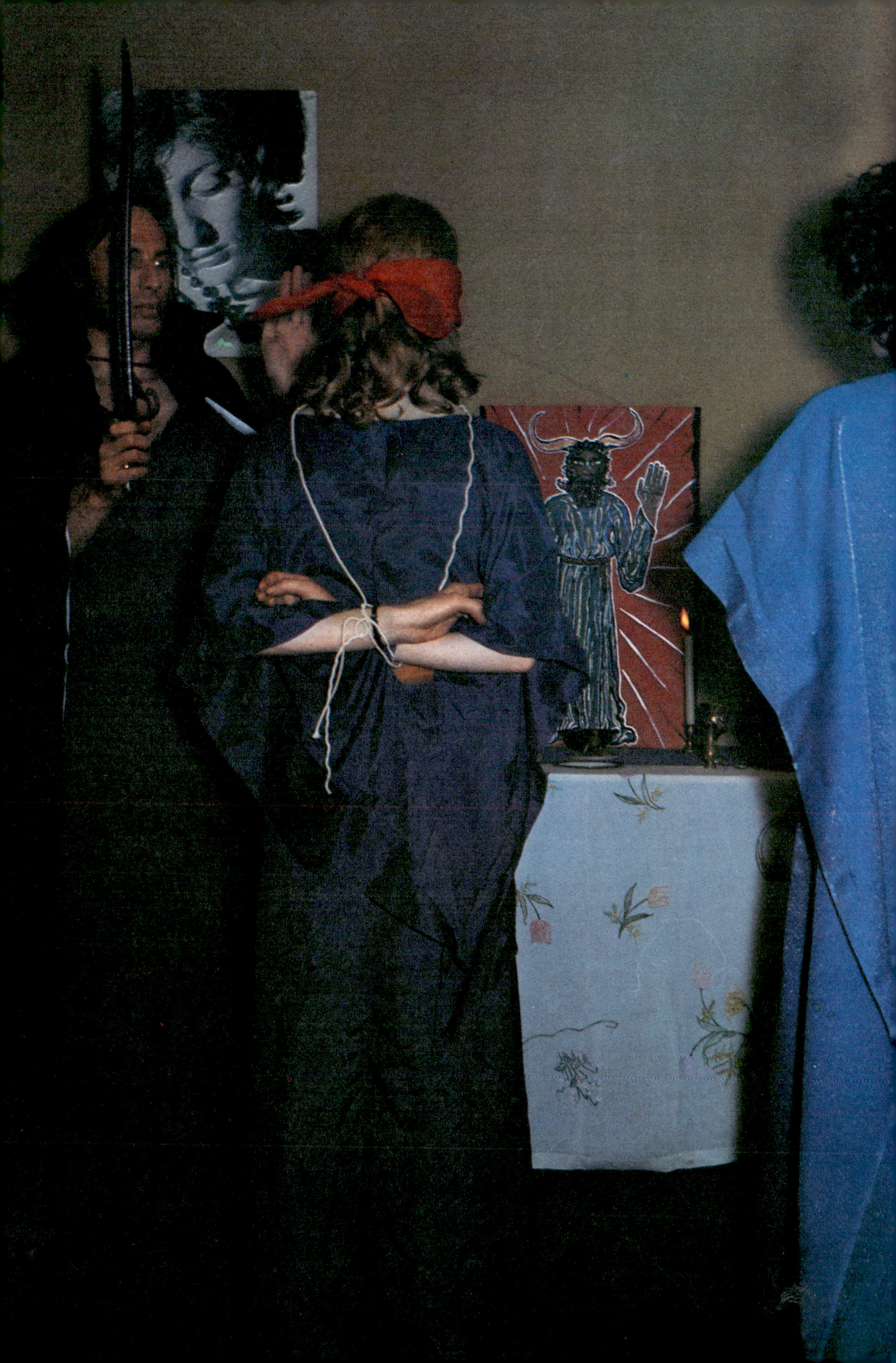

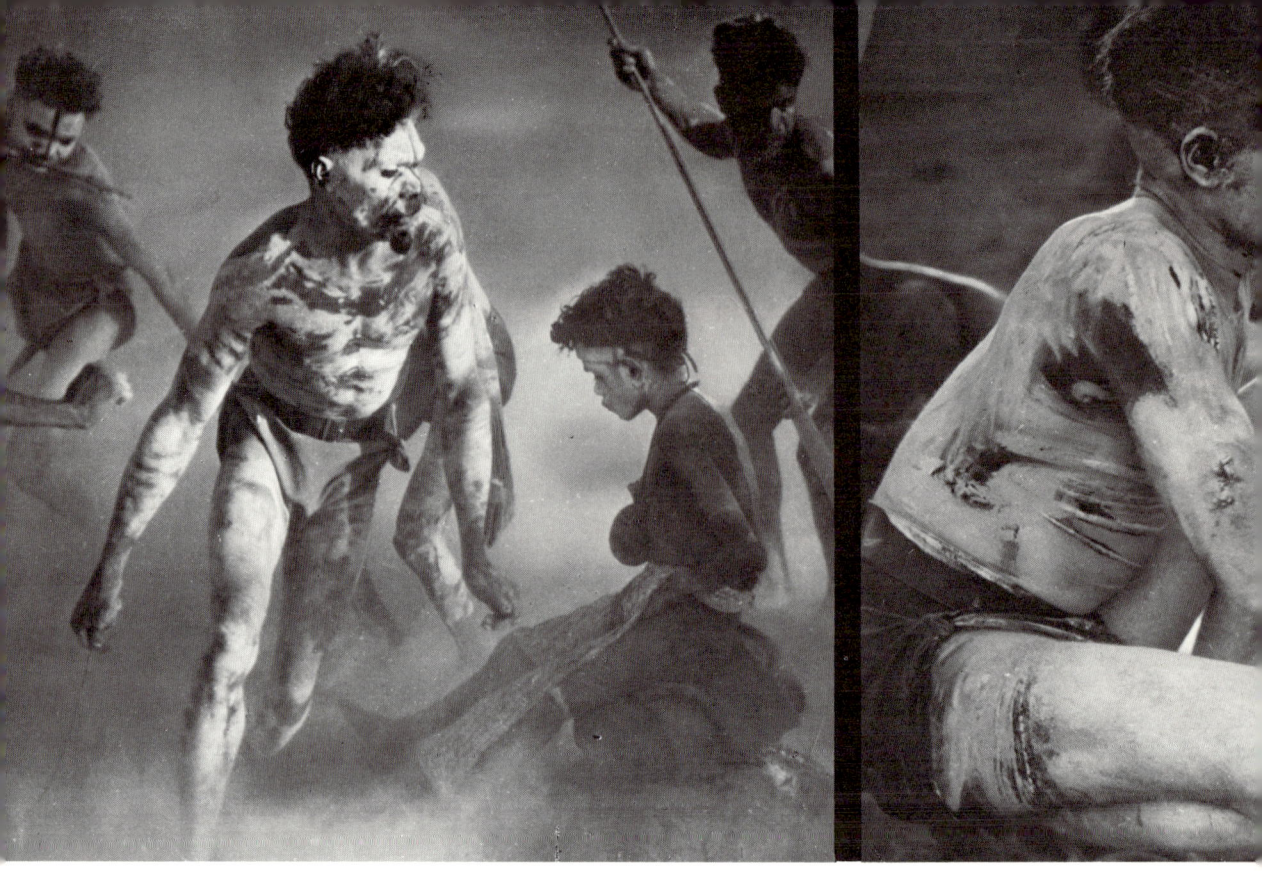

faster and faster around the novice and priestess, until the latter commands them to stop. The purpose of the dance is exactly the same as it is in dervish dancing: it is a means to work up excitement and mystical energy, creating what the witches call a cone of power in the circle. Standing in the centre of this power the priestess calls upon the great ones of the four elements in turn, asking them to receive the newcomer into their service.

A cakes and wine ceremony follows, during which small, crescent-shaped cakes are dedicated and distributed to those present, and the chalice of wine is passed from mouth to mouth. Witches vehemently deny that this is in any way an imitation of Christian communion. It is, they say, a thanksgiving for the grape and the grain. The ceremony ends with the closing of the circle and the 'dismissal' of the powers built up. The 'preparation, summoning, and dismissal' cycle, which also governs the necromantic rite, is complete.

But the initiation of a witch also contains the basic elements of the ritual of initiation into any group of society. The idea of rebirth, of changing and becoming part of a new group, is present in initiation ceremonies the world over. Indeed, according to the Kunapipi, an Australian aboriginal tribe, the young men about to become elders ceremonially 'enter the Mother, they go into the ring place, as happened in the beginning.' Inside a form of magic circle the boys undergo the ordeal of being hung from a pole for a set period. When that is over they are cut down and are symbolically reborn. Having survived the ordeal they are officially men. Rebirth through ordeal during initiation is common to many tribal systems in Asia, Africa, and North America. Among several plains Indian tribes, including the Comanches and the Cheyenne, the ordeal was real and extremely painful. To prove their manhood would-be warriors were suspended from bone hooks thrust through the skin of their chests and backs, and left to hang in the midday sun. In a Melanesian tribal custom bamboo shoots were thrust up the initiate's nostrils and urethra and twirled until he bled. If he managed to remain silent his manliness was proved.

Underlying each of these ordeals is the assumption that the tribal guardian spirits will help the initiates to conquer their pain and their fear. And by successfully undergoing the torture, the youths show that they have been approved by the 'powers.'

The humiliation and purification processes are universal. In parts of Brazil girls are cast out at puberty, left alone in huts isolated from the rest of the community

Initiation ceremonies throughout the world are linked by a basic theme: that of rebirth, change and acceptance by a new group. In the final stages of an Australian aborigine's initiation the youth sits over a sacred fire (far left) *while dancers, painted in ochre, ward off evil spirits. He is then presented with a ritual armband* (centre) *made from human hair which is thought to have the magical property of inducing courage and endurance. When the ceremony is over the boy is lifted up* (above) *and shown to his people.*

Death is surrounded by ritual which is intended to ease the passage of the soul from this life into the next, and protect the living from evil spirits. Above right *mourning Phillipine women; the chicken is thought to ward off evil spirits.* Below right *the dead woman is propped up in the death chair*

as ceremonial undesirables – neither child nor woman – until their first menstruation is over. Then they bathe themselves and walk back to the village centre, with their long hair brushed forward over their faces to indicate modesty in their new role as young adults. On the Luango coast of the Congo young men are painted white, to symbolize death and are taken out into the bush and circumcised. They are then 'buried' in a fetish hut for a period of fasting and meditation. The Plains Indians of North America were often specific in the matter of humiliation. Before the youths who were about to become braves set off for their first hunt or war-party, the women of the tribe would surround them, taunting them and jeering at their pretence to warrior status. The custom had the psychological effect of inspiring the young men to exert themselves more than they would otherwise have done.

These primitive rituals are paralleled in Western society by the initiation rites undergone by apprentices beginning work for the first time or on completion of their apprenticeship. A striking example from west Yorkshire, carried on until comparatively recently, could almost have been based on African or Asian customs. Boys beginning work in the wool mills, usually at the age of 14 or so, were carried off to a secluded corner by women weavers during their first day. They were de-bagged and their genitals smeared with oil and wool clippings. Their reaction to this traumatic treatment determined their future popularity in the mill.

Whether it is the joyful barmitzvah of a 13-year-old Jewish boy, or the oil-and-excrement smeared introduction of a novice to the Hell's Angels' motor cycle cults of California, initiation is only one of several rituals which mark man's passing through life. Others are concerned with birth, marriage, and death and, with initiation, they are known as rites of passage.

Rites of Passage

Like other rituals, rites of passage involve invoking supernatural aid, in their case at crisis points in the life of an individual. The underlying psychology in each rite is often universal. Birth rites, for instance, have the common theme of purity and dedication of the child's life to God; in the Christian baptismal service, the baby is anointed with water, the purifying and life-enhancing substance used in birth ceremonies from North America to Asia. A gift of silver, a pure metal, is also common, although in European countries the habit of crossing a baby's palm with silver has become a mere superstition. When a future chief or leader is baptized the child is often officially presented to God and to its people. Sioux chiefs held their heirs heavenwards on a shield to do this, in much the same way that Edward I of England is said to have placed his son, the Black Prince, on a shield and presented him to the people of Britain.

Death, when the soul passes from this life into the next, is also surrounded by rituals common to many peoples. The primitive practice of binding the hands and feet of a corpse so that the spirit cannot molest the

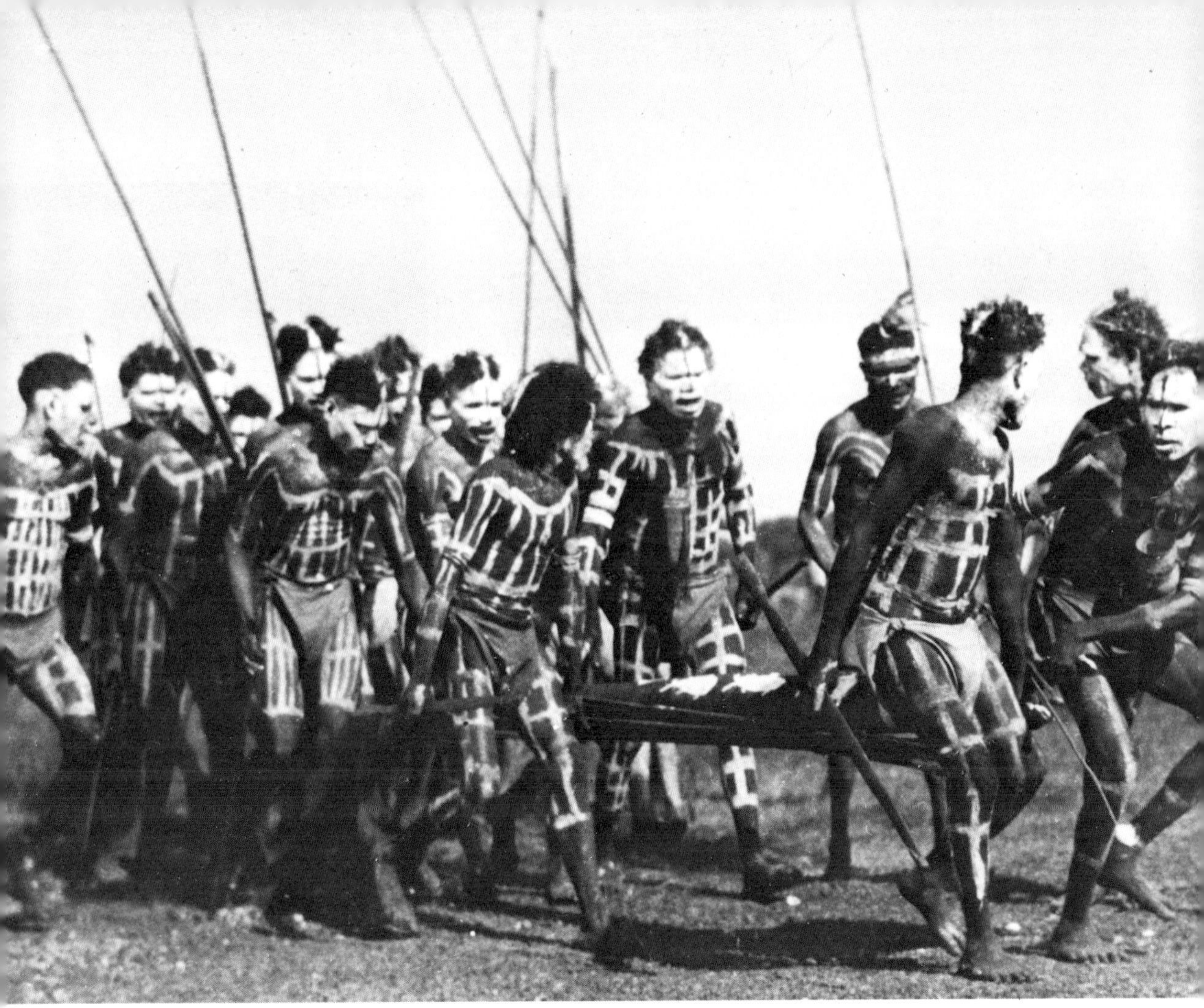

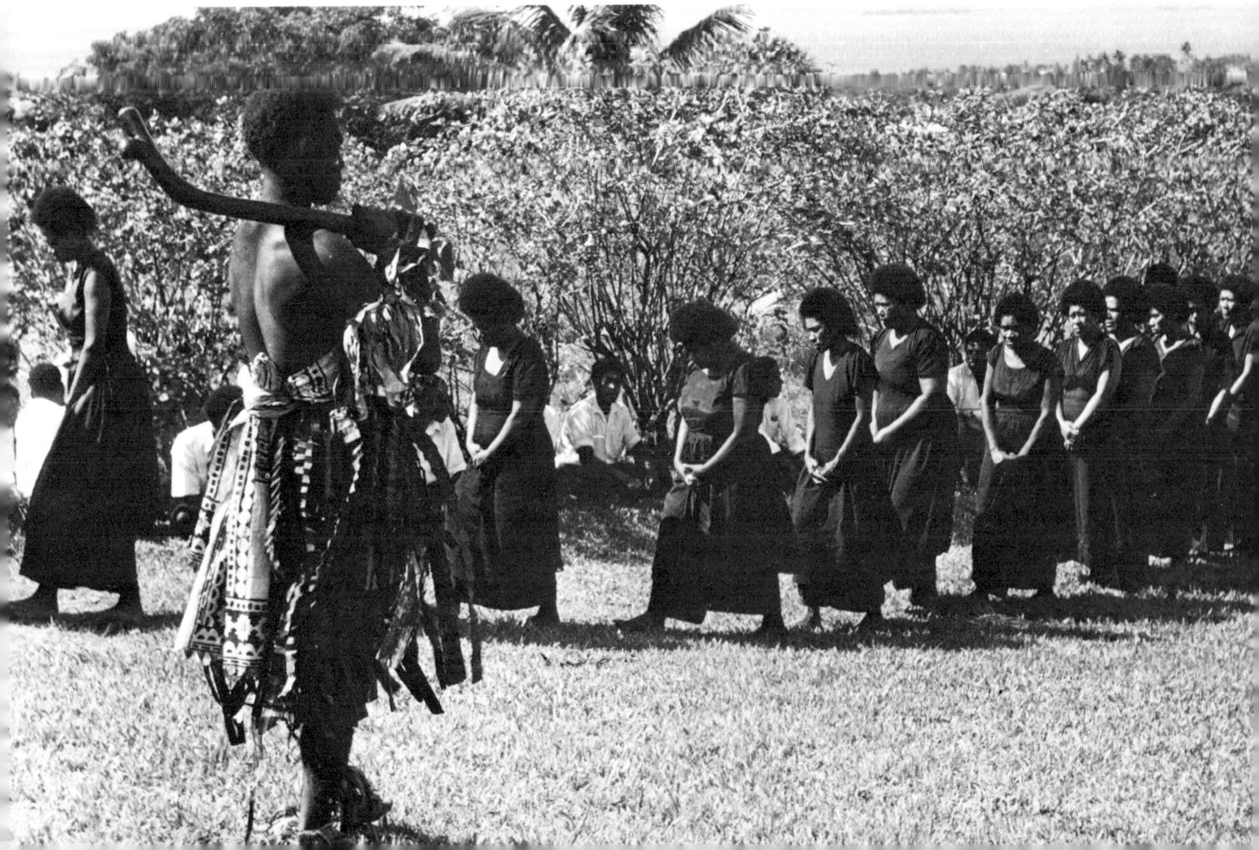

living is still traditional in many parts of Britain. Another old tradition, the placing of pennies on the eyes of the dead person recalls the practice, common since the days of ancient Greece, of furnishing the corpse with money to pay the boatman who will ferry his soul across the Styx into Hades.

Marriage customs, rites of passage which mark the couple's passing from the single state into the state of wedlock, are surrounded by fertility rites. In Europe, rice, a fertile food, is thrown over the couple; among the Apache Indians, the married pair are covered in pollen dust, another symbol of fertility.

These are examples of imitative magic, as are most fertility rituals. Modern witches, being members of what is basically a fertility cult, perform many rituals to induce the growth of crops, the reproduction of animals, and the return of the sun. Their four great seasonal sabbats are all attuned to Nature. In early spring they perform the dance of the wheel and cauldron, whirling sunwise around a fire, symbol of the sun, and leaping over a cauldron which itself is an ancient symbol of increase and plenty. The Mandan Indians performed an almost identical ceremony for the same purposes; like the witches, they felt that the sun had to be persuaded to return again to conquer the darkness and cold of winter.

Ceremonial copulation in pastureland or fields of crops was a universal piece of imitative magic of an explicit nature. Similarly urination on fields is common to many primitive peoples, imitative of the rain which they hope will fall to fertilize the earth. In Africa and on the North American plains, rainmaking dances are a vital part of the religious and symbolic life of the tribe, and in many cases a special, 'rainmaking' medicine-man, who is often also the chief, is responsible for inducing the required downpour. The rituals are often identical. The Kikuyu of Kenya, for instance, and the Cheyenne, both perform whirling dances around the figure of the medicine-man, who sprinkles water around him onto the dancers. Drums are beaten on the periphery of the circle to imitate thunder.

In the case of fertility rituals and rites of passage the powers invoked are basically good, enhancing life and bestowing fruitfulness. But because of the deep psychological implications involved, ritual is a powerful force

Facing page *although funeral rites vary according to local customs and traditions, death is always a solemn occasion. In Australia chanting tribesmen bear a pole coffin* (above). *Fijian women* (below), *wearing mourning clothes, file past a guard during the lying-in-state of their paramount chief*

Primitive initiation rites are paralleled in the West by the ordeals undergone by apprentices to a trade or craft Top *'Trussing the cooper', a ritual acknowledgment that an apprentice has completed his training* Above *Hell's Angels are traditionally smeared with oil and excrement during initiation*

Above the custom of placing coins on a corpse's eyes dates from classical Greece when a person who had died was provided with money to pay his passage to the underworld

Many religious ceremonies are based on the need to ensure growth of crops and reproduction of animals, while marriage customs are surrounded by fertility rites to encourage a fruitful union Above centre *a Muslim wedding in Malaya; the bridegroom is dressed in white.* Above right *a witch, her arms outstretched, stands in front of a flower-bedecked altar; modern witchcraft is basically a fertility religion* Right *a fertility festival in Nigeria*

when used for harmful purposes. Just as the quack doctor's 'medicine' made from coloured water may bring psychological benefits to a person who believes in its efficacy, so the same water, taken as a 'poison' may cause physical discomfort if someone believes in it strongly enough.

A classic example of evil ritual is the bone pointing, death-inducing ceremony of the Australian aborigine medicine-man. Belief in this rite is so powerful, even among educated Aborigines, that once the ceremony is performed (always with the knowledge of the victim) death almost invariably results.

In the late 1960s doctors in Melbourne were baffled by the case of a young aborigine who had accidentally disturbed a witch-doctor in the middle of a ceremony. The witch-doctor had pointed the death-bone at the young man, causing an invisible, supernatural snake to begin twining its coils around the latter's body. When the doctors were called in the young man was already paralysed in both legs. Despite the use of medication and hypnosis the paralysis crept up his body. First it caused stomach cramps so that he could not eat, then it compressed his lungs so that his breathing became laboured and shallow. Only when he was placed in an iron lung did the young man's breathing become nor-

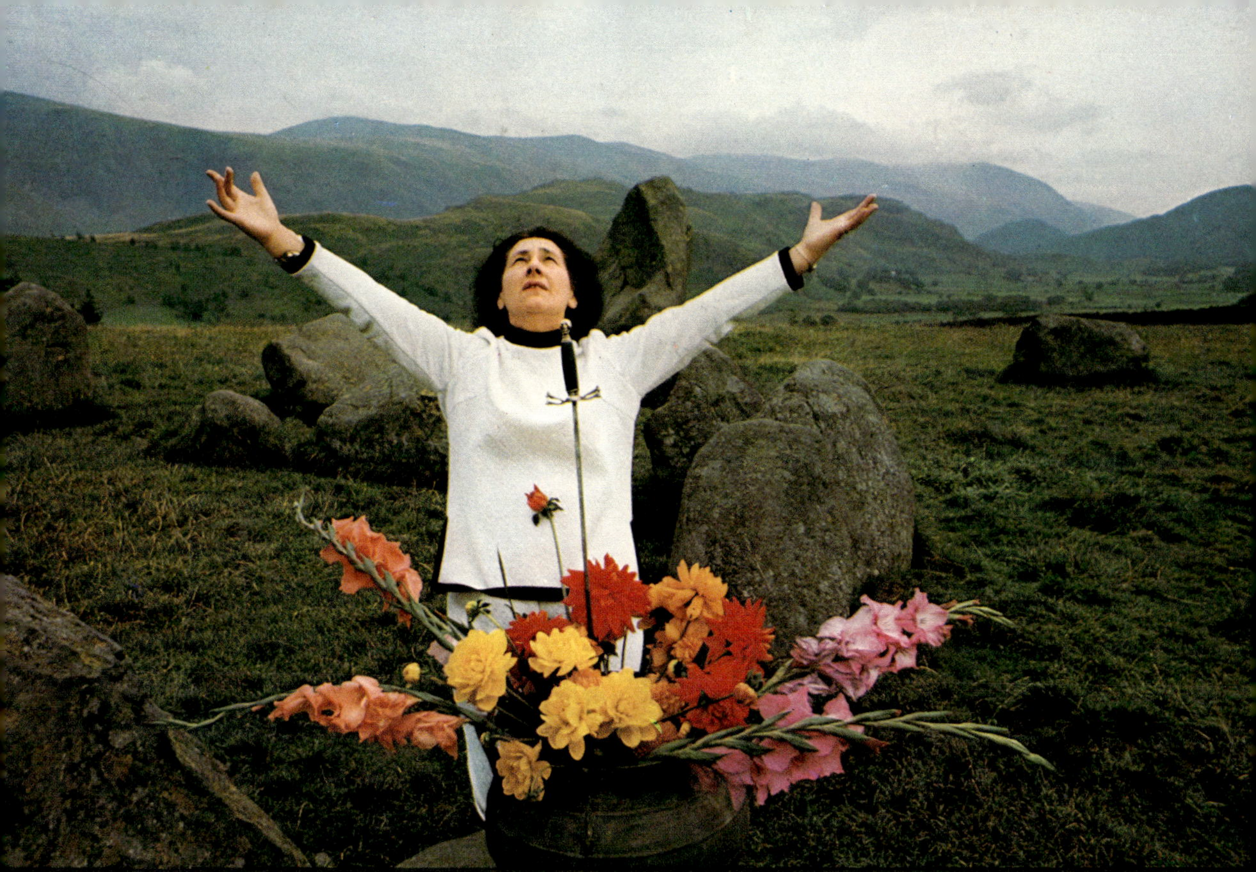

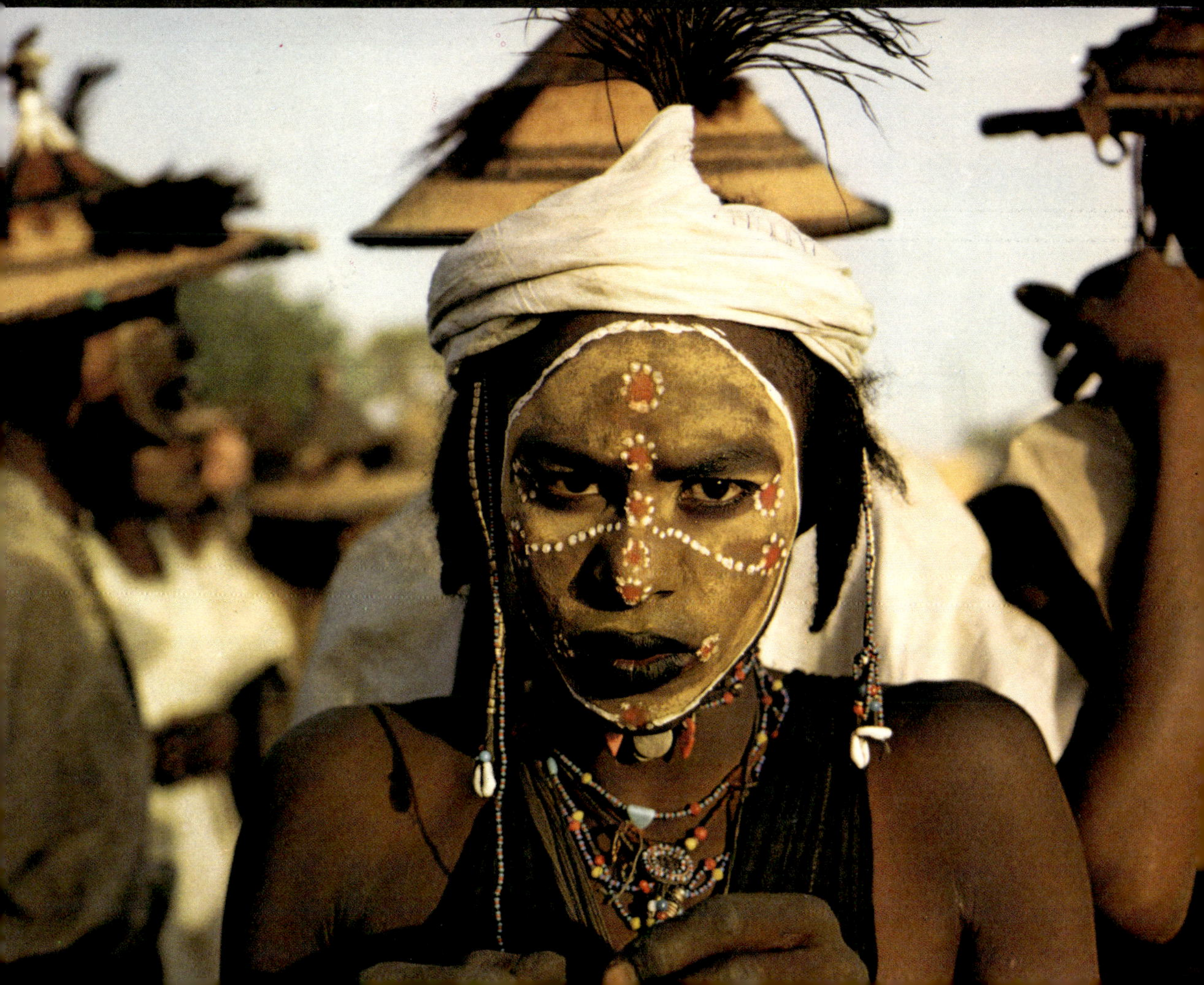

mal again. Convinced that the white man's magic was more powerful than the witch-doctor's death spell, he quickly recovered the permanent use of his limbs.

A common factor in all evil ritual, whether in Africa or in Western countries, is its psychosomatic effect. The victim is informed of what is going on; he knows that the witch is sticking pins into his wax image, and feels pain; he is aware of the magic serpent wrapping its inexorable coils around him, and loses the use of his legs. The actual ritual, with its irresistible occult element, is the force that works on his subconscious.

The idea of the Black Mass, basically the inversion of the Christian Mass as an act of worship to Satan, is one that sends a shiver of revulsion up Catholic spines, even though the ritual itself is a comparatively recent invention, first heard of in its modern form in the France of Louis XIV. Although it is a revolting ceremony of perverted sexuality and coprophagy, it is not in itself a

Because they celebrate life and new growth, fertility festivals are usually joyful and colourful occasions
Far left masked African dancers perform a fertility dance
Left participant in the Mardi Gras festival, New Orleans; like all spring festivals it celebrates returning fertility

malignant spell. The only example of the Christian Mass being used to malicious ends comes from medieval Gascony, where the Mass of St Secaire inspired terror and sometimes death. Unlike the Black Mass, the Mass of St Secaire involved no Devil worship; in essence it was a straightforward mass for the dead: with the frightening difference that it was said for a living person. St Secaire is not to be found in any calendar of saints; he or she is totally obscure in origin. As H.T.F. Rhodes points out in his book, *The Satanic Mass*, it may be significant that the Basque word *seka* or *sekha* means more than the French *sec* – 'dry' and can describe a fat man becoming thin, literally 'dwindling away.'

Certainly, someone who devoutly believed in the power of the real Mass, would literally be frightened to death if told that his name had been used, and that St Secaire had been invoked in a Mass to give his soul eternal rest.

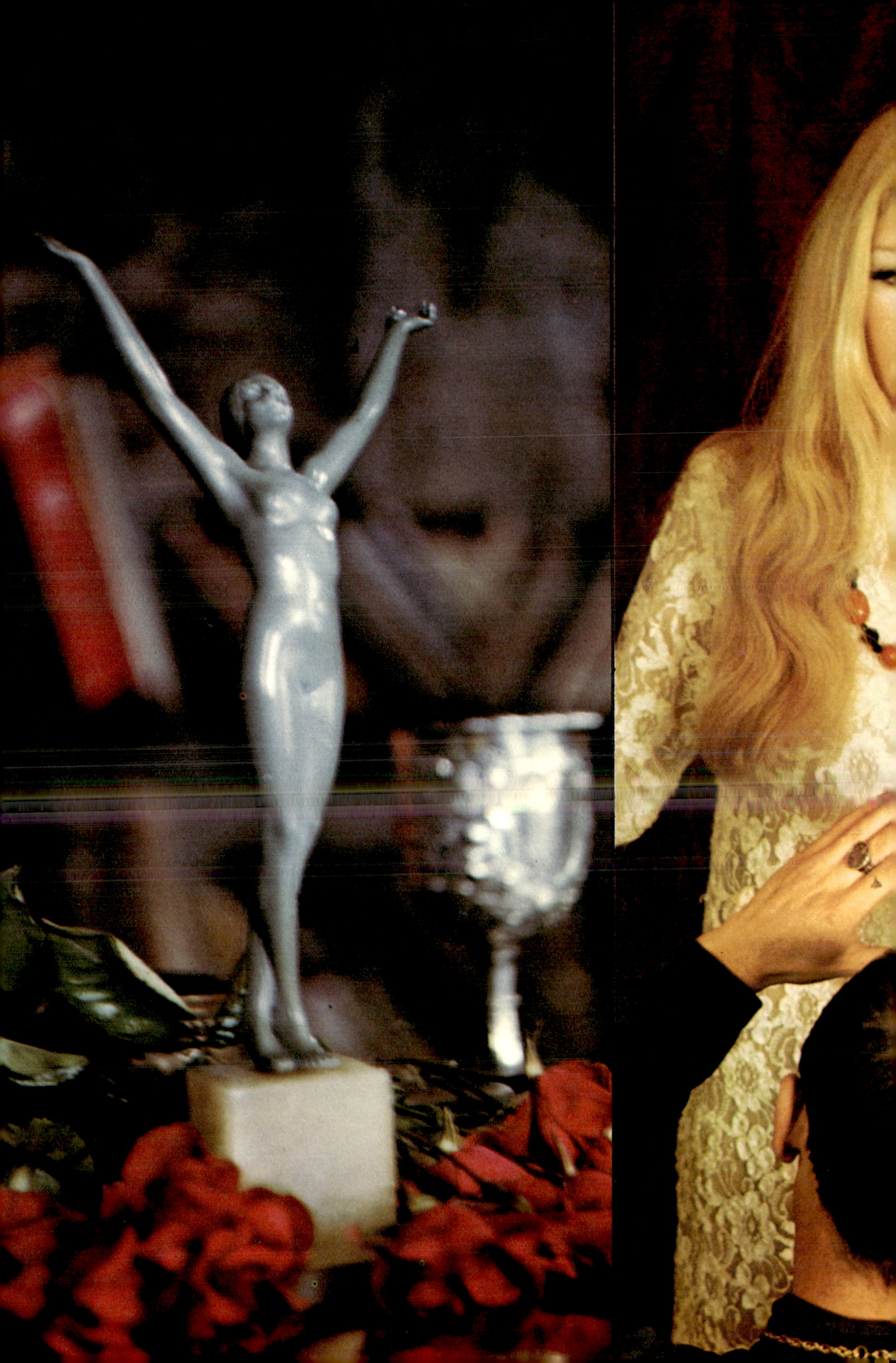

Magic in the Modern World

Previous pages *there is ample evidence of increasing interest in witchcraft in the modern world. In both the United States and Europe new covens are being formed and their members claim an affinity with the ways and practices of their witch ancestors. They call their craft 'wicca' and many claim to use their powers for good rather than evil ends*
Left *statue of a wicca goddess on an altar*
Centre *Alex Sanders, 'King of the Witches' and his wife and High Priestess, Maxine, in the ceremony of 'drawing down the moon'* **Right** *a naked witch lies prostrate. Modern witches hold their ceremonies in the nude believing that the flow of power is greater*

The immense technological advances of the past 70 years have done surprisingly little to dent man's deeply ingrained awe of the unknown. A dark, supernatural thread has run through the tapestry of the 20th century from its beginning. Today it has permeated all levels of society: 175,000 full-time astrologers thrive in the United States, two or three hundred witchcraft covens meet regularly in Britain, ouija boards and tarot cards enjoy steady sales, and there is a new interest in the old science of alchemy.

In 1900 only a handful of intellectuals carried on the occult traditions. Most of them were Theosophists, followers of Madame Helena Petrovna Blavatsky, whose powerful personality attracted disciples in both the United States and Britain before her death in 1891. But there were other groups too, believers, like the Theosophists, in mysterious secret chiefs who held wonderful stores of magical and Cabalist knowledge. One such group, certainly the most exclusive, was the Order of the Golden Dawn, which had many distinguished members in Britain and on the Continent. One of the most avid was William Butler Yeats, who even then was writing poetry steeped in the mystic Celtic traditions. Another was the Order's president, the writer McGregor Mathers, who translated several medieval grimoires. But the most important, potentially, was a young and wealthy brewer's son who felt that he was closer to the magical truths than Mathers himself. His name was Aleister Crowley, and it was his writing and activities that were to have most influence on the darker side of 20th century occult thinking.

Crowley was born in 1875 at Plymouth, Devon, where his family combined the knack of making money with intense, slightly cranky, religious piety. From an early age, Crowley felt drawn by the power of evil, so much so that his mother was moved to compare him with the 'Great Beast 666' of the Book of Revelations, –a title of which he was proud until the end of his life.

But it was as 'Brother Perdurabo'–'I will endure to the end'–that Crowley was initiated into the Golden Dawn. And endure he certainly did. From the beginning he determined that he would wear the magical mantle of such earlier magi as Eliphas Levi, and long before his death, worn out through drink, drugs, and general excess, he felt that it was secure on his shoulders.

After a disagreement with Mathers, Crowley grew disenchanted with the Golden Dawn, feeling that he had progressed in occult knowledge to the stage where he could start his own mystic organization, the *Ordo Templi Orientis*, or 'O.T.O.' a branch of which, apparently, still exists in New York today.

One of Crowley's wilder experiments, spreading his fame as the great beast to a delightedly horrified public between the two world wars, was to set up a monastery at Cefalu in Sicily, accompanied by various scarlet women and homosexual men. The principal rule was, 'Do what thou wilt shall be the whole of the law'; and Crowley indulged this regulation up to the hilt with black magic ceremonies, sexual perversions, animal sacrifices, and the alleged cannibalism of a young child. The British press heard about his activities and published speculative but probably well-founded stories of his evil doings. They blackened his name to such an extent that, when a libellous book was published about him later, the judge awarded him only one farthing in damages—a quarter of a cent.

There can be little doubt that Crowley was highly talented in several spheres of activity. At one point he made a name for himself as a mountain climber, and G.K. Chesterton compared his poems favourably with those of Swinburne. Despite the sensationalism with which he surrounded himself, and despite his sexual extravagances—he was polysexual—there was a brilliant, if twisted, vein to his thinking and writing which was recognized by only a few at the time of his death in 1947. Today, his works are read and published in Britain and the United States, and are treated with extreme seriousness by academics—a situation which would have amused but flattered him.

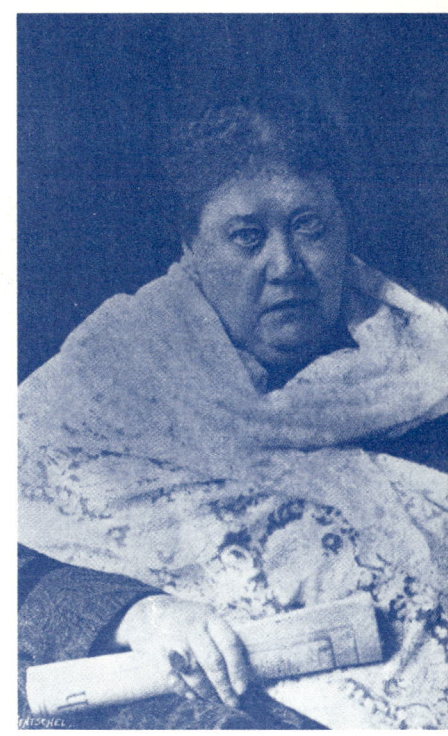

Top *Annie Besant with Krishnamurti seated to her left. Members of the Theosophist movement, one of whose founder members was Madame Helena Petrovna Blavatsky (above), they carried on the occult traditions in the early part of this century. Krishnamurti was hailed by Annie Besant as the new spiritual leader of the world*

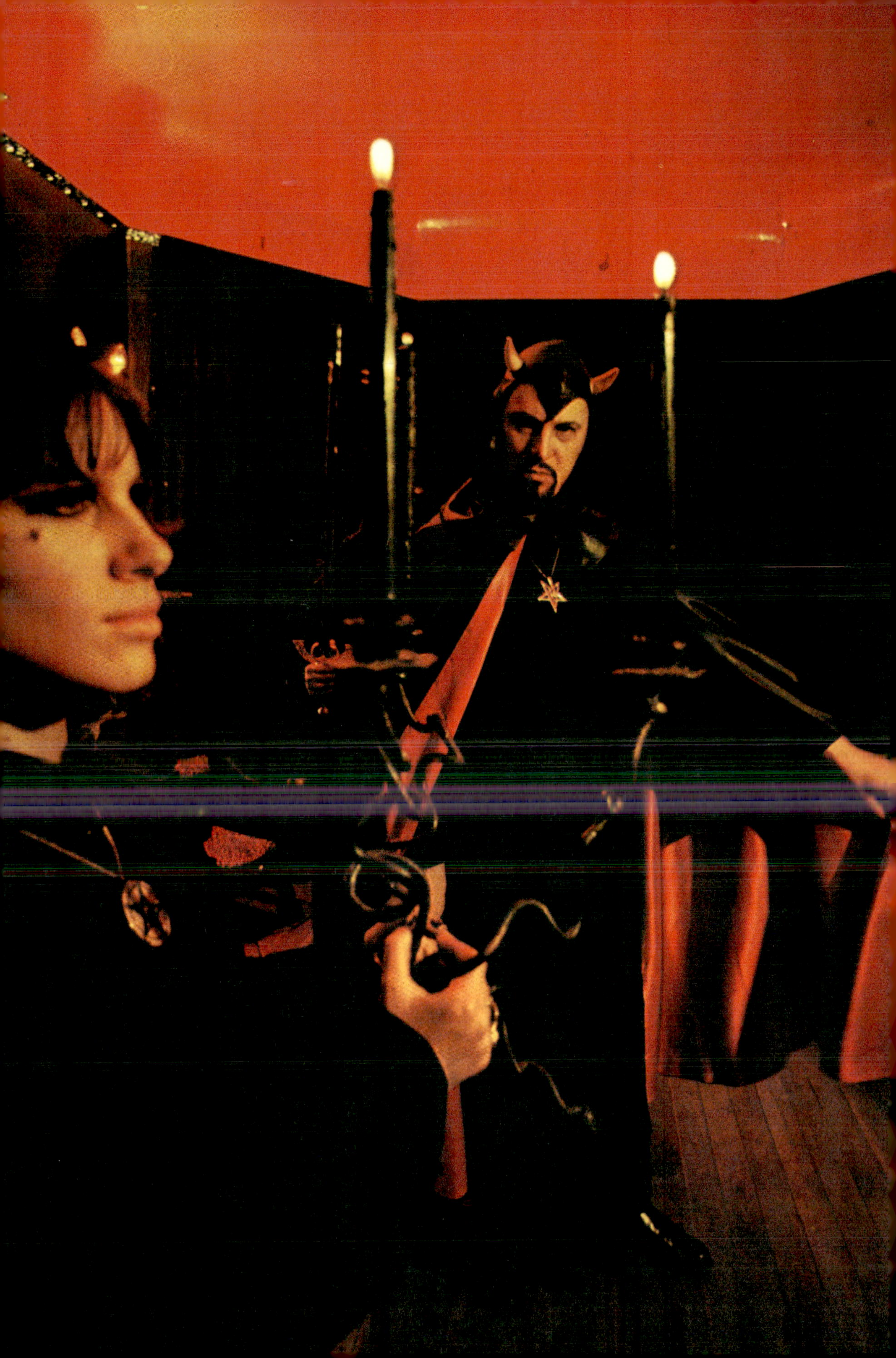

Left *black magic is usually practised at night and in strict secrecy, often in remote places*
Far left *and below* Anton La Vey, *leader of the Church of Satan together with some of his followers. La Vey wears a Devil's hood with horns and his followers often dress in animal heads. They claim that their religion is 'the celebration of man's animal powers and basic instincts'.*

Above *'the Great Beast 666' was the name given to Aleister Crowley* (below right), *undoubtedly the most notorious of modern magicians. He established his own mystic organization and conducted black magic ceremonies* (right). *He wrote several books on demonology and ceremonial magic and his principal rule was 'Do what thou wilt shall be the whole of the law'. An extract from his writings is shown* (far right)

Modern Witchcraft

Crowley's writing on subjects such as demonology, the mysteries of Eleusis, and ceremonial magic influence most contemporary magic groups, black and white. A combination of his work, and the work of an eccentric, though scholarly, English lady, named Dr Margaret Murray, form the basis for the current witchcraft revival. Dr Murray, sometime professor of Egyptology at the University of London, turned her archeological attentions nearer to home and published two books, *The Witch Cult in Western Europe* (1921) and *The God of the Witches* (1933). In these she attempted, and most modern scholars say failed, to equate the various horned god and mother goddess myths of Europe and the British Isles with the medieval 'man in black' whom so many so-called witches of the past confessed to having worshipped.

She argued that the cult of wicca was a survival from pre-Christian days, and that it had been practised in secret for many centuries after the establishment of the Church in England. One of her wilder but more fascinating theories was that the King of England was a high priest of witchcraft, and that the Order of the Garter, which has 26 members, was originally a double coven; a coven is traditionally composed of 13 people.

Dr Murray's ideas were greeted with varying degrees of scepticism by most critics. However, one man, a retired customs officer who was a student of mysticism and the works of Crowley, took her very seriously indeed. His name was Gerald Brosseau Gardner and in the Murray books he found just what he needed to satisfy his appetite for quasi-magical ceremonial and mystery. Gardner shared two common factors with his idol Crowley: he was the son of a wealthy businessman, and he had a strong urge for self-aggrandizement. He set out his general beliefs in two books, *Witchcraft Today* and *The Meaning of Witchcraft*. The full ceremonies appeared in a limited, privately printed edition, and circulated only among his trusted co-believers. Despite this, they are, with few changes, the rules by which covens in the United States and Britain operate today.

The alterations that have been made are mainly on the sexual side. Gardner was a flagellant, and his rituals originally involved mutual whipping and a great rite —sexual intercourse between the high priest and high

Liber LXXVII

Oz: "the law of the strong: this is our law and the joy of the world."
—AL. II. 21

"Do what thou wilt shall be the whole of the law."
—AL. I. 40

"thou hast no right but to do thy will. Do that, and no other shall say nay."—AL. I. 42-3.

"Every man and every woman is a star."—AL. I. 3.

There is no god but man.

1. Man has the right to live by his own law—
    to live in the way that he wills to do:
    to work as he will:
    to play as he will:
    to rest as he will:
    to die when and how he will.
2. Man has the the right to eat what he will:
    to drink what he will:
    to dwell where he will:
    to move as he will on the face of the earth.
3. Man has the right to think what he will:
    to speak what he will:
    to write what he will:
    to draw, paint, carve, etch, mould, build as he will:
    to dress as he will.
4. Man has the right to love as he will:—
    "take your fill and will of love as ye will,
    when, where, and with whom ye will.' —AL. I. 51.
5. Man has the right to kill those who would thwart these rights.
    "the slaves shall serve."—AL. II. 58.
    "Love is the law, love under will."—AL. I. 57.

Aleister Crowley

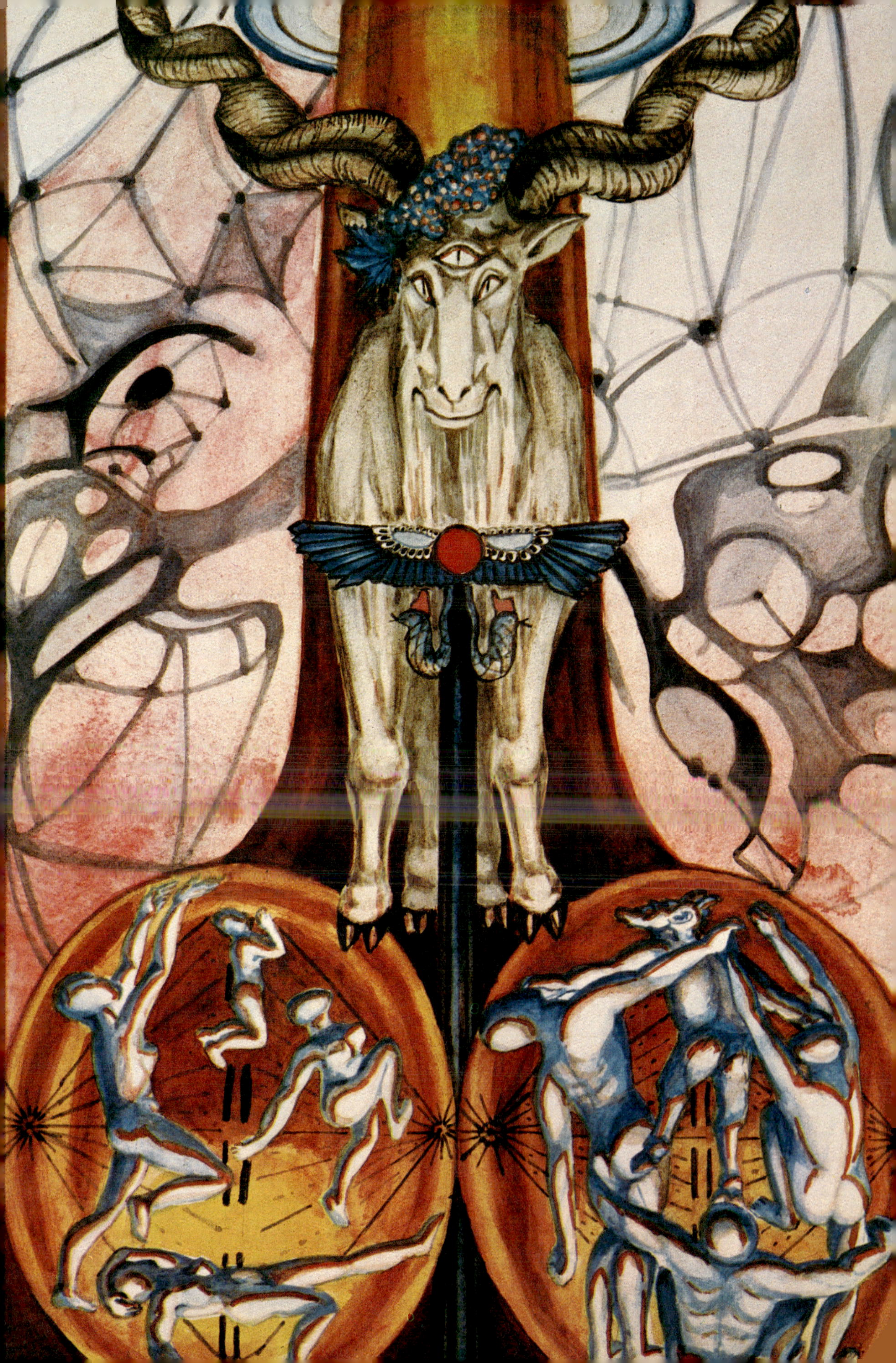

L∴ R∴ D∴ A∴ B∴ A∴

33°
GROSS-ORIENT
DES
ALTEN UND ANGENOMMENEN SCHOTTISCHEN RITUS
DER
FREIMAURER

DEUS MEUMQUE JUS

Souveränes Sanktuarium des Alten u. Primitif Ritus von Memphis u. Misraim in und für das Deutsche Reich.

FRIEDE – TOLERANZ – WAHRHEIT

An alle erleuchteten und erhabenen Freimaurer der Welt!

Unsern Gruss zuvor!

Hiermit wird beurkundet,

dass unser erleuchteter und erhabener Bruder **Eugen John Wieland of London** dessen Unterschrift nebenan steht

Ehrenmitglied der St. Johannis-Freimaurerloge zum "Heiligen Gral" im Or. von München

zum Chevalier Rose Croix und Inhaber des 18° A. A. Ritus proklamirt worden ist.

Wir befehlen allen Prinzen-Rittern und Meistern unserer Jurisdiction und wir bitten alle Brüder-Freimaurer der ganzen Welt ihn als **Prinz Maurer und Chevalier Rose Croix (18°) A. A. Ritus** anzuerkennen, und wir versprechen allen Brüdern ausserhalb unserer Jurisdiction, deren regelmässig beglaubigten Patente in unsern Logen, Kapiteln und Grossraten etc. gleichfalls anzuerkennen.

Urkundlich dessen ist gegenwärtiges Patent ausgefertigt, unterschrieben und gesiegelt worden im Gross-Orient und Souveränen Sanktuarium in und für das Deutsche Reich im Thale von Berlin und London am 18. Tage des Monats Hechir 000.000.000 d. e. 18. August 1912. E. V.

☩ Theodor Reuss 33°, 90°, 96°
Sovs. General Grossmeister ad Vitam
O.H.O. u. Fr. Superior des O.T.O. etc.

Henry Klein 33°, 95°
General Gross Registrar

Previous pages *the Devil,* (left) *a card from a Tarot pack designed for Aleister Crowley* (right) *a certificate of admission to the OTO, Ordo Templi Orientis, issued by Theodor Reuss, a German Freemason. Aleister Crowley played an active part in the formation of the British branch of this organization*

priestess, who represent the male and female elements of the witchcraft deity, in full view of their coven. Oddly enough, the permissive element of modern society tends to be suppressed in present-day Gardnerian covens. Almost without exception the whipping is done in token with a scourge made of sewing silk, and the great rite is performed only rarely. Aiden Kelly, a physics teacher from San Francisco, was one of the earliest Gardnerian witches in the United States. He calls his coven the 'New Reformed Orthodox Order of the Golden Dawn'. Kelly's group still adheres to most of the Gardnerian practices, but even Kelly seems a trifle squeamish about the third degree initation ceremony which involved the rite. 'Nobody in our coven,' he admitted to a newspaperman, 'has felt ready to take it.'

Not so Kelly's English equivalent, Alex Sanders, self-styled King of the Alexandrian witches. Sanders and his blonde wife Maxine frequently perform the great rite, at least in token, during the Thursday and Saturday evening gatherings at their flat—which is also the headquarters of their coven—in London's Notting Hill area. It is perhaps due more to Alex Sanders, with his gift for pop-style publicity than to Gerald Gardner, that witchcraft has become such a thriving cult in Britain.

Alex Sanders came to London in 1967 from his native Manchester, where he had already gained a certain notoriety, claiming that he was an hereditary witch descended from the legendary Welsh magician Owen Glendower. Cynical observers might say that the ancestry was apt; for in Shakespeare's *Henry IV*, when Glendower boasts: 'I can call spirits from the vasty deep,' Hotspur quickly retorts: 'Why so can I, and so can any man – but will they come when you do call for them?'

According to chief witch Sanders, they do come when he calls, especially a friendly if mischievous sprite named Michael, who is his spiritual bodyguard. Alex Sanders' more spectacular physical bodyguard is composed of blue-cloaked, sword-bearing Alexandrian Knights who frequently accompany him when he appears on television chat shows. They also assist in his magical rituals, some of which he has performed publicly on the stage.

Despite his sinister appearance–he is tall, thin and

balding, with a flat slow voice, a dry wit and dark, impenetrable glasses—Sanders is the most accommodating of witches, particularly where journalists and film crews are concerned. He has starred in one major film production, *Legend of the Witches* which, despite adverse comments from the film industry, enjoyed steady popularity when it was released in Britain. Unlike many of his counterparts both at home and abroad he has a certain compelling dignity. He has, however, still to fulfil his mysterious promise to 'make Aleister Crowley look like a Boy Scout'.

Most modern covens, whether Gardnerian or Alexandrian in origin, have many points in common. They base themselves on the medieval archetypes, but shun Devil-worship, claiming that they are paying homage to the forces of creation—the horned god and mother goddess, revered in ancient times as Isis and Osiris, Pan and Diana, Cernunnos and Arianrod. And they practise white magic, using it to do good, healing the sick, helping the growth of crops, and bringing about peace in the world.

However, not all modern witches belong to such groups. There are flamboyant individualists who are somehow more convincing than their whirling, dancing counterparts, because they have a basis in tradition, however tenuous. No social historian would deny the existence of the 'village wisewoman' in rural cultures;

Gerald Brosseau Gardner (left) *and Alex Sanders* (right) *two of the most influential witches of the twentieth century. The rules laid down by Gardner before his death are still followed by many witchcraft covens in the United States and Britain.*

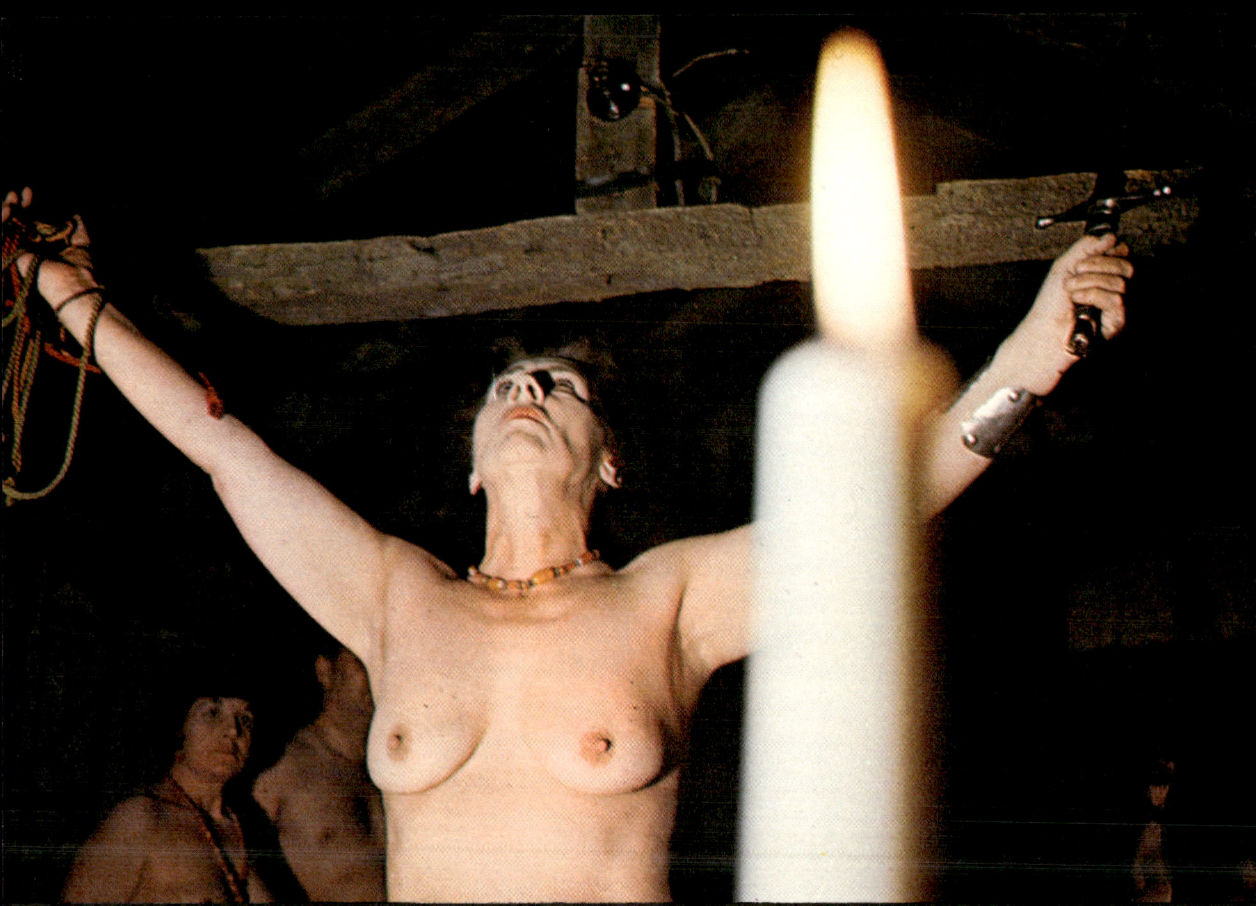

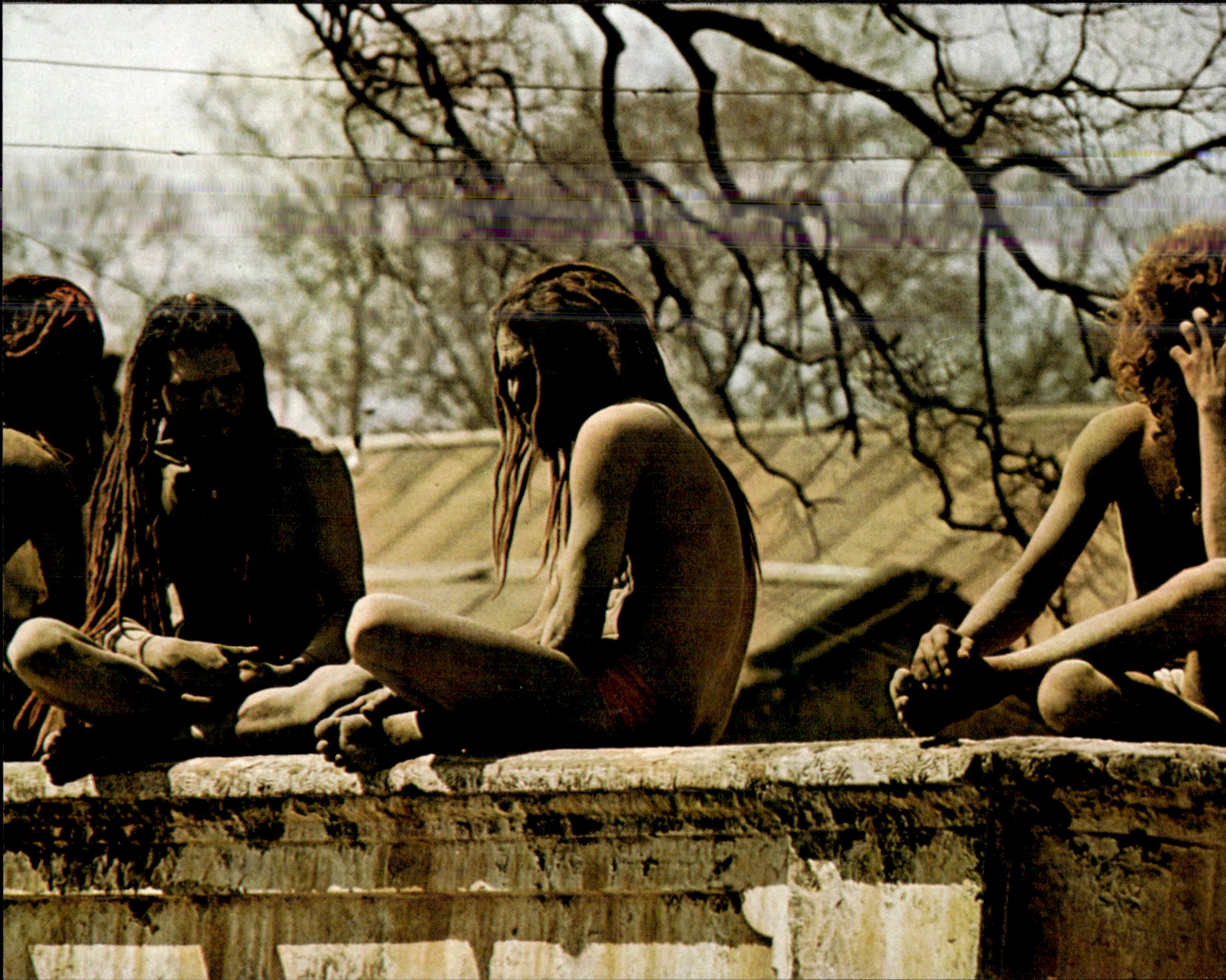

and it is in her footsteps that such loners as Sybil Leek, now an American citizen, and London's Madeline Montalban tread.

Sybil Leek was the first witch to gain widespread fame in the United States. She had operated for several years in her native village of Ringwood, in the New Forest area of Hampshire where she sold antiques by day and concocted spells by night. In the middle 1960s, however, her neighbours decided that the idea of a witch in their midst was too much for them. In 1967 Mrs Leek sold her property, gathered up her familiar, a jackdaw named Hotfoot Jackson, and set out for the New World. America, once so hard on the Salem witches, was good to Sybil Leek. As well as doing frequent radio and television interviews, she has had her own programme on both media, writes columns for *Ladies Home Journal*, designs dresses for a chain of stores, and lectures on occult matters. She became a strong rival to the Maharishi Mahesh Yogi during his brief period of fame by cornering the market in

In a changing world people often turn to alternative forms of religion to satisfy their spiritual needs. Many find comfort in the practice of modern witchcraft (left and below) *with its roots in the past and its present day emphasis on the working of good. Others turn to the mysticism of the East and seek to emulate the disciplines of the holy men* (below left)

Alex Sanders (right), *an English witch with his own coven in London, claims descent from the legendary Welsh magician Owen Glendover* (above)

American transcendental meditation. At one time she planned to start a recording company. As *Time* magazine remarked, she seems to have succeeded where the old alchemists failed, in turning base materials into gold.

Gold, or at least material wealth, is one of the principal objectives behind Madeline Montalban's magic, and she freely admits the fact. Miss Montalban writes regularly in Britain's leading occult journal *Prediction*. But for the last fifteen years or so her main income has come from selling spells for all occasions, teaching Chaldean magic by post, and gambling on the Stock Exchange with the aid of astrology and magical ritual. She lives in an expensive London apartment, wears flowing, fairy queen-like robes that glitter and swirl as she moves, chain-smokes, and drinks sherry from silver goblets. She admires Mrs Leek for her success, but believes herself to be superior in magical power. 'Magic is magic,' she explains, 'black or white, what's the difference? You still use the same powers and you use them for what you want—to do otherwise would be rather silly wouldn't it? Aleister Crowley taught me that when I was a young girl: a sweet man, Aleister... He failed ultimately to become a true *magus* because of his lack of knowledge of astrology. He could never master it properly, poor dear.'

If all modern occultists were like Sybil Leek and Madeline Montalban, they would long ago have become part of the Western establishment. But, of course, they are not. The dark side of the occult has always been the more fascinating, hypnotizing the casual dabbler, and more often than not ensnaring the fervent practitioner in a way that the powers of modern psychology cannot explain.

Some years ago I interviewed a well-to-do photographer in the South of England who lived in a moderate-sized house with a large garden on the coast of Kent. He had a private yacht, a witty and vivacious wife, and a number of friends who were interested in satanism. At the time of the interview the photographer had been dabbling with Black Masses of his own composition, and had performed several necromantic rituals. He was partly sceptical, partly nervous, but said he felt compelled to continue with what seemed to be absurd and unpleasant experiments. Two years later

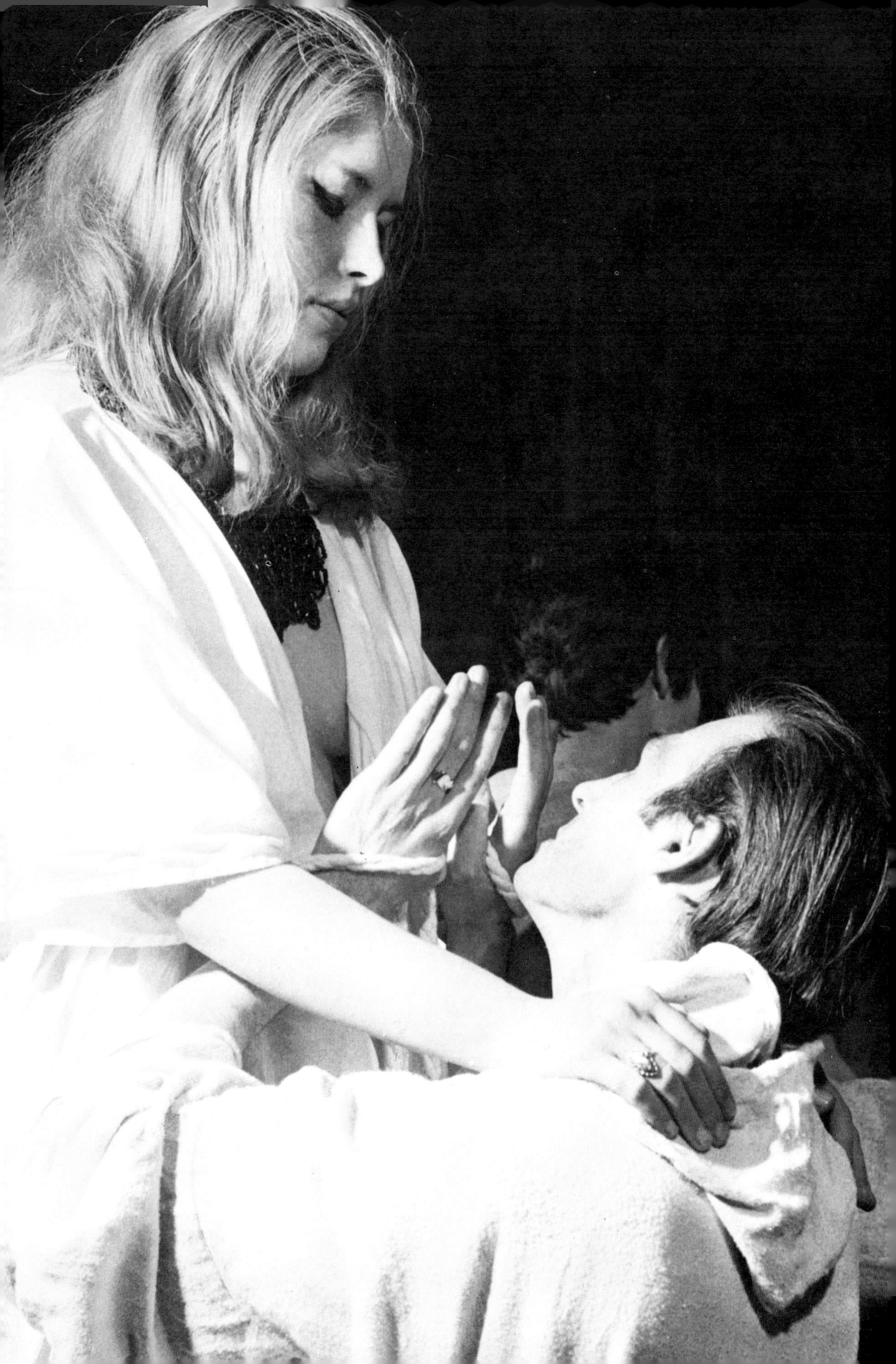

his house had twice been struck by lightning, fire had destroyed his studio and all his equipment, he had suffered a nervous breakdown, his boat was wrecked in a storm and, worst of all, his wife, swearing that she was being pursued by evil powers, had killed herself.

To those who believe in the black arts, such occurrences are far from suprising. Denis Wheatley, the occult thriller writer, always prefaces his books with a warning against interfering in black magic. Most responsible writers on necromancy, however sceptical they may be, advise their readers of the unpleasantness that these rituals entail.

Undoubtedly there are secret satanist cults in Britain but, by and large, they remain secret, shunning all publicity and operating strictly by night. On the few occasions that such groups have come to light the reason for secrecy has immediately been obvious: the members tend to be wealthy businessmen and their principal objective is usually bizarre group sex.

In the United States perhaps the best-known of all occult groups is the San Franciso-based Church of Satan, led by Anton Szandor La Vey, who legally registered his cult under Californian law in 1966. La Vey openly proselytizes for his outfit, which in the words of *Time* magazine, 'offers a mirror-image of most of the beliefs and ethics of traditional Christianity'. La Vey has so far written and published two books, *The Satanic Bible* and *The Compleat Witch* and his newsletter *Cloven Hoof*, edited by an American army officer, has a wide but private circulation. La Vey and his followers dress in animal heads and richly decorated cloaks, and La Vey wears a Devil hood with plastic horns. They recently spurned any belief in the actual existence of demonic power. Instead they claim that their 'religion' is the celebration of man's animal powers and basic instincts. Might, says La Vey, is right: 'Blessed are the strong, for they shall possess the earth. If a man smite you on one cheek, smash him on the other!'

It is more than possible that La Vey's much publicized cult influenced Charles Manson, although La Vey has denied that any of the Manson 'family' were ever members of the Church of Satan. But the mass-killer and his brood were certainly influenced by the idea of satanism itself and it is more than likely that they in turn inspired other ritual killers who have appeared

Above *Anton La Vey, leader of the San Francisco-based Church of Satan*
Left *a black magic ceremony. The links with traditional religion are obvious but the symbols are reversed. The altar is draped in black and the candles are black; the cross, symbol of Christianity and good, is inverted.*

The novice witch is presented with the working tools. This forms part of a witch's first degree initiation. The High Priest presents her with the athame, the most important ritual tool and she has just received the pentacle, a metal disc inscribed with symbols in the United States in recent years. There can be no better, or worse, justification for the warnings of such writers as Denis Wheatley.

New Horizons of the Supernatural
The world of the occult revival covers more than just witchcraft and magical and satanist groups. People in search of new religious commitment also turn to the older, orthodox religions and tailor them to their own needs. The Jesus Freaks, for instance, took the old Holy Roller concept of Christianity and mounted it in a

modern pop setting, achieving considerable success throughout the Western world. Even more popular is the Hare Krishna movement, boosted by George Harrison's records *Hare Krishna* and *My Sweet Lord*. The International Society of Krishna Consciousness, to give the movement its full title, was founded as far back as 1944 by Swami Praphupad, an Asian guru who felt that the world needed a spiritual weapon against the age of Kali or discord. For over 20 years his organization met with only modest success, until after the flower-power era when the occult-minded youth of America adopted his teachings. Today there are 33 Sri Sri Radha Krishna Temples in the United States, Canada, Australia, Japan, West Germany, France and Britain; the sight of the saffron robes, the shaved heads and the bare feet of the chanting followers of Krishna has become a familiar one in the streets of most major cities.

Eastern religious movements have played an important part in the spiritual revival of recent years. Orthodox Buddhism has recruited hundreds of new adherents in the West, while new religions based on Tibetan religious practice abound. In North America, the move towards Tibetanism started with the popularity of a curious book by a man calling himself Tuesday Lobsang Rampa. In his first volume of alleged autobiography, *The Third Eye*, and in its sequels, Rampa claimed that he was the reincarnation of a high lama, sent to save the West from its follies. Even when Lobsang Rampa was revealed to be a former City of London clerk called Cyril Hoskins, the Rampa saga continued unabated. His books still sell in millions.

While Rampa-Hoskins writes his books in his secluded flat in Montreal, a movement which would probably meet with his approval is gradually growing in Britain. The 'Re-Formed Golden Order of Lamaistic Buddhism' is headed by another ex-clerk, Roger Curtis, who is known as Senge Rimposhe, or Brave Lion to his followers. A serious young man in his twenties, Curtis shuns alcohol, drugs and meat-eating, and claims that he and his principal followers are the reincarnations of lamas killed during the Chinese invasion of Tibet in 1950. Curtis's object is to set up a self-supporting teaching monastery in England's West Country, which will also be a rehabilitation centre for drug addicts.

New cults based on old concepts, and old religions

Following pages *in recent years young people have been greatly attracted by the mystical teachings of Eastern religions. Followers of the Hare Krishna Movement (left above and below), dressed in Eastern robes and with their heads shaved can be seen chanting and shuffling along the streets of most major cities. Sometimes attention is focused on the teachings of a particular holy man (centre bottom) or the guru is regarded by his followers as an incarnation of a deity. This is the case with the 15-year-old Guru Maharaj Ji (top centre and far right)*

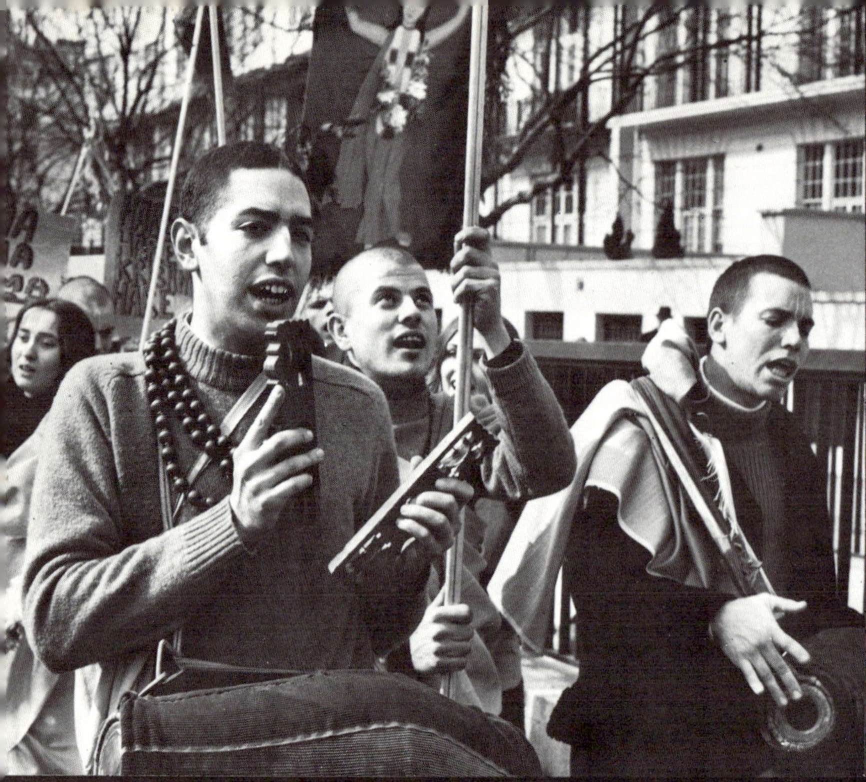

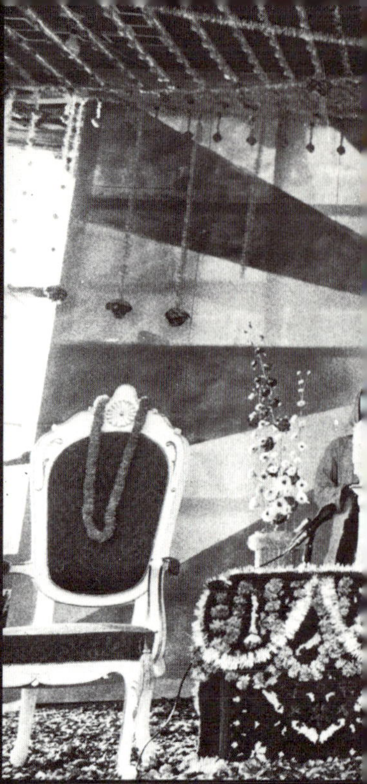

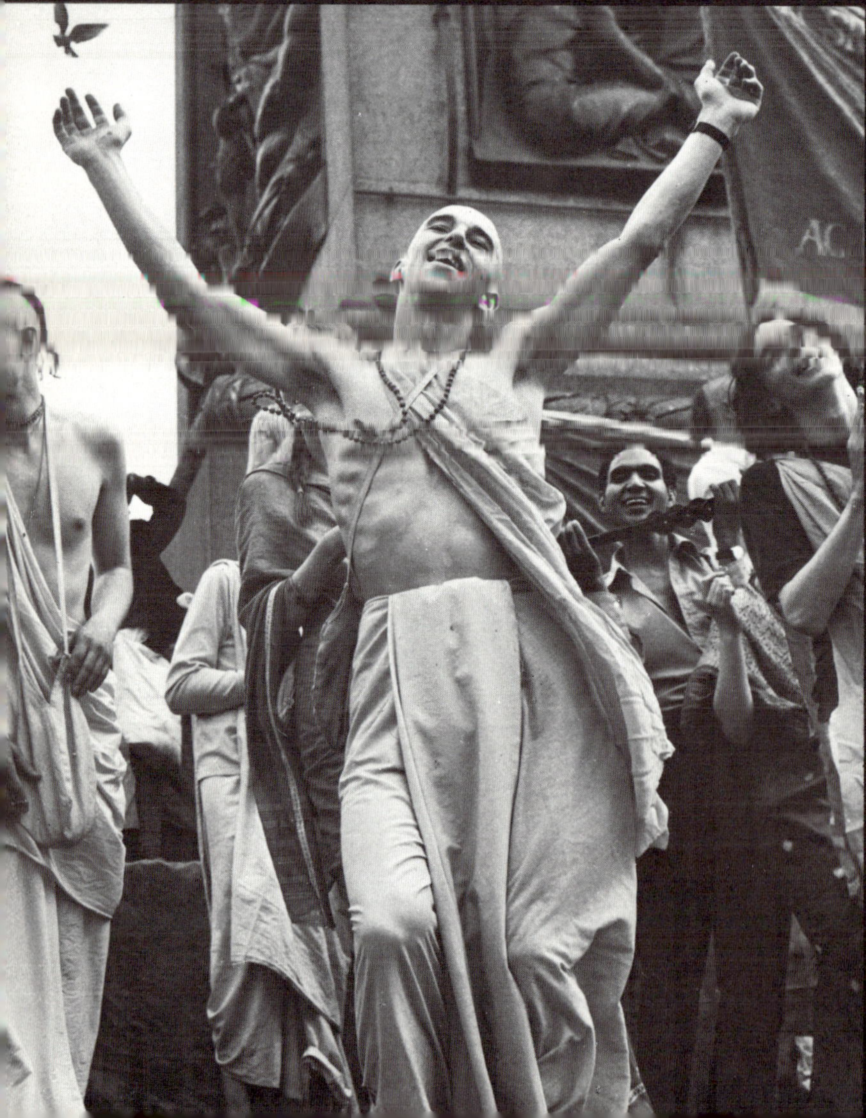

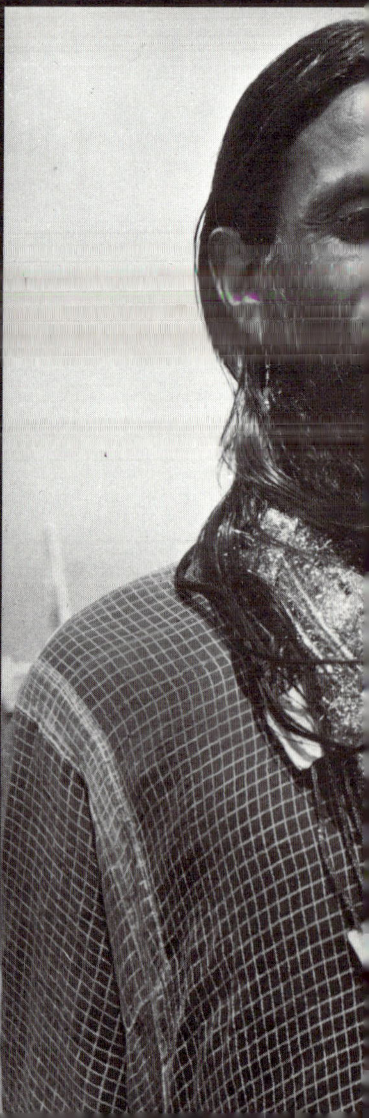

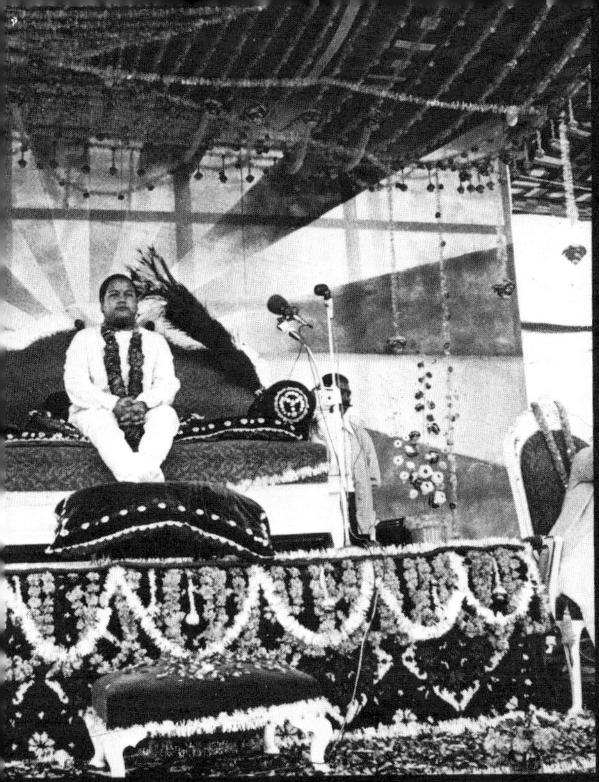
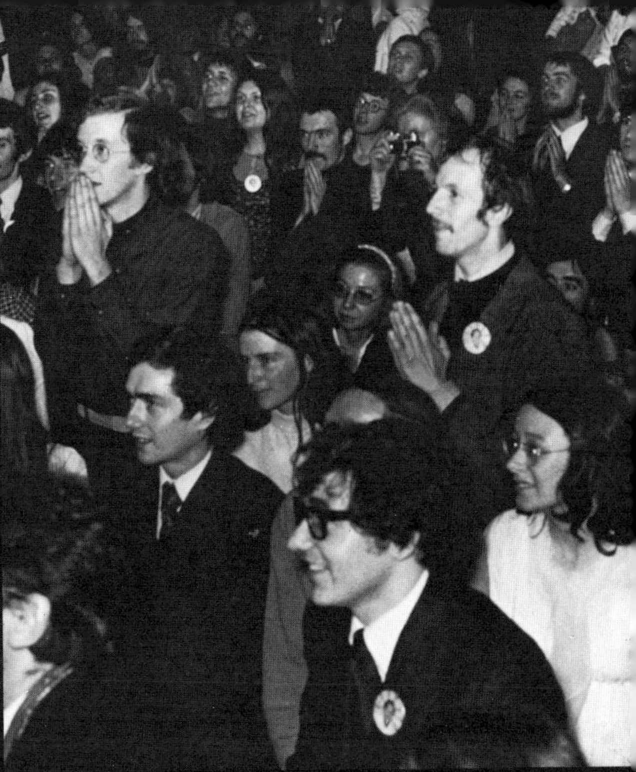
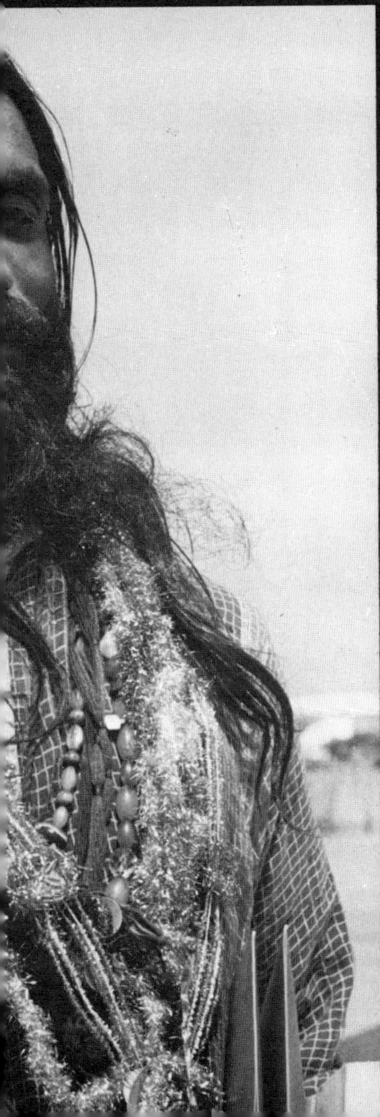
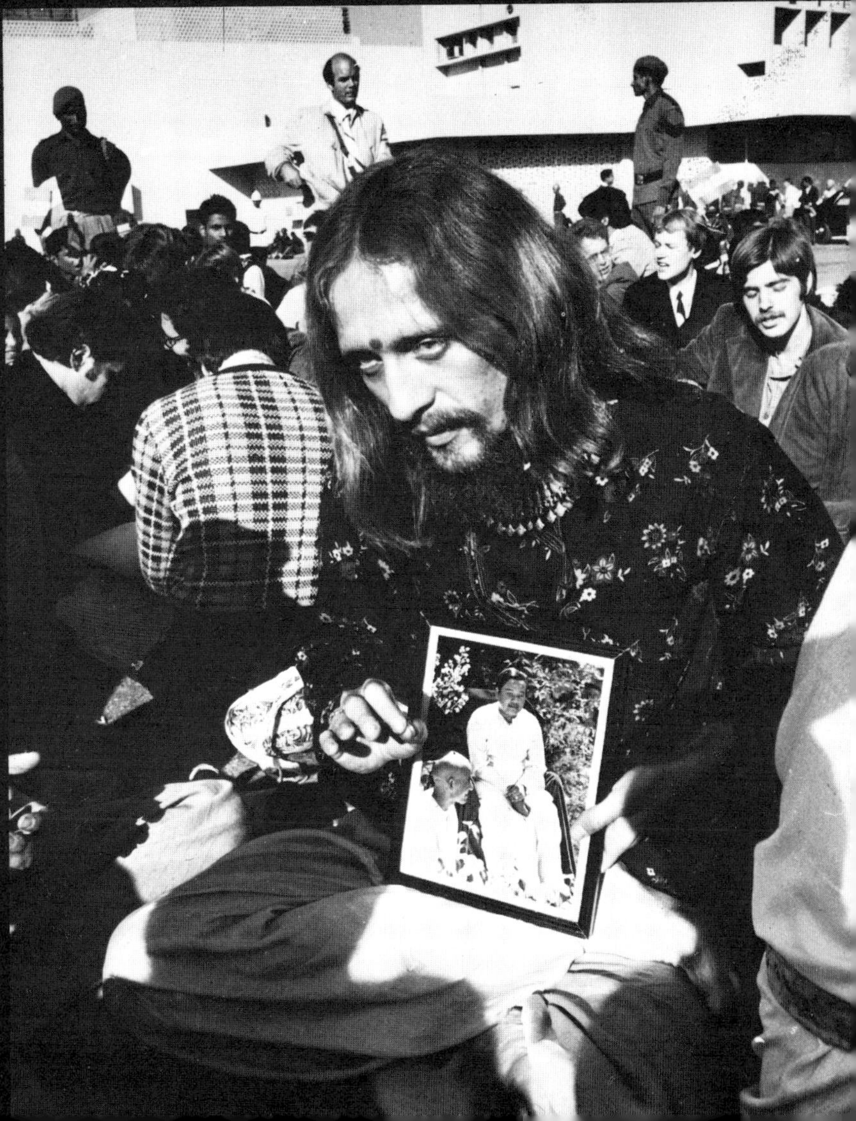

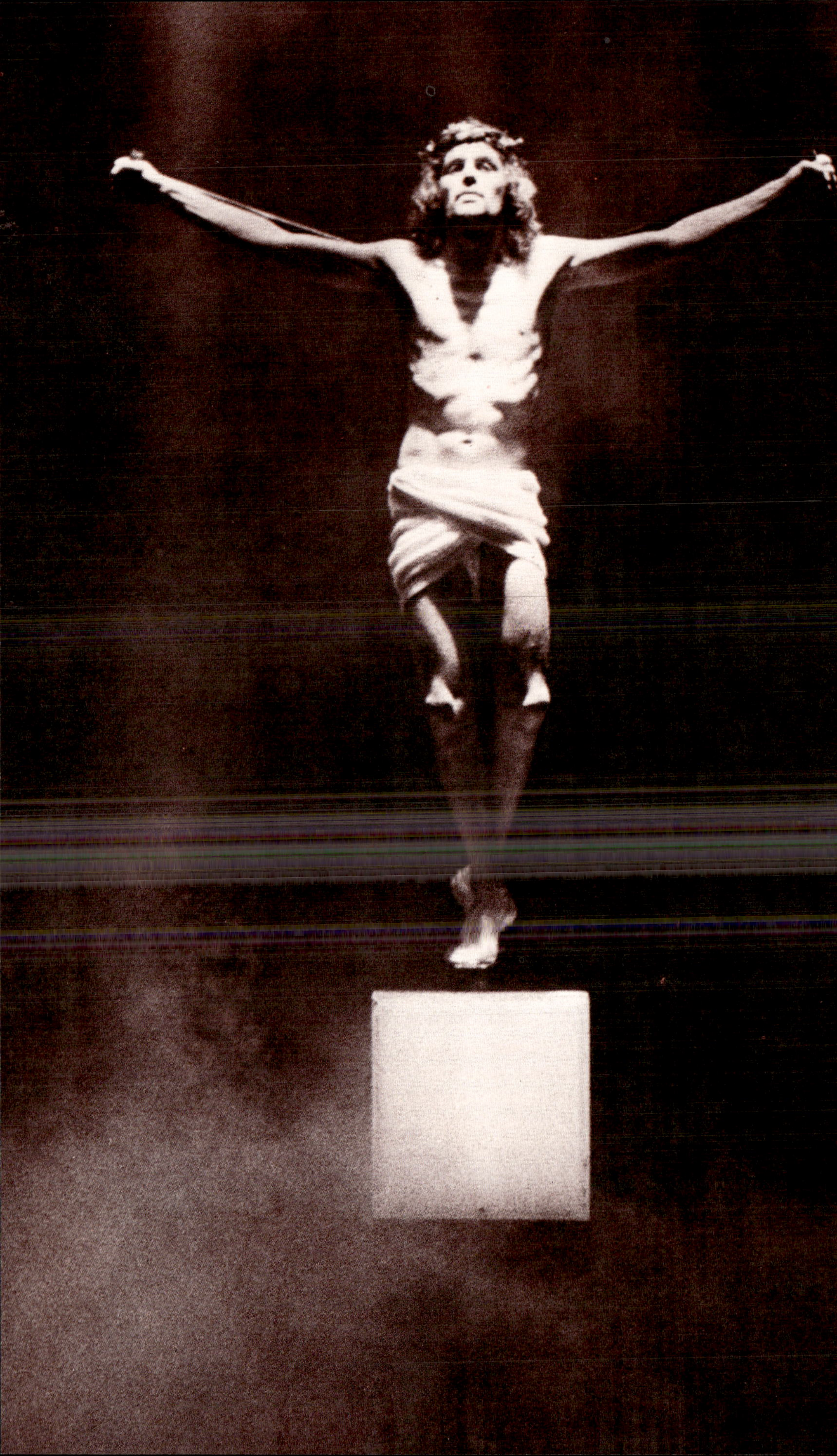

given a novel twist are intriguing, but the question most often asked by the casual observer of the occult or supernatural scene is simply: 'Is there anything in it?' The answer is largely a matter of individual belief, but it is undeniable that psychic phenomena do exist. There is Edgar Cayce, an occult diagnostician and spiritual healer from Kentucky who, at the time of his death in 1945, had over 30,000 successful – and well-attested – cures to his credit. And José Pedro de Freitas, a Brazilian peasant farmer who performed operations in a trance, relying on rusty scissors, kitchen knives, and faith in his spirit guide.

At the height of his fame in the mid-1960s de Freitas, also known as 'Arigo', performed several complex operations each week. He was observed by distinguished members of the Brazilian and American medical profession, who said he was 'totally impressive' but 'inexplicable'. He removed tumours, performed hysterectomies, and carried out delicate eye operations all at high speed, and without ever making a slip, or failing either to cure or ease the condition of his patients. Unfortunately, while the world's medical authorities debated the issue of Arigo, a Brazilian judge gaoled him for practising medicine illegally, and for professing 'witchcraft'.

Scientists in Russia, the United States and Britain have started to do research in the field of psychic phenomena, and it is possible that before the century is out the mysterious powers of Cayce and Arigo, telepathy, extra-sensory perception and precognition will no longer be as mysterious as they are at present. Witchcraft and magic may be proved, after all, to be based not in the supernatural, but in scientific fact.

Left *A scene from the recent production of* Jesus Christ Superstar. *Established religions have received a new lease of life*

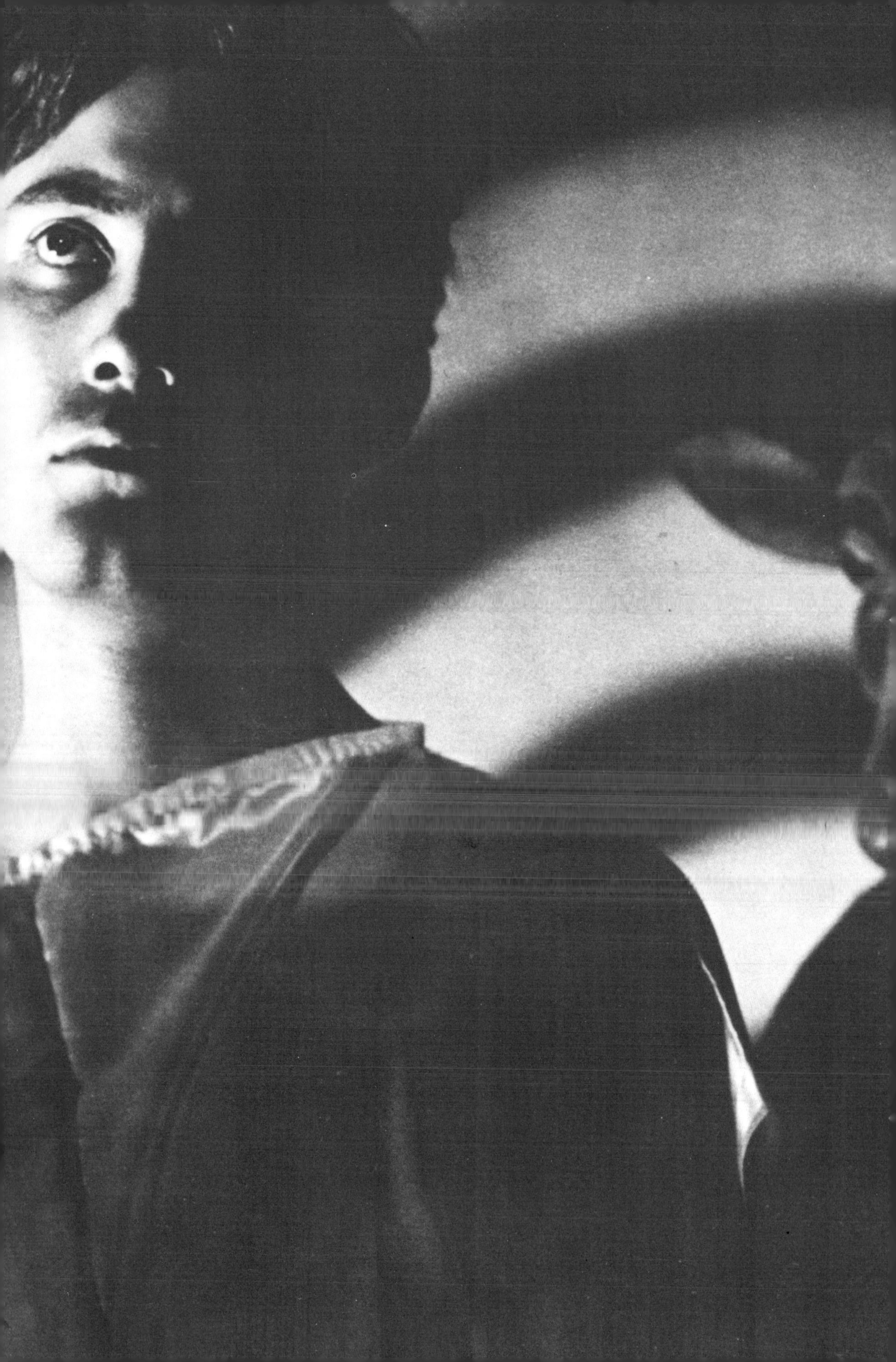

Further Reading

The Black Arts, R. Cavendish. Routledge, 1967
The Domain of Devils, Eric Maple. Hale, 1966
Encyclopedia of Superstitions, Christina Hole. Hutchinson, 1961
Encyclopedia of Witchcraft and Demonology, R.H. Robbins. Peter Nevill, 1959
Lost Worlds of Africa, James Wellard. Hutchinson, 1967
The Magical Arts, C.A. Burland. Barker, 1966
Magic, Medicine and Quackery, Eric Maple. Hale, 1968
Magic: an Occult Primer, David Conway. Cape, 1971
Politics, Law and Ritual in Tribal Society, Max Gluckman. Blackwell, Oxford, 1965
The Satanic Mass, H.T.F. Rhodes. Rider, 1954
The Sufis, Idries Shah. W.H. Allen, 1964
The Supernatural, Douglas Hill and Pat Williams. Aldus Books, 1964
Witchcraft, Pennethorne Hughes. Penguin, 1965
The Witch-Cult in Western Europe, Margaret Murray. Clarendon Press, 1967
Witchcraft in Old and New England, G.L. Kittredge. Harvard University Press, 1909
Witchcraft at Salem, Chadwick Hansen. Brazillier N.Y., 1969
Witchcraft and Sorcery, M.G. Marwick. Penguin, 1971

A scene from the film
Legend of the Witches

Acknowledgments

The authors and publishers are grateful to the following for allowing them to reproduce the magnificent illustrations in this book:

Abbey Museum/Michael Holford: Page 50(top left)
Allied Press Services: Page 26(top)
Joe Bangay: Page 170
Barnaby's Picture Library: Pages 9(top right), 19, 26(bottom left), 76(top), 114–15, 168(left, top & bottom)
Border Film Production: Pages 172–3
BPC Picture Library: Pages 20(bottom), 25(top), 49, 52, 53, 57, 60, 64(bottom), 77(top left), 86, 88(bottom), 95, 104(top), 133, 145(top), 160(top)
British Museum: Page 115
British Museum/Michael Holford: Pages 17(top), 27(top), 58(bottom left), 61, 68(bottom left), 112(top left), 123(bottom), 132
British Tourist Authority: Page 76(bottom)
Buckland Museum: Pages 27(bottom), 148(left)
Camera Press Ltd.: Pages 4, 16, 17(bottom left & right), 26(bottom right), 29(bottom), 31, 32(top), 41(top), 44(left & right), 45(bottom) 62–3, 67(top & bottom), 78, 79, 82, 83, 84, 85, 87(left), 92, 98(top & bottom left), 106(top), 120(bottom left), 122, 123(top), 138–9, 142(top & bottom), 146(top & bottom), 149, 150(left), 151, 155(top), 168–9(centre top, left top & bottom)
Daily Telegraph Colour Library: Pages 34(top), 98, 152, 153(bottom)
Ursula Edelmann/Goethe Museum, Frankfurt: Page 59
Robert Estall: Pages 13(top), 33(bottom), 108–9, 112(top right)
Mary Evans Picture Library: Pages 88(top), 89, 93(bottom right), 103(top), 127
Stewart Farrar: Pages 23(bottom left), 30, 45(top), 74(top & bottom), 90, 106(left), 107, 130, 134, 148(centre), 166
Werner Forman: Page 72(bottom left)
Alan Frank: Page 98(bottom right)
Kenneth Grant: Pages 154, 155(top right & bottom)
Collection of Kenneth Grant/Michael Holford: 39, 97
Ray Halin: Pages 6–7, 11, 80(inset), 116–17, 141(top & bottom)
Sonia Halliday: Pages 34–5(bottom), 35(top), 58(top left & right), 77(bottom)

Helga Photo Studio Inc.: Page 64(top)
Michael Holford: Pages 28, 105
Horniman Museum/Michael Holford: Pages 15(bottom), 29(top)
Anne Horton: Pages 24(bottom), 25(bottom), 37(left & right), 103(bottom), 118(bottom), 151(top & bottom), 155(top right)
Pat Keene: Pages 32(bottom), 126
Keystone Press Agency: Pages 91(left), 118(top), 143(top & bottom), 168–9(centre bottom)
Serge Kordeiv: Pages 69, 104(bottom), 136, 137(top & bottom), 153(top), 165(bottom)
William MacQuitty: Pages 2–3, 51, 58(bottom right)
The Mansell Collection: Pages 1, 8, 9(top left & bottom), 21, 33(top), 40, 41(bottom), 71, 87(right), 91(right), 102, 111, 114, 162
John Moss: Pages 23(top left), 129
Musée Guimet, Paris/Michael Holford: Page 80
Museum of the American Indian, New York: Pages 99(left & right), 121
Museum of Archaeology and Ethnography, Cambridge/Michael Holford: Page 72(top)
Axel Poignant: Page 68(bottom right)
Prado Museum, Madrid: Pages 46–7
Jean Roubier: Pages 18, 56
Rex Features Ltd: Pages 106(bottom), 159(right), 163
Scala: Pages 50(bottom), 100–1
Snark International: Pages 42, 94–5
Spectrum Colour Library: Pages 10, 14, 15(top right), 23(right, top & bottom), 50(top right), 65(bottom), 77(top right), 110–1, 112 (bottom), 120(top & bottom right), 125, 144(right), 145(bottom), 160(bottom)
G. Tomsich: Pages 24(top), 68(top), 72(bottom right), 73, 108(inset), 110
Transworld Feature Syndicate: Pages 13(bottom), 144(left)
Victoria & Albert Museum/Michael Holford: Pages 54, 55, 124(left)
Voelkerkunde Museum, Munich/Michael Holford: Page 15(top left)
Warburg Institute/Michael Holford: Pages 43, 156
Warner Bros. Film: Page 93(left & top right)
Collection of Gerald Yorke/Michael Holford: Pages 65(top), 124(right), 157

Index

Abbots Bromley 75
Africa 29, 91
Agrippa, Cornelius 83, 85, 88
Aloes 110
Amber 113
Amethyst 113
Amulet 68, *68*, 70
Animals 114
Apple 109
Arabia 48, 99
Ash 110
Astrology 19, 20, 22, 52
Australian Aborigine *8*, 22, 25, *75*, 79, *123*, 139, *139*, *143*, 144
Barrett, Francis *133*
Basil 111
Bat 114
Bay 111
Bear 114
Beardsley, Aubrey *103*
Birch 109
Birds 115
Black Mass 29–30, 36, 122, 146–47
Blake, William *55*
Bosch, Hieronymus *48*
Brazil *86*, 140
Britain 18, 30, 32, 44, 115, 141, 143, 150, 154, *159*
British Columbia 18
Buddha *15*, 79
Cagliostro, Count 86, *88*
Cameroons *8*
Canada 18
Carnelian 113
Cat 114
Chinese 64, 70, 113
Christianity 29–30, 37, 40, 42, 56–57, 75, 133
Clairvoyance 22, 24, 111
Clover 110
Cock *28*, 115
Congo *52*, 140
Conway, David 74
Coven 42, *91*, 99, 103, *107*, 135, 150, *150*, 154, 158–59
Crow 115
Crowley, Aleister 36, *42*, 81, *126*, 131, 150–51, 154, *154*, 158–59, 162
Crystal gazing 21, *22*
Cuckoo 115
Cup tossing *21*
Dahomey *119*
Dance 75, *75*, 79, *81*, *85*, 136–37, 143
Dashwood Sir Francis *33*

Demon 8, 12, *12*, 22, 27, 33, *35*, 48–49, 52, *52*, 56, *56*, 57, *60*, 82, 85–86, 128
Diamond 74, 113
Dill 68, 111
Dog 114
Dove 115
Egypt *68*, 70, 75, 79, 96
Elder 109
Emerald 113
Endor, Witch of 88, 126, 133
Ethiopia *86*
Evil Eye 24–25, 40, 111, 114–15
Faith Healer 27
Familiar 32, *37*, 114–15, *115*
Fennel 111
Fern 110
Fertility 104, 109–10, 113–14, 143, *144*, 147
Fir 109
Fish 115
Flowers 110
Forget-me-not 110
Fortune telling 19, 21, *21*, 22, *42*
France 32, *35*, *58*, *92*, 147
Freitas, Jose Pedro de 171
Frog 114
Fuseli *58*
Gardner, Gerald Brosseau 154, *159*
Garlic 111
Geranium 110
Germany 32
Ghana *44*
Gluckman, Max 119
Goat 114
Gold 113
Golden Dawn, Order of 150–51, 158
Goya *37*, *99*
Grandier, Urbain *93*
Greece 19, 96, 143, *144*
Grimoire 81, 122, 131
Guazzo, Francesco-Maria 88
Haiti *33*, 85
Hawthorn 109, *109*
Healing 25, 37
Herbs 68, 94, 111
Herring 115
Hong Kong *12*
Horse 114
Hungary *66*
Inanimate objects 25, *27*
Inca 22
Incantation 75, 127
India 22, 70, 79, *81*, 96, 113

Initiation, Rites of 135, 136, *136*, 137–39, *139*, 140, *166*
Italy 25
Japan *21*, 52
Jewels 74, 113
Kali 49, *55*, 167
Katmandu *15*, *58*, *64*
Kelly, Aidan 158
Kenya 143
Kraken 115
Krishna, Hare 167
La Vey, Anton *35*, 36, *153*, 164, *165*
Leek, Sybil 37, 161–62
Lemon Balm 111
Levi, Eliphas 88, *88*, 150
Lilith 49
Lotus 110
Lovage 111
Magic 64, 66, 68, 70, 75, 81–82, 96, 98, *104*, *135*, 146
   Black 29–30, 33, *35*, *37*, 48, *133*, *153*, *154*, 162, *165*
   Imitative 96, 99, *99*, 111, 143
   Sympathetic 95, 98
   White 29, 37, *44*, 128, 159
Magician 27, *60*, 66, *66*, 70, *75*, 81, 83, 85, 122–23, 126, 128, 131, 133, 135
Malaya 52, 57, *144*
Mandrake 70, 111, *111*
Maori 70
Marigold 110
Mathers, McGregor 57, 150–51
Medicine-man 22, 27, *99*, 143–44
Medium 22, *24*, *27*, *86*
Medmenham Abbey 30
Melanesia *15*, 95
Mesopotamia 20, 96
Mexico 68
Montalban, Madeline 161–62
Mountain Ash 109
Murray, Margaret 154
Myrtle 68
Myth 8, 12, *18*, 19
Necromancy 126–28, 131, 162, 164
New Guinea 22, *29*, 81
New Zealand 74
Nigeria *8*, *144*
North American Indian *18*, 27, 48, 57, *75*, *99*, *119*, 139–40, 143
Numbers 67–68
Oak 109
Osman Spare, Austin *96*, *104*

Owl 115

Papua 29
Paracelsus 83, *87*
Parsley 111
Passage, Rites of 140-41, 143
Peacock 115
Pearl 74, 113
Peony 110
Pig 114
Plants 68, 110
Poppy 110
Precognition 22, *24*

Raven 115
Rhodesia *18*
Ritual 18-20, 22, 25, 27, 41, *104*, 116-47, 154
Rhodes, H. T. F. 147
Rome 19, *24*, 96
Rose 68, 110
Rosemary 111
Rowan 109
Ruby 113

Sabbat *91*, *95*, 113-14, 135, 143

Sage 111
Salem witches *41*
Sanders, Alex 158-59, *159*, *162*
Sapphire 113
Satanism 33, *35*, 36-37, *37*, *44*, 164
Scone, Stone of 113
Scotland *12*, 13, 32
Shaman 22, *27*, 29, 92
Shah, Idries 103
Signorelli *52*
Silver 113
Singapore *12*, 52
Snake 114, *114*
South America 29
Spain 32
Spell 31, 68, 81
Spirits 8, 12, *12*, *15*, *19*, 27, 29, 48, 52, 60
Stork 115
Stones 113
Superstition 18-19, 24
Sweden 68
Symbolism 122, 135, *135*

Taboo 18
Talisman 68, 70, 74, *74*
Tibetanism 167
Topaz 74
Torture 32, 40
Totem poles *16*
Trees 109
United States 13, 19-20, 37, 70, 114, 150, *150*, 154, 158, *159*, 164
Voodoo 22, *33*, 81-82, *82*, *83*, 92
Water 113
Wicca 42, 150, 135
Willow 109
Witch 22, 30, *31*, *35*, 37, 40, 40-42, 44, *44*, 66, 68, 88, *91*, 92, *92*, 94-95, *96*, 99, *99*, *104*, 107, *107*, 114, *115*, *128*, 135-37, 143, *144*, *150*, 154, 159, *159*, 161
Witch-hunt 30-33
Witchdoctor *8*, *31*, 82, *91*, 95, 144
Yew 109

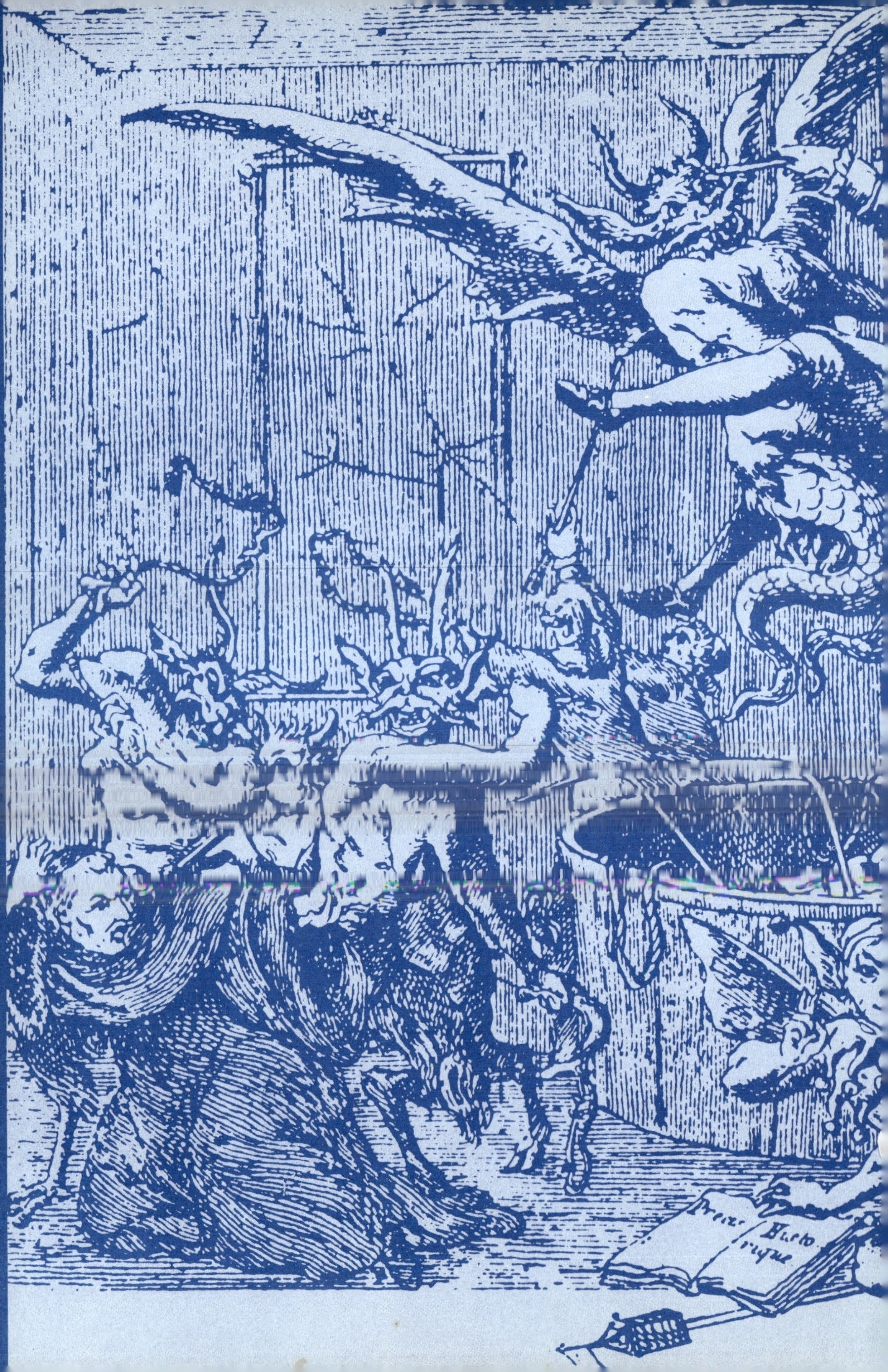